# PEOPLE, PRODUCTION AND THE ENVIRONMENT

## Mark Crundwell, David Horsfall, Gill Miller
### Edited by Glennis Copnall

Hodder & Stoughton

A MEMBER OF THE HODDER HEADLINE GROUP

# Acknowledgements

The publishers would like to thank the following for permission to reproduce copyright photographs in this book: Life File, Figure 1.7, Figure 4.16b, Hulton-Deutsch, Figure 4.16a; Aerofilms, Figure 5.32a; Port of Tyne Authority, Figure 5.34a, b. All other photos provided by the authors.

The publishers would also like to thank Oxfam and Ordnance Survey for permission to reproduce copyright materials.

Every effort has been made to contact the holders of copyright material used in this book, but if any has been overlooked, the publishers will be pleased to make the necessary alterations at the first opportunity.

Orders: please contact Bookpoint Ltd, 39 Milton Park, Abingdon, Oxon OX14 4TD. Telephone: (44) 01235 400414, Fax: (44) 01235 400454. Lines are open from 9.00–6.00, Monday to Saturday, with a 24 hour message answering service. Email address: orders@bookpoint.co.uk

*British Library Cataloguing in Publication Data*
A catalogue record for this title is available from The British Library

ISBN 0 340 72448 X

First published 1999
Impression number   10 9 8 7 6 5 4 3 2 1
Year                      2004 2003 2002 2001 2000 1999

Copyright © 1999 Mark Crundwell, David Horsfall and Gill Miller

Typeset by Fakenham Photosetting Limited, Fakenham Norfolk NR21 8NL
Printed in China for Hodder & Stoughton Educational, a division of Hodder Headline Plc, 338 Euston Road, London NW1 3BH by Sun Fung Offset Binding Co., Ltd.

# Contents

# INTRODUCTION

**People, Production and the Environment** is an up-to-date look at Economic Geography. The book considers economic development, the use of physical and human resources and some resulting issues. The authors draw attention to globalisation, interdependence and sustainability as key concepts which affect all our lives. Each chapter provides through text, data, diagrams, maps, and case studies, knowledge and understanding of these concepts. You can also develop your geographical and examination skills by completing the tasks and using the following geographical questions as a framework to your studies. By the end of the book you should be able to answer the questions below in depth and breadth and with located examples. Each question will enable you to demonstrate not only the knowledge and understanding, but the skills, required by A level geography specifications.

## A Study Framework of Key Questions and Key Skills

*Q. Where and why are there spatial variations in economic activity?*
*Task: Try this as a research task. Produce a written answer supported by facts and data. [Skill: to recognise a pattern]*

Survival at either the subsistence or commercial level requires utilisation of resources from physical and human environments. The world's resources vary in location, amount, and characteristics. The result is a spatial **pattern** of economic activity, the variations of which occur at a range of scales. The case studies in the book draw attention to those variations at different scales from farm to nation, enterprise zone to world city.

*Q. How and why do these variations change through time?*
*Task: Use a range of graphic and cartographic techniques to illustrate changes through time. [Skill: to identify a trend]*

Temporal variations also occur. Changes in resource bases, technology, markets and government policies mean that in any one location the characteristics of economic activity **change** as economic systems evolve. Yesterday's hive of activity can be today's ghost town or rust belt. Characteristics of economic activity therefore change in both time and space.

*Q. What do we mean by development? By what criteria can development be classified?*
*Task: Discuss why there might be a range of answers to this questions. [Skill: to sort and classify by criteria]*

Economic geography often uses the terms Less and More Economically Developed Countries to draw attention to the global **inequalities** which exist. However this is a very narrow view of development. At all scales there are also inequalities of human development and opportunity.

*Q. Where and why does physical, human and environmental exploitation take place?*
*Task: Research and examine different types of exploitation. [Skill: to demonstrate knowledge of places, understanding of processes]*

Physical and human resources are used as inputs to maintain the outputs of the 'economic' system. Many parts of physical and human environments currently are being misused or even abused. How can we understand the current processes to predict and plan for **sustainable** social, economic and environmental development to meet the needs of the next generation?

*Q. To what extent are we all in this together?*
*Task: Use the Internet and daily papers, to identify items which illustrate economic interdependence at a range of scales, global to local community. [Skill: to evaluate evidence]*

In all aspects of economic activity, we are increasingly **interdependent**. Within countries, urban and rural lives are linked. Across the world rural lives of one country are linked with urban lives in another. In primary production, manufacturing and service activity; globalisation is the dominating trend. Environmental impacts have global implications and are of global concern.

*Q. Can you illustrate economic patterns, processes and issues with reference to your own experience and your own local area?*
*Task: Apply your knowledge and understanding to an area you can visit. Use a range of skills: Annotated diagrams and photographs, sketch maps and data, to produce a report on the economic activity of the area. Develop an awareness of the part you yourself play in the **local, regional, national and global economic system**. [Skill: to apply and exemplify appropriately]*

# FURTHER READING

**Industrialisation and Development** (ed.) Hewitt, Johnson & Wield (OUP 1995)

**Human Development Reports** UNCP

**Population, Resources and Development**, Chrispin and Jegede (Collins 1996)

**The World Guide 1997/8** New Internationalist Pubs

**Global Shift: transforming the world economy**, Dicken (Paul Chapman 1998)

**New Patterns: Process and Change in Human Geography**, Carr (Nelson 1997)

**A Geography of the Third World**, Dickenson (Routledge 1996)

**People and Environments: Issues and Enquiries**, Slater (Collins Educational 1986)

**Services and Space**, Marshall and Wood (Longman, 1995)

**Location and Change**, Healey and Ilberry (OUP 1990)

**Services in World Economy**, Daniels (Blackwell, 1993)

**The Global Economy in Transition**, Daniels and Lever (Longman, 1996)

*Debt, the Philippines and the World Bank*, **Geography Review**, Vol 12, No 4, March 1999

*Industrial change in Central and Eastern Europe*, **Geography Review**, Vol 10, No 2, November 1996

*Regional inequalities in the EU*, **Geography Review**, Vol 11, No 4, March 1998

*Falling Tigers*, **Geography Review**, Vol 12, No 3, January 1999

*Globalisation and employment in Europe*, **Geography Review**, Vol 11, No 9, May 1998

*Sustaining the soil*, **People and the Planet**, Vol 7, No 1

# 1
# THE GLOBAL ECONOMIC SYSTEM

*'We're in this together'*

## The Global Economic System

Have you ever been abroad and seen any of these familiar logos? What do they tell you? That the goods we enjoy at home are available all over the world, and in many cases are produced by very large international companies. In fact most of our everyday and commonplace items have some connection with other parts of the world. The major decisions of companies in the US for instance can affect factories in Britain or Indonesia. The factories producing microchips or wiring can supply a number of other factories all around the world, and in turn they supply the famous names in the high street. All these connections or linkages are part of the **global economic system**. There is very little that we do in Britain that does not have some impact elsewhere. Economic geography helps us to understand the linkages between people, production and the environment.

---

**STUDENT ACTIVITY 1:**
**HOW GLOBAL ARE YOU?**

Take a look at yourself.
Where are your trainers made?
Where were your clothes manufactured?
What have you eaten today? Where was it produced?
If you eat out, where do you eat or drink?

---

The world economic system is not an invention of the twentieth century. Trade between countries has been carried out since early Chinese, Greek and Egyptian civilisations. Brand names reflect the steady growth of international trade since the nineteenth century. Successful companies in Britain and Europe wanted to expand and found new markets overseas and new products to sell at home. The political colonial expansion was matched in the nineteenth and early twentieth centuries by economic expansion of firms into Asia, South America and Africa. Many companies traded on the open market for raw materials and agricultural products from the colonies, and companies such as Brooke Bond, Tate & Lyle, Fray Bentos and Lever

Try to visualise some of these international trade marks:

## Pepsi  Microsoft

## Virgin  Kodak

## McDonald's

## Kellogg's  Nike

## Calvin Klein

## Visa

FIGURE 1.1 International names are instantly recognisable.

developed their own resources for export to sell in Europe (see Figure 1.2). Manufactured products were then made in Europe and exported back to new, growing markets in the colonies. Japan emerged in a similar relationship with South East Asia in the early twentieth century while at the same time US business expanded into Asia, Latin America and Europe. The pattern of world trade was a response to **comparative advantage**.

| Company | Product | Principal location of activity |
|---|---|---|
| Brooke Bond | tea | Kenya |
| Lever | palm oil | Nigeria, West Africa |
| Fray Bentos | meat | Argentina |
| Tate & Lyle | sugar | Caribbean |
| Fyffe's | bananas | Caribbean |
| De Beers | diamonds | South Africa |
| Royal Dutch Shell | oil | Far East, Nigeria |

FIGURE 1.2 The colonial origins of familiar products

## The Principle of Comparative Advantage

The pattern of world trade is based on the different resources of each country. Trade will occur between two countries if each one specialises in the production/manufacturing which it does most effectively, and in which it makes more profit compared to the other i.e. it has a **comparative advantage**. This advantage may stem from physical, technical, capital or labour resources.

For example, some countries such as the UK and Germany have capital resources and produce and export machinery and equipment. Others use their rich land resources to export raw materials or develop tourism, or use their cheap labour resources to produce labour-intensive products. Each country can use its resources to trade wherever it appears to have a comparative advantage over another nation. The principle of comparative advantage therefore helps to explain geographical differences in production and trade within and between countries.

This historical development of international trade led to the fundamental global contrast in wealth between the European/North American industrialised nations who became wealthy through dealing in manufactured goods, and the Asian/African/South American nations who concentrated on exporting raw materials/foodstuffs and were without the technology to evolve manufacturing exports themselves. The pattern was one of mutual dependence – the raw material producers became dependent on the advanced nations to buy their resources in order to earn some foreign income to pay for the manufactured goods they needed in order to develop.

> **Internationalisation**: the geographical spread of economic activities across national boundaries
> **Globalisation**: the functional and financial integration between internationally dispersed activities.

At the end of the twentieth century that contrast still exists between the More Economically Developed Countries (MEDCs) and Less Economically Developed Countries (LEDCs) but **globalisation** and **internationalisation** have transformed relationships between countries into a complicated web of interdependence – countries relying on each other to varying degrees.

The fundamental differences today are the *rate* at which the global system is evolving, and the *size* of the global system itself. No single country remains isolated. Each has economic connections of some kind with other countries. At the same time levels of inequality between and within nations have increased sharply. This issue is addressed in later chapters of this book.

FIGURE 1.3 Population, economic and environmental indices for selected countries

| Country | Population indices | | | | Economic indices (a) | | (b) | | | Environmental indices | | (c) |
| --- | --- | --- | --- | --- | --- | --- | --- | --- | --- | --- | --- | --- |
| | Population '000s 1995 | Pop growth rate % year | Life expectancy at birth | Infant Mortality rate | GNP per capita $ (1995) | Net flow of Aid $ per capita | Energy Use kg per capita 1994 | % pop in Agriculture 1990 | % pop in Industry 1990 | $CO_2$ emissions per capita | Annual deforest-ation % 1980–90 | HDI |
| Argentina | 34 665 | 1.3 | 73 | 22 | 8030 | 7 | 1504 | 12 | 32 | 3.5 | 0.1 | 0.884 |
| Bangladesh | 119 768 | 2.0 | 58 | 79 | 240 | 15 | 64 | 64 | 16 | 0.2 | 4.1 | 0.368 |
| Brazil | 159 222 | 1.6 | 67 | 44 | 3640 | 2 | 718 | 23 | 23 | 1.6 | 0.6 | 0.783 |
| Chile | 14 225 | 1.6 | 72 | 12 | 4160 | 11 | 1012 | 19 | 25 | 2.6 | −0.1 | 0.891 |
| China | 1 200 241 | 1.3 | 69 | 34 | 620 | 3 | 664 | 74 | 15 | 2.3 | 0.7 | 0.626 |
| Egypt | 58 800 | 2.2 | 63 | 56 | 790 | 47 | 600 | 43 | 23 | 1.5 | 0.0 | 0.614 |
| Ethiopia | 56 404 | 2.6 | 49 | 112 | 100 | 20 | 22 | 80 | 2 | 0.1 | 0.3 | 0.244 |
| France | 58 060 | 0.5 | 78 | 6 | 24 999 | na | 4042 | 5 | 29 | 6.3 | −0.1 | 0.946 |
| Germany | 81 869 | 0.5 | 76 | 6 | 27 510 | na | 4128 | 4 | 38 | 10.9 | −0.4 | 0.924 |
| Hong Kong | 6190 | 1.3 | 79 | 5 | 22 990 | 4 | 2185 | 1 | 37 | 5.0 | −0.5 | 0.914 |
| India | 929 358 | 1.9 | 62 | 68 | 340 | 3 | 248 | 64 | 16 | 0.9 | 0.6 | 0.446 |
| Indonesia | 193 277 | 1.7 | 64 | 51 | 980 | 9 | 366 | 57 | 14 | 1.0 | 1.1 | 0.668 |
| Japan | 125 213 | 0.4 | 80 | 4 | 39 640 | na | 3856 | 7 | 34 | 8.8 | 0.0 | 0.940 |
| Kenya | 26 688 | 2.9 | 58 | 58 | 280 | 26 | 110 | 80 | 7 | 0.2 | 0.6 | 0.463 |
| Nigeria | 111 273 | 2.9 | 53 | 80 | 260 | 2 | 162 | 43 | 8 | 0.9 | 0.7 | 0.393 |
| Pakistan | 129 905 | 3.0 | 60 | 90 | 460 | 13 | 254 | 26 | 31 | 0.6 | 3.5 | 0.445 |
| Poland | 38 612 | 0.4 | 70 | 14 | 2790 | 47 | 2401 | 27 | 36 | 8.9 | −0.1 | 0.834 |
| Saudi Arabia | 18 979 | 4.3 | 70 | 21 | 7040 | 1 | 4566 | 20 | 20 | 13.1 | 0.0 | 0.784 |
| South Africa | 41 457 | 2.3 | 64 | 50 | 3150 | 7 | 2146 | 14 | 32 | 7.5 | −0.8 | 0.716 |
| Thailand | 58 242 | 1.3 | 69 | 35 | 2740 | 10 | 769 | 64 | 14 | 2.0 | 3.5 | 0.833 |
| UK | 58 533 | 0.3 | 77 | 6 | 18 700 | na | 3722 | 2 | 29 | 9.8 | −1.1 | 0.931 |
| USA | 236 119 | 0.9 | 77 | 8 | 26 980 | na | 7819 | 3 | 28 | 19.1 | 0.1 | 0.942 |
| Venezuela | 21 671 | 2.4 | 71 | 23 | 3020 | 1 | 2186 | 12 | 28 | 5.7 | 1.2 | 0.861 |
| Zambia | 8978 | 2.6 | 46 | 109 | 3605 | 78 | 149 | 75 | 9 | 0.3 | 1.1 | 0.369 |

(a) Incoming aid minus outgoing aid
(b) Energy used equivalent to kgs.oil/capita
(c) Human Development Index (see page 77)

(Source: World Bank Atlas 1997, na – not applicable)

The historical developments of trade and colonial expansion have led to global contrasts in wealth and in rates of economic growth. These contrasts lead Geographers and Economists to *classify* countries into groups. We identify *criteria* to define an MEDC or an LEDC and look at the world pattern of MEDCs and LEDCs. We analyse the *changes* in that pattern over time.

We can use a variety of indicator data on population, social and economic activity, environmental activity which together can give a summary picture of the levels of development around the world.

The contrast between MEDCs and LEDCs can be stark. According to the World Bank, MEDCs have 17 per cent of world population, 64 per cent of world manufacturing industry and consume over 50 per cent of world energy. LEDCs have 80 per cent of world population, 14 per cent of world manufacturing and consume only 25 per cent of world energy. While these contrasts suggest a simple economic divide, they really emphasise the difference between the very rich and the very poor. Fig 1.3 shows the range of wealth indicators around the world.

There is a middle group of countries whose economic indices suggest a move towards the levels of MEDCs. These countries, often referred to as economic 'Tigers', are developing sizeable manufacturing bases forming a group of **Newly Industrialising Countries**, mainly located in Latin America and Asia. In the 1950s these countries were poor, with no industry and a low GNP. Now the original four 'Tigers' (Hong Kong, Singapore, Taiwan and South Korea) have reached Western levels of development, and the second wave are all well on their way (Malaysia, Thailand, Indonesia, Mexico and Brazil). It is in the LEDCs of Sub-Saharan Africa where there is less than 0.5 per cent of world manufacturing and where the highest levels of poverty occur.

---

**STUDENT ACTIVITY 2**

Look carefully at the data in Fig 1.3 which shows a number of population, economic and environmental indices for selected countries.
**1** Attempt to classify every country in the table into a small number of groups (between 3 and 5).
**2** Describe the characteristics of each group and justify your choice of criteria for each one.
**3** Justify your selection of countries into each group.
**4** Represent your groups of countries on a copy of the world map, Fig 1.4.
**5** Make three geographical statements about the map you have drawn.

---

## Trans-National Companies (TNCs)

The concept of globalisation has been generated by **transnational companies** i.e. those who engage in activities of all kinds in several countries. Their impact has been significant in both global and local terms. Many TNCs have a turnover larger than the GNP of some nations. General Motors, for instance, has a turnover of US$169 billion (see Figure 1.5). Most TNCs concentrate two-thirds of their activities in their home country, and many of the famous household names have clearly identifiable national identities. Governments and politicians cannot afford to ignore TNCs, and their complicated interrelationships with each other and national governments have created the **global economic system**. Decisions about long term global strategies of a company can be made in the US, Japan or Europe and have a crucial impact at a local level in South Wales, Sao Paulo or Bangkok.

FIGURE 1.4  World map

# It's bigger than Turkey, Thailand or Denmark – but it's not a country ...

In the late Seventies, a French civil servant declared that IBM had all the attributes it needed to become a world power.

But the truth is that, even diminished, IBM is *still* a world power. Its 1995 sales of $71.9 billion were greater than the GDP of all but 40 nation states – about the same as the Philippines and half as much again as Iran or Ireland.

IBM is just 18th among the world's biggest corporations. The real corporate leviathans – Japan's Mitsubishi and Mitsui, with sales of more than $180bn each – just miss the world's economic top 20, not far behind Indonesia and Sweden. Economically speaking, Mitsubishi is more than half the size of Russia or Australia.

This is not just abstract power. One commentator has written: 'By making ordinary business decisions, managers now have more power than most sovereign governments to determine where people will live; what work they will do – if any; what they will eat, drink and wear; what sorts of knowledge they will accumulate; and what kinds of society their children will inherit.'

In the conventional economic model, size doesn't matter so long as the company is accountable to the market.

But this doesn't work any more. Beyond a certain size companies are too big to be allowed to go bust.

Size *does* matter. None of these great corporate entities is accountable to those whose lives they affect, as the vast majority of national entities are.

*Observer 8.3.98*

Figure 1.5 The world's top economic entities

| Country/company by GDP/sales | $bn |
|---|---|
| 1 United States | 7100 |
| 2 Japan | 4964 |
| 3 Germany | 2252 |
| 4 France | 1451 |
| 5 United Kingdom | 1095 |
| 6 Italy | 1088 |
| 7 China | 745 |
| 8 Brazil | 580 |
| 9 Canada | 574 |
| 10 Spain | 532 |
| 11 South Korea | 435 |
| 12 Netherlands | 371 |
| 13 Australia | 338 |
| 14 Russia | 332 |
| 15 India | 320 |
| 16 Mexico | 305 |
| 17 Switzerland | 286 |
| 18 Argentina | 278 |
| 19 Taiwan | 260 |
| 20 Belgium | 251 |
| 21 Austria | 217 |
| 22 Sweden | 210 |
| 23 Indonesia | 190 |
| 24 Mitsubishi (Japan) | 184 |
| 25 Mitsui (Japan) | 181 |
| 26 Itochu (Japan) | 169 |
| 27 Turkey | 169 |
| 28 General Motors (US) | 169 |
| 29 Sumitomo (Japan) | 168 |
| 30 Marubeni (Japan) | 161 |

Figure 1.6 The influence of large transnational corporations

# Globalisation

Globalisation has been the outcome of the complex interactions between transnational corporations and nation-states in our technological age. The globalisation of production involves both governments and TNCs with foreign investment. It has changed not only the products we buy but their composition. The same product may be produced in a number of countries with the same characteristics and may also be assembled using components from several different countries.

The concept of globalisation is associated with the development of Newly Industrialised Countries and what has been called the **New International Division of Labour** (NIDL). This term relates both to manufacturing and to service industries. New products which require research and development are established in the countries with rich resources of capital and technology. When the product is ready for the global market it is often mass produced in another location where costs are lower i.e. there is some comparative advantage in that location. For instance cheap labour can reduce the cost of the product so much that it is cost-effective to transfer production thousands of miles to a new factory.

Since the 1980s this labour market has been found principally in South East Asia, hence the origin of the clothes, shoes, and goods we use. As factory and service workers earn more money, they themselves form a market for all kinds of products. China and India now present the greatest market opportunity ever seen as their expanding middle class populations with gradually rising disposable income are seeking western consumer goods. The influence of the West has led to demand for 'westernised' products such as telephones and computers, a change of diet to 'westernised' fast foods see Figs 1.7 and 1.8, and increasing expectations of continuing education into university.

In some cases international firms become firmly rooted in the national economy through joint ventures (where a company has a partnership with local firms or government concerns), then begin to produce specifically for a particular market.

Hewlett Packard began its first overseas expansion with a joint venture in Japan in 1963 with Yokogawa Electric Works. HP then identified items specifically for the Japanese market by working inside Japan.

MCDONALD'S Maharaja Mac does not figure in The Economist's Big Mac index. Being made of mutton, and not beef, it challenges the premise of purchasing-power parity: that a Big Mac is identical the world over, and therefore should cost the same in all countries. The McDonald's formula, hugely successful as it is, was always going to have to be adapted to a place where killing cows is sacrilege. But burger joints are not the only ones that need to be careful: other western firms tempted by India's growing middle class have had to be sensitive to the country's very definite tastes. McDonald's, which now has seven restaurants in India, was launched there a year ago. It has had to deal with a market that is 40% vegetarian; with the aversion to either beef or pork among meat-eaters; with a hostility to frozen meat and fish; with the general Indian fondness for spice with everything.

To satisfy such tastes, McDonald's has discovered that it needs to do more than provide the right burgers. Customers buying vegetarian burgers want to be sure that these are cooked in a separate area in the kitchen using separate utensils. Sauces like McMasala and McImli are on offer to satisfy the Indian taste for spice. McDonald's promises to introduce a spiced version of its fries soon.

Source: *The Economist*

FIGURE 1.8 A McDonald's outlet in S.E. Asia

FIGURE 1.7 Global McDonald's

## CASE STUDY

### Hewlett Packard

| | |
|---|---|
| Type: | Global electronics company – computer products, medical and engineering products, high value, world leaders |
| Home base: | Palo Alto in Silicon Valley, California |
| Production: | in 25 countries |
| Subsidiaries: | in over 120 countries |
| Size: | Revenue: $42.9 billion. 121 900 employees worldwide |
| Organisation: | decentralised to allow flexible responses to local situations |
| Key factors: | **Labour** – assembly plants in cheap labour locations, India/China. Skilled activities (Research and development (R&D)) in US |
| | **Markets** – factories in major markets to reduce transport costs. Fast response to customers. Opportunities to exploit local demands. |
| | Protectionism – national governments can limit imports therefore develop joint ventures. |
| | **Costs** – labour less than 2% value of product. Main costs are buying materials, organising manufacturing, efficient R&D |
| Strategies: | Intense global competition therefore collaboration with other electronic companies e.g. Hitachi. |

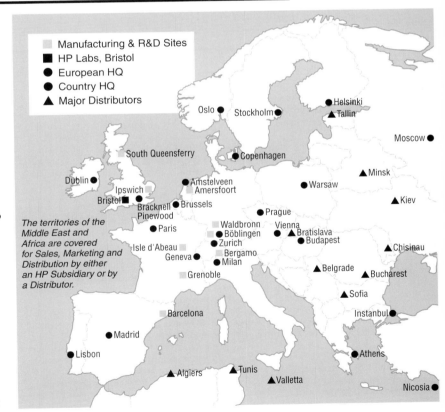

FIGURE 1.9 Location of Hewlett Packard operations in Europe

### STUDENT ACTIVITY 3

Comment and suggest reasons for the distribution of Hewlett Packard operations in
a) Europe (Fig 1.9)
b) the world (Fig 1.10)

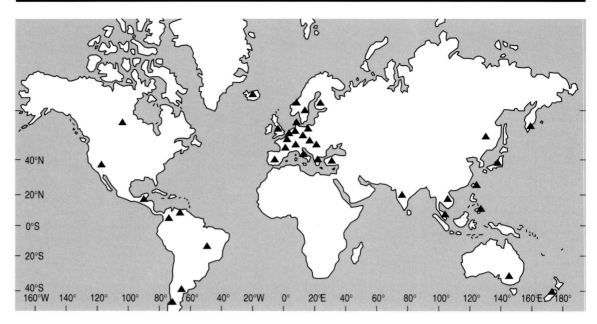

Strong commitment to research and development, plus ability to manufacture and market new technology quickly means that new products are constantly available. In 1996 over half company orders were for products introduced during the previous 2 years.

FIGURE 1.10  Location of Hewlett Packard operations worldwide

# Cheap labour at the end of a phone line

The European Commission and trade unions are beginning to worry about changes at a more global level. Swissair's ticket accounting, computer entry queries and discount scheme is carried out by 370 staff in one office – in Bombay.

The same centre is also doing the ticketing for Austrian Airlines, and the intention is to move more tasks there from Swissair's head office in Zurich. Behind the geographical shift is some hard-edged accounting: operations transferred to the office have achieved 50 per cent savings.

Similarly, Lufthansa and British Airways have transferred some of their data processing to areas with lower wage costs. BA has had a small unit in New Delhi since 1990 to overcome recruitment problems in the UK.

A number of big airlines have established Third World divisions to operate their administration in moves that seem certain to be copied in other industries that rely heavily on data processing. Trade unions contend that some large corporations are using Third World teleworkers, particularly in India, because of the much lower rates of pay.

American Airlines has much of its data processing undertaken in Barbados and the Dominican Republic.

'Ticket bookings will stay in the country of the passenger,' predicts Stuart Howard, secretary of the civil aviation section of the International Transport Workers' Federation. 'Other functions can be located anywhere. It is the kind of thing that other industries, such as garments and the auto industry, have been doing for some time, using electronic communications to enable them to relocate functions.'

Organised by the Labour Telematics teletrading will grow significantly as many large corporations cut their staffing, using the international labour market and part-time workers to create a more flexible workforce.

Examples of teletrade have so far mostly involved data processing, where comparatively low-paid work can be sent abroad to even lower-paid workers. It is predicted, though, that the greatest growth will be in occupations that attract higher salaries, such as accountancy and computer programming, where much greater cost savings can be achieved. A recent large contract for programming awarded by the Royal Bank of Scotland was won by Tatar, an India-based company.

*Independent 3.8.95*

The idea that comparative advantage stimulates trade is also seen in the service industries. The combination of cheaper labour and telecommunications has allowed many clerical tasks to be completed hundreds of miles from their originators. Textbooks may be written and sold in the US/UK with Hodder & Stoughton but have been printed in Hong Kong. A local call to an airline to check reservations may well be directed to Bombay where clerical workers have access to the same information on computer as their British counterparts but can be paid more cheaply (Fig 1.11).

---

### STUDENT ACTIVITY 4

Internet exercise: choose 2 or 3 transnational companies dealing in different products and search their web sites to identify their global operations. Map their global operations on a world map. Can you explain the world patterns you discover?

Try searching the following:

http://www.dupont.com/corp/world.html
http://www.shell.com/i/i.html
http://www.glaxowellcome.co.uk/world/research.html
http://www.hilton.com/sitemap/map.html
http://www.kimberly-clarke.com/who/scope
http://www.pg.com/about/overview/world.htm
http://www.cadburyschweppes.com/company-business/history-details.html

FIGURE 1.11  Unexpected locations for the West's office work

Banking and financial services are truly global. The world's key financial cities are Hong Kong, Singapore, Tokyo, London and New York and despite the time zones they trade 24 hours a day. Instant global communications have generated huge empires based on dealings in stocks and shares and speculation in the currency markets. Vast sums from one country are quickly invested in another yet equally rapidly withdrawn, creating great instability. Our interdependence is illustrated by the extent that financial crises can send alarm bells around the world. During the 1980s and 1990s there were waves of international panic generated by the Latin American Debt crisis in Mexico in 1982, the collapse of the BCCI (Bank of Credit Commerce International), the Yamaichi Securities scandal in Japan in 1997, and the International Monetary Fund support to keep Indonesia solvent in 1997/98.

# Economic change and employment

National economies evolve through time with changing characteristics of economic activity and employment. This evolution is shown in the **Sector Model** which identifies different sectors which change in size and relative importance (see Figure 1.12). **Primary sector** employment refers to those employed in the exploitation of naturally occurring resources. These would include extractive activities and agriculture. The **Secondary sector** includes manufacturing and construction, in which value is added to the materials produced by the primary sector. The **Tertiary sector** is concerned with a varied range of services. The sector includes consumer, producer and public services. Typical categories of services include retailing, distribution, and tourism. The most recent sector to be identified is the **Quaternary sector**. This specialises in the handling of information and organisation of business. It includes the professions, solicitors, accountants, and intellectual services, such as education and research and development.

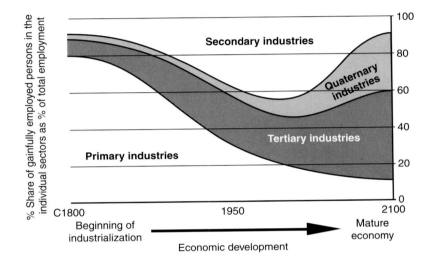

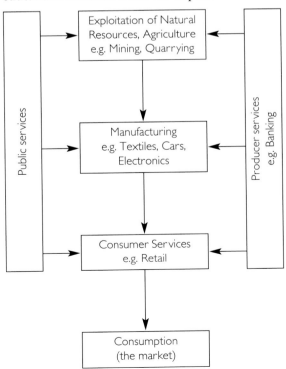

FIGURE 1.13 Inter-relationships of Economic Sectors

FIGURE 1.12 The sector model of economic development

The sector model emphasises the growth of the service sector and its significance in today's economies. However as economies have become more complex, recognition of clearly defined employment sectors is more difficult. For example a lawyer may be working for the research and development section of a large food processing firm. Fig 1.13 shows a way of illustrating the links between today's employment sectors, and the manner in which services to link to 'primary', 'secondary' and 'tertiary' sectors.

All countries pass through economic cycles of growth and decline. Even the wildly successful 'Tiger' economies have progressed through a similar pattern of growth and change and, despite all their best intentions, have also experienced recession. Industrialisation appeared to be the only path to development in the 1960s and 1970s but now it is apparent that it has created as many problems as it has solved. In MEDCs more people are employed in services and the decline of heavy industries has taken a heavy toll on communities particularly those established around steel and shipbuilding. The legacy of old industrial sites and contamination is one which MEDCs are finding difficult and expensive to deal with. In the NICs history is in danger of repeating itself but governments are unsure as to how to manage this threat to their new economic independence.

## Why do countries industrialise?

In order to increase national wealth and raise living standards, countries need to industrialise by using their resources and creating higher value manufactured products. Few experts would question whether industrialisation is the only way forward for national economies, and global patterns of the nineteenth and twentieth centuries lead to the conclusion that raw material/agricultural based economies have struggled to increase their GNP at the same rate as industrialising countries.

## Global inequalities

As countries develop, their industrial production patterns change and this tends to widen the gap between industrial and non-industrial economies. MEDCs have become more specialist and technically oriented, needing fewer workers and leading to increased unemployment. Specialist jobs require increased levels of education and training which are rewarded by higher salaries, and in turn that encourages local consumer industries. As the production process becomes more expensive, higher levels of investment are required, therefore larger firms (often TNCs) can dominate the market. The 'Tiger' economies of East Asia have also easily embraced new production patterns albeit with substantial financial government support.

FIGURE 1.14  The impact of influential global companies on local producers

In Eastern Europe countries such as Poland struggle to bring their economies into the global arena following the break up of the Comecon (Soviet) trading bloc. Here production patterns have been characterised by labour intensive/low technology, heavy industry, with inefficient production methods and a poorly trained and badly equipped workforce but there are visible signs of changing economies which should integrate Eastern Europe into the global system. Many foreign firms are concentrated in car making, such as Audi, Opel and VW and the industry has successfully adapted to western techniques. Audi and Opel aim to supply car components to assembly plants in Western Europe and are rapidly expanding their suppliers from within Eastern Europe. Labour costs are the big attraction. They make up only 1 per cent of the engine costs in Hungary compared with 8 per cent in Western Europe; there is less beaurocracy; 7-day working; cheap subcontracting of other services such as payroll, catering and security. Although economic prospects are good however, the principal factor limiting growth is the lack of a trained, qualified workforce – an issue which needs to be addressed by substantial government funding of education.

There is some underlying unease within Eastern Europe that foreigners may treat the region as 'Europe's Mexico' and become insensitive to social issues. Optimists see foreign investment as the most visible sign of the region's integration into the world economy and expect that it will be quickly overshadowed by the new generation of local companies set up since 1989. The case of Poland illustrates the tensions typical within these economies as they seek to raise productivity and standards of living, while at the same time improve conditions for everyone (Fig 1.14).

Sub-Saharan Africa takes least part in the global trading system. Competitive exchange rates, availability of foreign exchange and a reliable transport infrastructure are key elements in the expansion of trade, all of which are noticeably absent from several African nations. Only two-fifths of all foreign direct investment goes to LEDCs. Despite global trends, the volume of trade between Sub-Saharan Africa and the rest of the world fell in the mid 1980s and 1990s.

There is also disparity in countries' ability to attract foreign capital. Despite a ten-fold increase worldwide in capital flows, developing regions have fared unequally, with most expansion going to East Asia and Latin America. The World Bank estimates that more than half the population of the developing world remains untouched by this aspect of globalisation. China now receives the most foreign investment of all LEDCs, having received almost none in 1980. Direct investment in LEDCs used to be focused on extraction of natural resources, especially oil, but now the focus is on local consumer markets. As people become wealthier they can afford products such as cars and computers so TNCs place their investment in

# Poland's sweet smell of success

To hear Ronald Lauder tell it, the decision to open a high-profile boutique in Warsaw was nothing more than another of the intuitive moves that have made his family-owned **Estée Lauder** Companies a global force in the cosmetics and personal care products industry.

The Lauder store joins established company-operated boutiques, including Dior and Guerlain, in brightening up the grey streets of Warsaw.

According to the US Foreign Commercial Service in Warsaw, imports made up more than half of the estimated $110 million which Polish women spent last year on cosmetics. That figure is expected to increase despite high tariffs and competition from lower priced domestically produced creams, face powders and toiletry items.

Pressure from imports has thrown domestic producers into a scramble to retain their market shares and bring their products up to the standard of manufacturers in the West. Further still, those firms have had to cope with a loss of markets to the East. Poland was a leading cosmetic manufacturer among countries of the former Soviet Bloc.

The result has forced some collective producers out of the market while others have formed strategic partnerships with western companies.

'The influence of international companies is very big and it is becoming more competitive all the time', said Dariusz Grabowski, whose Cosmex firm rang up $2 million in sales last year.

Source: *The European* 19/11/93

growing markets such as Asia and Latin America. Africa, despite its rich natural resources, has received very little foreign investment because its consumers are so poor. The problems of mass illiteracy and high graduate unemployment hinder the development of a broad middle class that is the economic 'motor' in other emerging markets. Nevertheless, in the cities of Morocco and Egypt there are people with mobile phones and *Gucci* suits. Perhaps North Africa will become the emerging market of the early twenty-first century.

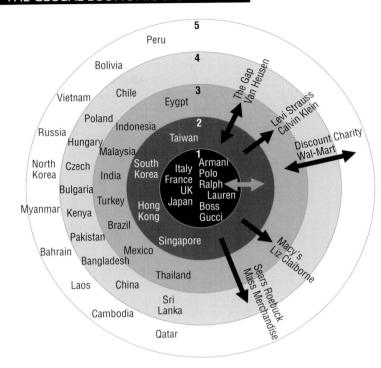

FIGURE 1.15 Clothing companies and retailers and their global sourcing

## CASE STUDY

### *Poland*

'Poland the first European Tiger: the reform process is secure and the economy is roaring ahead.'
*CBI news*, May 1994

'The reform process has been very good for the speculators and a few foreign firms. But large parts of the economy are in ruins and society groans under the onslaught of misdirected liberalism. We must not give away the national assets it took Poland 40 years to build.'
Editorial in *Gazeta Wyborcza*, 19 September 1994

*Before 1990* the State controlled 80 per cent of output, 70 per cent employment as well as sales of houses, food, and industrial goods. Heavy industry with huge, outdated plants dominated the economy; queues and shortages were common; the black market thrived; inflation reached 2000 per cent per year.

*In 1990* Poland's 'Big Bang' broke the ties with its communist past and its insularity from global markets, to be followed by economic growth, declining inflation and reduction in unemployment. The economic reforms have transformed much of Poland's economy particularly in food processing, construction and trade, as it opened up to international trade and investment. There was a rapid shift to the private sector with many foreign investments so that in 1993 and 1994 Poland had

Europe's highest GDP growth rate, and the world's best stock market performance. The private sector now produces over 50 per cent of GDP.

*But* while new investment and technology was dramatically changing the patterns of light industry, the huge state owned firms failed to respond even when foreign trade was encouraged to make state firms more competitive. Employees in private firms learned new skills, increased their productivity and wages gradually rose. These workers have formed the new consumer spending boom leaving workers in state industries far behind.

Krosno's glass factory is typical: old machines produced poor quality jugs, vases and glasses with very high energy costs, and with a dwindling market. The Government hesitated to close the factory, finding it easier to give more subsidies than increase unemployment. Although the glass workers took a cut in pay to stay in work ultimately that reduced some consumer spending power within Poland and restricted the growth of consumer industries.

Similar problems were occurring in the textile factories of Lodz, and state-owned steel mills near Krakow. Ultimately the inefficient businesses will not survive international competition and there will be increasing inequality between employees in modernised firms and those in state companies.

## Global trends

Liberalisation of trade and investment laws have contributed to a huge increase in the volume of world trade and foreign investment. Multilateral and regional agreements have led to market expansion and economic interdependence. As economies evolve at the millennium, different strands of change have emerged affecting patterns of production.

### The move towards globalisation of consumption

Products like Pepsi, McDonald's, Nike are consumed worldwide. The TNCs involved have created powerful and instantly recognisable brand names/logos by heavy advertising and marketing expenditure. This can effectively limit the success of small local producers who cannot match the advertising expenditure of the large company or sustain financial loss by selling at discount prices. In other words the TNC protects its position by creating 'barriers to entry'. This trade-led industrialisation is typical of labour intensive, consumer goods companies such as Nike, Reebok and Toys R Us, where there are complex networks to manufacture, package and ship from around the world.

### The move towards standardisation of products for mass consumption

High research and development costs can be recouped by making one product suitable for a world wide market. This is often the case with multinationals who specialise in providing components for big brand-name manufacturers. Intel's microchip and Bosch carburettors are typical examples. Production here is controlled by the producer and is typical of capital-intensive and technology-intensive industries such as cars, aircraft, computers, and electrical machinery.

### The move towards 'niche' marketing

In the affluent Developed countries individuals who have all their basic requirements can afford to buy exclusive goods. Those who are short of time can purchase convenience services. The small and select haute couture fashion market meets the demand of the wealthy to buy distinctive clothes with designer labels at very high prices. The aim here is conspicuous consumption. Value can be added to relatively cheap and ordinary products such as ready peeled oranges or packaged salads packaged with salad dressing and a knife and fork for the office worker.

### The move towards globalisation of economic policy

This has been particularly relevant since the 1980s when policies in China and Eastern Europe became unacceptable when they largely failed to deliver promised economic development. A second influence has been the overturning of state-led capitalism in favour of policies which emphasise free markets in goods and services.

Both moves have allowed greater independence to companies, particularly TNCs, to conduct business without constraints in a competitive climate, and to increase global investment and interdependence.

International agencies such as the IMF (International Monetary Fund) and the World Bank have also adopted a changed role. They have made Aid dependent upon the application of free market policies. In practice this has meant increased privatisation, freer financial markets, reducing government deficits and cutting back on barriers to international trade. The overall effect of these policies has been to make industries of all kinds more competitive, but has severely disadvantaged those countries who have little comparative advantage. The African nations are typical examples of countries who have been hard hit by global economic policy.

# The Global Economic System and the environment

The links between global development and the environment have become clearer over the last decade and as countries strive for economic growth the cost to the environment has been high. This problem is exacerbated by the fact the environmental cost is often not on our doorsteps in the developed world, and is frequently seen as someone else's problem. It is a paradox that physical resources, capital, labour, and technology are clearly identified as global but the environmental problems which have resulted from their exploitation are generally not.

The key issues are at both global and local scales. Climatic change, loss of biodiversity and protection of international waters attract global attention.

Equally important are the more local issues such as urban air and water pollution, deforestation, and soil degradation which occur in so many locations worldwide. Solutions to these environmental problems flounder because of the wide range of vested interests at stake, and because environmental protection is not necessarily cheap. However, sustainability of the environment requires cooperation at the highest levels, and the increase in the number of international agreements gives some cause for optimism.

One issue which caught the headlines in 1997–8 was 'Smog in South East Asia' caused by the extensive fires in tropical forests. It was not the slash and burn farmers who had been blamed in

1994, but plantation owners who cleared forests to produce palm oil and pulp and paper. The situation was made worse by the El Niño event of 1997–8 when seasonal rains and persistent light winds failed to disperse the intense smoke. While ASEAN has experienced rapid industrial globalisation and development, its governments remain politically weak and patriarchal, and wealthy businessmen, such as loggers, can hold significant influence over government actions. Many governments have yet to prove that they are taking their environmental responsibilities seriously.

Trans-national companies shoulder some of the blame for global environmental degradation. They are responsible for many of the world's ecological disasters such as the oil spill caused by Exxon Valdez in Prince William Sound, Alaska. In one of its latest reports UNCTC (the UN Centre for Trans National Corporations) disclosed that half of the gases responsible for the greenhouse effect were created by TNCs.

The issue of resource depletion is also waiting to be addressed. MEDCs have spent nearly 200 years depleting natural resources which formed the basis of much of their industrial development. Britain, among others, now has no iron ore, limited reserves of coal and oil, and is dependent on imports. Of all resources, energy without which modern economies cannot function, is the most critical. Often these resources are in inhospitable areas, underpopulated and isolated. Wilderness regions such as the Amazon Basin, Siberia, the Canadian Shield can provide a wealth of raw materials but on entering the twenty-first century their exploitation has environmental as well as economic implications. LEDCs are trapped between exploiting their resources for their own manufacturing development and feeding the insatiable demand from MEDCs, while at the same time trying to protect the environment. To balance these demands requires money – something that LEDCs don't have and that MEDCs are not prepared to spend.

The Earth Summit in Rio in 1992 and Kobe 1997 illustrate the double standards of wealthy nations. They would like the world environmental system to be protected and sustained, but appear to be unwilling to take the unpopular steps at home to reduce resource depletion and environmental damage, while heaping blame on LEDCs themselves for their high levels of environmental destruction and pollutants. The limited income earned by LEDCs does not enable them to take appropriate environmental protection measures and they are particularly worried that environmental issues may slow their economic growth. LEDCs also complain that richer nations have so far failed to help them either through Aid or technology.

However despite gloomy forecasts of environmental collapse there have been some local successes. Mexico is set to eliminate the sale of leaded petrol and Thailand is trying to phase out the 2-stroke motorcycles that account for over 50 per cent of the dirt in Bangkok's air. Water quality is improving, world health and life expectancy have increased, fertility rates and global emissions of lead, soot and CFCs have decreased.

# Summary

The global economic system affects every facet of human activity. On one hand, it draws economies together through very complex financial and manufacturing connections, and allows similar products and services to be marketed worldwide. On the other hand it increases inequality both within and between countries and creates new problems to be solved at the national, regional and global scale. The complex phenomenon of globalisation identifies and successfully utilises physical resources, capital, labour and world technology at the global scale. Whilst the attendant problems of hunger, disease, poverty, exploitation and environmental degradation have been identified, global action to provide solutions has been only partial.

# Key Ideas

- Globalisation is a dominant feature of current economic systems
- Geographical differences within the global economic system are explained by the principle of comparative advantage
- Globalisation has increased economic, social and spatial inequalities
- Globalisation has created new global scale organisations; Trans-National Companies
- Development of the Global economic system has implications for the global environment

# 2
# RURAL ENVIRONMENTS

## Primary Production Systems

FIGURE 2.1 Rural-based primary production systems

| System | Physical inputs | + | Process impacts | = | Outputs |
|---|---|---|---|---|---|
| Farming | climate/soil | | control plants/animals | | food/raw materials |
| Forestry | tree stands | | afforestation/deforestation | | timber/pulp |
| Mines/quarries | rocks/minerals | | sinking/stripping/cutting | | fuels/minerals |
| Water | rivers/lakes | | storage and abstraction | | domestic/industrial |

FIGURE 2.2 Landscape types

| Rural urban fringe | Farmscape | Marginal fringe | Wildscape |
|---|---|---|---|
| Inner rural | Inner rural | Outer rural | Outer rural |
| *penetration by* | *farm systems at* | *several competing* | *environmental* |
| *urban elements* | *varied intensities* | *extensive land-uses* | *limitations evident* |
| housing estates | satellite villages | isolated village | hamlets and farms |

Definition: landscape is a part of the earth's surface which we can comprehend in a single view – usually an air-photograph and/or map.

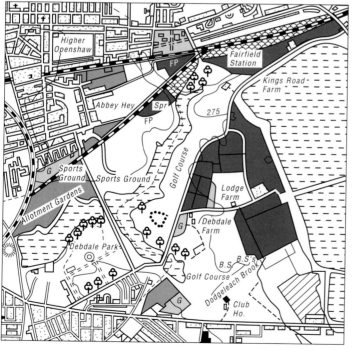

Settlement Commercial and residential

Allotment Gardens

Rough land

G   Grass moor

Unvegetated

Grassland

Open space tended but unproductive land

Water

Industry public utilities

Transport port areas airfield

0 ⊢———————⊢———————⊣ 1/2 mile   1Km

**Rural regions** are home to several vital **primary production** systems. Each region is a land-use 'jigsaw' of production systems and settlements, all competing for land. Where the physical environment offers opportunities for primary production and resource development – fossil fuels, softwood timber, alluvial soils, water surplus catchments – a focus for investment and production may develop, making an impact on the landscape. To these fixed physical inputs are added human economic ones: capital – to buy land and machinery; labour – to operate the system; transport networks – connecting production to the demand of the markets; and so production starts, jobs are generated and impacts appear. Rural regions are increasingly attractive to leisure and tourist investments, as well as return migrants.

## Rural regions – landscapes in the UK

The variety of rural regions can be understood by linking photographs and OS maps to a classification developed by Alice Coleman.

FIGURE 2.3 Rural urban fringe where town and country meet

FIGURE 2.4 Wildscape
and marginal fringe:
Mynydd Hiraethog

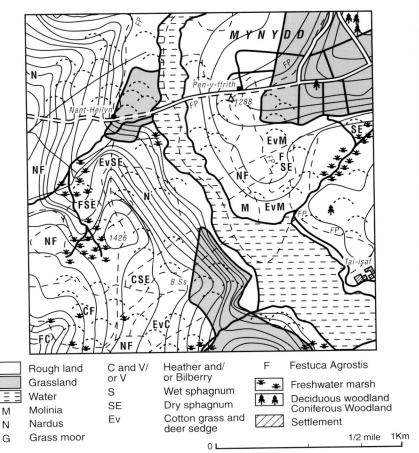

## Wildscape – the natural environment is dominant

This is land dominated by natural or partially modified vegetation. Trees are stunted and grass is in tussocks. It is distinct from areas where the results of human activities are dominant. Large areas are often undrained and there are no clear boundaries. Upper slopes may be characteristically exposed rock while below are screes of loose rock. Increasingly in the UK these areas are used for leisure, and this has distinctive impacts. Developments such as the Aviemore ski-centre may provide local employment but the stimulus is mainly investment from distant urban centres. Such uses present a problem of definition. If the land is used seasonally, is it truly wild? Wildscape differs from farmscape because although it is used, it is not created for use, as are the richer lowland farmscapes areas and, to a lesser extent, the marginal fringe.

## Marginal fringe – 'tamed' wildscape

This is a 'zone of transition' between farmscape and wildscape. Visually it presents a face of improved and unimproved land where forestry, water resources and quarrying compete for space. Individual farms are few and widely dispersed. Settlements are hamlets rather than villages. The isolated village will tend to have a higher proportion of second homes, perhaps unused in off-season periods. These changes are clearly observed in Upland Britain.

## Farmscape – out into the countryside

This category dominates our perception and imagery of rural landscape. Visually it is full of farming, although there may be other non-agricultural elements, for example reservoirs and quarries. The landscape has clearly been improved for effective and efficient operation of these production systems. This is most evident in the **field system**. This formal arrangement or layout and use of the fields is a synthesis of physical conditions – relief and drainage, and climate and soils, the land tenure system – who owns the land and how it is divided up legally. The influence of farming on rural settlements has declined markedly. For example mechanisation of farm processes means fewer farm-hands while the number of commuters, in **gentrified** villages, has increased.

FIGURE 2.5 Farmscape:
Sutton in Derwent

The **satellite village** has a housing stock, released by farm amalgamations, and now available for commuters. Not all low-order settlements are based on farming. For example in the South-West many prospered from tin mining (Camborne) and others from fishing (Newlyn).

### Rural urban fringe – on the edge of town

The city casts a shadow over this zone. The landscape may appear largely rural to the eye, but it contains economic features, related to the extension of the city, and it could also be described as a 'zone of transition'. The conversion of the landscape is clearly recognisable. A predominantly rural area may contain evidence of urban economic systems. Public services such as hospitals and sewage works, estates of retail, industrial and residential activity are developed on 'greenfield' sites. Leisure services are common. Farmland may become golf courses and attract leisure centres. The comparative advantage of proximity to the urban centre and efficient infrastructure of by-passes and motorway links may encourage the rural fringe to be so dominated by urban elements it is incorporated into the town or city 'economic system'.

## Rural regions cannot be separated economically from urban areas

As economic development continues, the influence of cities grows. Industrialisation also revolutionises life in **rural regions**. Changes occur in rural production – new non-agricultural jobs and skills replace declining trades. Population structure changes as newcomers 'rub shoulders' with locals. Settlement sizes and functions alter as farming villages become satellite suburbs.

In towns and cities much more expensive land is a platform for commerce and manufacturing, rather than a working part of an economic system. In the countryside primary production is tied to the land.

Rural regions may be contrasted with urban areas as parts of a country where the major production systems are dominated by fixed inputs of land e.g. farming/forestry/water supply.'

The rural situation is becoming more complex. Adding to the primary production base is a rapidly developing service sector in leisure and tourism.

# Farming – the main primary production system in rural environments

Farms can be described as systems and grouped into categories by their most important enterprise (pastoral/livestock, arable or cropping, and mixed), and further classified by input level, process mode and output location.

Farming regions develop where a particular system has a **comparative advantage**. In this way associations between production and location build up, for example mechanised cereal production in mid-latitude grasslands.

Each form of agricultural activity has optimum environmental conditions, which often occur in several global locations. Away from the cores of these areas, productivity will decline as the comparative advantages diminish. Eventually a point is reached where the income from farming drops to the level of production costs. Economic rent (income from farming) is then zero, and the logical **margin of production** has been reached. In practice precise logical boundaries of production are rare. An output is likely to come out of production before the economic margin is reached. The reason for this is that alternative land-uses become more profitable, since land may be economically marginal for one type of production but not all types. (See 'Land-use theories'.)

Land may also be marginal in a biological or environmental sense, where conditions are beyond the normal tolerance of a crop or livestock. For example attempts have been made to extend cereal production into areas most suited to extensive livestock rearing. In Australia, the south west USA and former USSR (during the Virgin lands campaign) cereals were grown where the environment was physically marginal i.e. close to the limits of crop tolerance. Production was possible but eventually abandoned because yields were so low that farming was unprofitable. Margins may be pressurised by policies, grants and subsidies.

---

**STUDENT ACTIVITY**

**1** Study Figure 2.6 which shows the relative importance of inputs, processes and outputs in contrasting **global locations**.
**2** Using these concepts (inputs, processes and outputs) develop contrasting systems diagrams for **UK locations**, e.g. livestock farming on Dartmoor and agribusiness in East Anglia or The Fens (see 'Rural environments and the role of Agriculture' – contrasting case studies).

The sizes of the boxes suggests their relative importance

FIGURE 2.6 Farms as systems

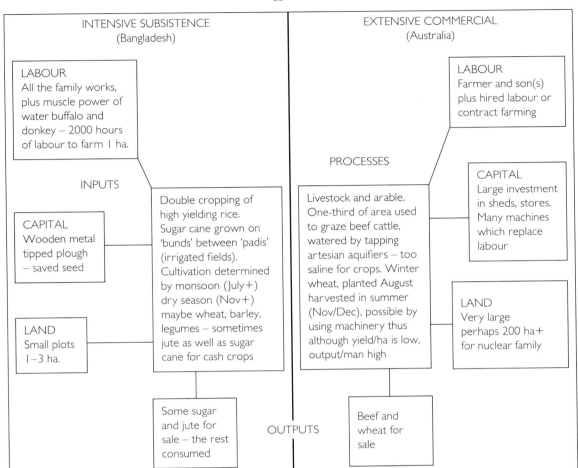

In a good year the subsistence farmer may have a small cash surplus. In a bad year hunger may give way to famine. Usually outputs balance inputs so there is stability, but no possibility of introducing change by the purchase of superior inputs. Various concepts are used to describe this situation. The farmer is said to be in a vicious circle – the system has negative feedback – attitudes are conservative and the mode of production is satisficing. Most years the commercial farmer will be able to

contemplate changes in order to improve the system. Much will depend on experience, but innovations may come via advisory services and perhaps state and government initiatives. Change is normal except in unusual circumstances such as losses due to natural hazards. The farmer is in a virtuous cycle – the system has positive feedback. Open attitudes favour change to optimise production.

FIGURE 2.7 Farm systems and key concepts

| SYSTEMS APPROACH | KEY CONCEPTS | | |
|---|---|---|---|
| **I. INPUT LEVEL**<br>determined by resource value<br>e.g. fertile/infertile soils | **INTENSIVE**<br>high levels of inputs<br>especially capital or labour | OR | **EXTENSIVE**<br>low levels of inputs<br>especially labour |
| **2. PROCESS MODE**<br>related to level of economic<br>development (MEDC/LEDC) | **COMMERCIAL**<br>outputs for sale<br>ie marketed | OR | **SUBSISTENCE**<br>outputs retained<br>ie consumed |
| **OUTPUT LOCATIONS**<br>combining I & 2<br>in contrasting environmental<br>zonal locations | **TEMPERATE**<br>e.g. *intensive commercial*<br>pig farming in<br>*temperate* Denmark<br>or<br>e.g. extensive commercial<br>ranching in Australia | OR | **TROPICAL**<br>e.g. *extensive subsistence*<br>nomadism in the<br>*tropical* Sahel<br>or<br>intensive commercial<br>sugar growing in Brazil |

| GROUPS | | | | | |
|---|---|---|---|---|---|
| **C R O P P I N G** | TEMPERATE | Commercial | Intensive | glasshouse production of salad vegetables on Dutch polderlands |
| | | | Extensive | mechanised cereal production in American mid-west |
| | | Subsistence | Intensive | Scottish crofting movement |
| | | | Extensive | no examples |
| | TROPICAL | Commercial | Intensive | rubber plantations in Malaysia |
| | | | Extensive | no examples |
| | | Subsistence | Intensive | irrigated (padi) rice-cultivation in SE Asia |
| | | | Extensive | shifting cultivation in less accessible areas of rainforest |
| **L I V E S T O C K** | TEMPERATE | Commercial | Intensive | dairy farming in the Irish republic (Eire) |
| | | | Extensive | cattle ranching on the High Plains of the American West (Wyoming) |
| | | Subsistence | Intensive | no examples |
| | | | Extensive | Lapland reindeer herding |
| | TROPICAL | Commercial | Intensive | dairy farming in the Kenyan highlands |
| | | | Extensive | beef cattle in Australian outback (Queensland & N. Territories) |
| | | Subsistence | Intensive | no examples |
| | | | Extensive | nomadic cattle rearing in West (Fulani) and East (Masai) Africa |
| **M I X E D** | TEMPERATE | Commercial | Intensive | 'hogging-down' corn in US mid-West |
| | | | Extensive | wheat/sheep farming in South Australia |
| | | Subsistence | Intensive | no examples |
| | | | Extensive | no examples |
| | TROPICAL | Commercial | Intensive | communes in Southern China |
| | | | Extensive | no examples |
| | | Subsistence | Intensive | shifting garden production (taro/sweet potatoes/pork) Solomon islands |
| | | | Extensive | no examples |

## MEDC Farm systems – England & Wales

Look at Figures 2.9 and 2.10
Each system has particular physical inputs which link it to the rural environment, and each is dominant in different regions see Figs 2.11 and 2.12.

■ **Livestock farming (beef cattle and sheep) covers the largest area**
It is the preferred option in marginal land where there is less choice of alternatives so it is associated with upland Britain, for example Dartmoor. These systems are *severely CONSTRAINED in output by the physical inputs* – steep slopes, higher altitude therefore lower temperatures/shorter growing season, heavy rainfall with high totals, which reduce sunlight, immature soils which are often thin and infertile

■ **Dairy farming (dairy cattle) is a regional specialisation**
The system is regionally *CONFINED by the distribution of key physical inputs*. There is a longer growing season in the milder West, plus a high water-table resulting from adequate regular rainfall, so grass grows best in the West.

FIGURE 2.8  Key concepts used to develop a classification

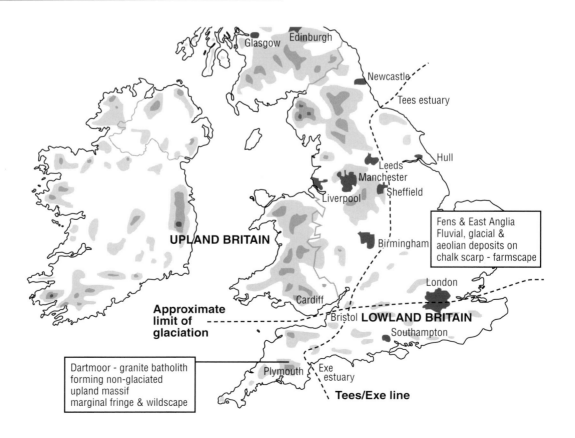

Fens & East Anglia
Fluvial, glacial & aeolian deposits on chalk scarp - farmscape

UPLAND BRITAIN

LOWLAND BRITAIN

Approximate limit of glaciation

Dartmoor - granite batholith forming non-glaciated upland massif marginal fringe & wildscape

Tees/Exe line

Glasgow  Edinburgh  Newcastle  Tees estuary  Hull  Leeds  Manchester  Sheffield  Liverpool  Birmingham  London  Cardiff  Bristol  Southampton  Plymouth  Exe estuary

FIGURE 2.9a  Farm systems in England and Wales

FIGURE 2.9b
Environmental contrasts
in England and Wales

## UPLAND ENVIRONMENTS

old hard resistant rocks
igneous & metamorphic
old sedimentaries up to & including
Carboniferous series (coal & limestone)

dominated by upland relief of moors
& mountains – flat summits and steep
sides – lowland in river valleys and
along coasts – use of machines very limited

relief precipitation and lower temperatures
high cloud amounts – high incidence of frost
shorter growing season – livestock better
option than cropping

soil poorly developed – formation slow
glacial erosion – high levels of acidity

## LOWLAND ENVIRONMENTS

newer less-resistant rocks
younger (post-Carboniferous) sedimentaries
folded into basins and anticlines emphasised
by relative resistance to erosion

dominated by ridges of low hills (escarpments)
separated by clay vales. In East Anglia this
base is masked by a variety of deposits,
varied soils but responsive to working

rain-shadow of upland Britain, drier
warmer continental influences result in
higher summer temperatures. This plus low
relief & soils makes cropping attractive

South of maximum glaciation, soils follow
scarpland catena patterns

These advantages would be of little value without effective marketing mechanisms such as Milk Marque, the privatised version of the Milk Marketing Board, whose blanket pricing system effectively subsidises production in more remote locations.

These human factors enable farmers to take advantage of the physical environment.

■ **Crop farming** has much greater variety of outputs than dairying – *the characteristics of the systems are CONDITIONED* by the physical environment rather than constrained (livestock) or confined (dairying).

Compare West and East in both North and South. This shows the difference between. moderate maritime influences in the West and continental influences in the East plus the general effect of latitude.

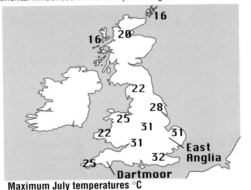

Maximum July temperatures °C

FIGURE 2.10 Temperature
contrast in the British
Isles

FIGURE 2.11 Features of
British and Welsh
farming

| Dominant systems | Environment elements | Production elements |
|---|---|---|
| (I) **Livestock** – beef/sheep dominant in upland upland e.g. Dartmoor *relief dominant* | more exposed – higher, wetter, cooler, shorter growing season steep slopes – leached thin soils, mechanisation limited | extensive – cheap land inaccessible, marginal for farming – alternative land-uses e.g. forestry |
| (ii) **Cropping**/arable dominant lowland areas e.g. Cambridgeshire and E. Anglia and the Fens *continental climatic influences dominant* | sheltered in rain-shadow of upland Britain, drier, warmer, longer growing season, mature soils respond to inputs – 'prairie' landscape enables fully mechanised systems | intensive – valuable accessible land – attractive to agribusiness profitable for a wide variety of products, strongly linked to supermarkets and food processing industries |
| (iii) **Dairy farming** dominant lowland areas of West, where growing season is lengthened *maritime climatic influences dominant* | higher average winter temps reliable regular rainfall = high water table in colluvial soils encourages pasture and fodder mechanised milking traditional landscape-hedges | intensive–investment in stock overshadows machinery – fresh milk marketing depends on accessibility – dairy products (weight-loss) marketed via creameries and supermarket chains |
| (iv) **Mixed farming** loosely aligned along NW/SE urban axis between pastoral West and arable East regions | inside many counties is a wide variety of soils, relief and climate – local adaptation results in a 'tailoring' of systems to detail e.g. aspect | location balanced between environmental constraints of West and economic opportunities of East, proximity to urban markets and food processors |

**Crop Combinations**

**L** = livestock
     (sheep, beef cattle)
**D** = diary farming
**C** = crops

**P** = pigs/poultry
**H** = horticulture/
     market gardening
**M** = mixed

**Dominant Enterprise**

☐ Livestock
≡ Cropping
┄ Dairy farming
■ Mixed

FIGURE 2.12 Farm
production in England
and Wales

*Inorganic chemical fertilisers* were developed to
replace the nutrients removed by harvesting in
agro-ecosystems. Crops require nutrients chiefly
varying quantities of six major elements – calcium,
magnesium, sulphur and especially nitrogen,
phosphorous and potassium – as well as smaller
amounts of trace elements. Traditional use of
organic substances such as manure has been
replaced, by the application of artificial fertilisers,
in the pursuit of increased production.

*Hybrid seeds* are developed by cross-breeding to
achieve improved hardiness, growth rate or yield.
This technique which began in the American mid-
West with maize, has worldwide application. The
success of hybridisation techniques strengthens the
arguments for genetic conservation and biodiversity
– the retention of plants and animals for the
purpose of safeguarding their genetic information.

*Selective breeding* has similar aims to hybridisation
but is more generalised in approach and includes
livestock. New genetic lines with desirable
inheritable characteristics are achieved by means of
crossbreeding, using natural and artificial
fertilisation. Desirable characteristics are those
which aid selling, for example standard-sized pigs
and poultry, produced in minimum time in
batteries or on feedlots.

*Genetic engineering or modification* (GM) involves
mixing genes across species in a way unknown in
nature. It is not therefore a continuation of selective
breeding but a radical new technology creating a
highly sensitive issue. GM crops produce GM foods
which one supermarket (Iceland) has pledged not to
sell. Monsanto, the US-based multinational most
responsible for the genetics revolution, has
launched a £1 million advertising campaign to
shore up its image. Surveys in Britain indicate that
three-quarters of consumers want a moratorium on
the planting of GM crops until further research has
been done, and nearly two-thirds do not want to eat
GM foods. GM is perceived as being unnatural
selection.

## MEDCs – changes and issues

Rural production systems, especially farming, have
been revolutionised by the development process.

*Input changes – Appliance of science and
technology*

FIGURE 2.13

| Inputs changes | Processes changes | Output changes |
|---|---|---|
| *Applied science & technology:* | *Intensification:* | *From supply to demand:* |
| *Inorganic chemical fertilisers* | *Mechanisation* | *Market forces* |
| *Hybrids* and *selective breeding* | *Specialist production* | *Government food* |
| *Genetic engineering* | and *environmental controls* | *policies (CAP)* |

| Input issues | Process issues | Output issues |
|---|---|---|
| *Environmental concerns:* | *The costs of change:* | *Future of the countryside:* |
| *Soil erosion* | *Economies of scale* | *Environmental adaptation* |
| *Water pollution* | *Food and health* | *Long-term management* |
| | *Organic farming* | |

## Input issues – Environmental concerns

*Soil erosion* – intensive cropping methods deplete plant nutrients, so humus, which binds soil and is provided by natural manure, becomes scarce. Soil structure deteriorates and there is a risk of both water and wind erosion especially in enlarged fields, on lighter soils, in spells of drier weather.

*Water pollution* – Chemicals also infiltrate aquifers and groundwater. Slow rates of seepage may result in long-term problems affecting the quality of drinking water. High levels of nitrate in drinking water have been linked to stomach cancer, hypertension in children and birth defects.

## Process changes – Intensification

**Intensive agriculture** describes systems with high levels of inputs which achieve high levels of outputs/production from each unit of land.

- productivity may be measured as output per unit of input (land/labour/capital),
- productivity measured in output per unit of land area is referred to as yield.

Intensive methods tend to encourage concentration of investment in the better suited areas (for example East Anglia and Region 2, Zimbabwe) at the expense of marginal or peripheral areas. Within the favoured areas farms tend to specialise in the most profitable enterprise. Market gardening and dairy farming are both typical MEDC intensive systems (see Fig 2.15 and related Student Activity).

*Mechanisation* – reduces labour costs, increases yields and results in greater productivity. As development continues farming tends to shift from labour (people) intensive to capital (machine) intensive methods. Historically, the spread of tractors and combine harvesters have been bench-marks in this trend. For example:

| Western Europe before 1939 | 20 000 tractors |
| Western Europe mid-1950 | 2 millions |
| European Union by 1983 | 5.4 million |

## Specialist production

- *Glasshouses* provide a sheltered environment in which physical inputs can be closely controlled. By regulating the physical inputs (moisture, ventilation, carbon dioxide enrichment and artificial heating) high quality produce can be grown out-of-season when prices are higher.
- *Hydroponics* takes this trend further. Plants are grown, under glass, in peat or gravel through which nutrient-rich solutions are pumped. The growing season is minimised, plant densities are maximised

and so unit costs are reduced. Production is continuous and automated resembling a factory.

- *Factory farming* methods have been most widely adopted in the production of pigs and poultry (sometimes called battery farming). Specialised buildings house high densities of animals, especially chickens. Temperatures, ventilation and lighting are carefully controlled. Feeding is computer controlled and developed for the stock in question. By reducing the land area needed and controlling the production processes, the system is optimised.
- *Feedlots* are relatively small areas of land for fattening or finishing off animals, usually cattle. The stocking densities are very high. Fodder is brought in as concentrates and roughages to promote rapid weight gain and lean meat. The spread of this fattening technique is linked to the development of high-yielding cereals, which keep the price of fodder down.

The development of technology and growth of **scientific knowledge** encourages and enables production systems to achieve the best possible economic return. This optimising approach may be contrasted with a more traditional satisfier outlook.

## Process issues – the costs of change

*Economies of scale* – machines achieve greater reductions in cost when they operate on larger fields, an economy of scale. Removing hedges is a logical production response, but the consequences for the environment are:
- loss of hedgerow habitats;
- loss of the sheltering effects of hedges, promoting wind and water erosion, especially with spring-sown crops.

Moreover modern machines are very heavy and soils suffer. Peds are compressed, porosity is reduced and runoff increases. Ploughing up permanent pasture has similar consequences.

*Food and health* – the demand for basic foods has decreased with the rise in standards of living. Advertising seeks to create demand by linking food to diet and health issues. Sales can be markedly affected by the media, for example salmonella in eggs and the BSE issue which highlights the dangers involved in interfering with the food chain. The growth of organic farming is in part a consumer-led reaction. Many people are worried about chemical residues in food and therefore switch to food produced by what is perceived to be a healthier system. Thus a market niche has developed despite higher food prices.

FIGURE 2.14

| Optimiser – Agribusiness | Satisficer – Traditionalist |
| --- | --- |
| maximising yields for greatest profit | profit sufficient to meet needs |
| investment, conscious application of science | adaptation to main perceived trends |
| forward-looking and innovative | practical, conventional but efficient |
| main priority wealth creation | main priority stability and continuity |

■ *Organic farming* is a more recent trend based on a return to sustainable production methods which use less energy, natural fertilisers and no artificial stimulants to growth. Organic farmers tend to be owner-occupiers of smaller holdings. Many are first time farmers. In the UK, they are geographically concentrated in the South-West and West Wales, nowhere are they an important regional enterprise. Only about 0.3 per cent of Britain's farmland is under organic cultivation, and is increasing at 11 per cent per annum. Other EU member are converting much more quickly – for example in Austria 11.5 per cent of the land is organically farmed and the area is doubling each year. Organic production is less efficient. Yields are lower (10 to 20 per cent) because it is less intensive and uses few chemical inputs and profitability is questionable.

### Output changes – from supply to demand

*Market forces* – development and larger changes in society have shifted our perception of agriculture from a supply to a demand led system. The link between farm and supermarket shelf is all important. For example in 1988 at Whitehall farm in the Cambridgeshire fens, Hassey Carrot Growers was set up to guarantee 'soil to supermarket' supply within 24 hours. The efficiency of this service is maintained by using imported carrots if necessary. Many farms produce high quality outputs. In the UK over 60 per cent of agricultural production is carried out under contract to food-processing firms and supermarket chains. The farm is becoming an element in a larger agro-industrial system controlled by corporate business with a high degree of vertical linkage.

*Government food policies* – The success and continuity of agricultural production systems in MEDCs is often affected by government policies. Food policies in Europe and North America are mainly concerned with market regulation of outputs rather than concerning themselves with issues arising from inputs and production processes. The main reasons for this have been to secure domestic food supply and encourage efficiency of production. Their success has led to rising costs for the taxpayer, food surpluses and taking the land out of production. For example, the EU Common Agricultural Policy (CAP) is by far the most expensive item of the EU budget. Initially CAP had four main protective aims:

■ to secure food supplies – threatened in the Second World War;
■ to enable EU countries to supply and feed themselves if possible;
■ to stabilise production using:
   guaranteed prices
   intervention buying to keep prices up
   storage of resulting surpluses
   subsidies on farm inputs and operating costs.
■ to ensure a fair standard of living for farmers who were more numerous and politically important in the 1950s than today (20 per cent of labour force in 1957, now 4–5 per cent) with a legacy of rural deprivation.

In the 1990s there has been a shift towards policies which prevent surpluses arising rather than disposing of them – for example:

■ reduction of price support – for example cereals and beef prices dropped 29 per cent and 19 per cent respectively between 1993 and 1996;
■ set-aside – payments for taking land out of production, similar to US soil banks;
■ quota changes – for example milk quotas reduced by 2 per cent;
■ financial support for other land-uses, i.e. diversification of business into leisure and tourism (golf and holiday homes).

### Output issues – the future of the countryside

#### Environmental adaptation

*Large-scale modification* – while extension of cultivated areas was a continuous theme of early development, the impact of modern farming goes beyond the destruction of local habitats and soil structures to much larger regional scales of landscape modification. Examples include the reclamation of the Dutch polderlands and extension of irrigation along the Colorado river in the south west US.

*Partial modification* – in areas of existing farmland which has suffered from physical and economic dereliction co-ordinating policies may be used to change the land use as a means of economic regeneration. In south eastern USA, the Tennessee Valley Authority has pioneered conservation techniques of shelter belts and afforestation of watersheds, contour ploughing and soil banks (a form of set-aside), dry and 'trash' farming techniques. Similar remedial measures have been applied in problem rural regions such as the Mezzogiorno of Southern Italy.

---

### STUDENT ACTIVITY

'Agribusiness essentially involves the application of modern methods of organisation and technology, to the creation of vertically-integrated enterprises handling agricultural products from the farm to the consumer. Multinational agribusiness is concerned not only with the production, processing, packing and transport of goods from their sources of origin, but also with marketing and distribution, usually in the developed world.'

1  Using examples, describe briefly three important characteristics of 'agribusiness'.
2  Choose two different agricultural systems and show how each might be affected by the development of agribusiness
3  Consider the environmental and social costs and benefits which have arisen from intensification.

*Longer term management*

The distinction between urban and rural is not clear anymore. Development and accessibility are remodelling settlements and production systems in rural regions. Suburban features (greenfield sites, industrial and housing estates), usually associated with the fringe of city-regions, are now replicated where practicable in farmscape locations, for example the market towns of East Anglia. The translation of these urban elements to rural locations accompanies counterurbanisation, the decentralisation of urban regions. This means that jobs and homes in rural regions are no longer dominated by primary production systems. In marginal fringes, leisure and tourism have expanded, adding and linking service occupations to primary production systems – for example purpose-built 'timeshare' homes in the afforested areas of National Parks (Lake District) and the development of sailing facilities on Water Authority reservoirs (Kielder, Northumberland).

The diversification of farming is a part of these economic adaptations as farmers search for a stable national economic role in the countryside. At the purely local scale farmers may well become guardians of the countryside, whose function could be to smooth the rough edges of modern farm technology, supported by stewardship grants.

## LEDCs – Rural economies

More than two-thirds of the world's population live in LEDCs and the majority of them are engaged in agriculture. Their systems are not nearly so productive, see Fig 2.15.

Much of LEDC farming is in subsistence mode, so production does not affect **AGDP** (Agricultural Gross Domestic Product). Food shortages are common, locally caused by famines, wars and refugees, but generally caused by:

- high population growth, itself the result of – declining death rates, coupled with high fertility rates, since many LEDC populations are in the early (2) or late expanding (3) stages of population transition;
- climate failure drought (especially in Africa South of the Sahara) and desertification
- environmental hazards such as flooding and pests;

- poor quality of inputs to farm systems – linked to land shortages;
- instability – civil wars and refugees.

However commercial agriculture is increasing, especially in the more stable countries where the general development of other sectors is taking place – for example Venezuela, an OPEC member, has developed commercial beef rearing on the Llanos, in the outer periphery of the Orinoco valley. Despite the endemic problems of tropical grasslands such as the rainfall unreliability and seasonal concentration and flooding of the riverine pastures, better quality production is now well established and there is a limited export trade. Comparisons with MEDCs are difficult because protectionist measures inflate AGDP, as for example in the EU.

At the macro-scale regional contrasts are evident, see Fig 2.16.

- extensive systems dominate much of tropical Africa pastoral nomadism and shifting cultivation cover large areas of grassland and forest producing low output levels. Large areas of Africa are difficult to farm, for example the Sahel and the dry veld of Western Zimbabwe – (Region 4).
   exceptions include highland areas such as Eastern Zimbabwe (Region 2), where investment has been attracted to the more favourable environmental conditions.
- Intensive systems dominate SE Asia – irrigated rice cultivation is the most important system dominating the river valleys throughout this most densely populated region – exceptions include Cambodia and Laos
- Latin America has a small proportion of cultivated land, but a high proportion of grazing.

---

**STUDENT ACTIVITY**

Look at Fig 2.15
1   Draw a scattergraph to illustrate the relationship between the two sets of figures.
2   Give reasons for the main differences
   (a)  between the major groups
   (b)  within the LEDC group.
3   What problems are created if fewer people are employed in agriculture?

---

FIGURE 2.15

| Major continental regions | | People/1000 ha of agricultural land | Value per person (US$) employed in agriculture |
|---|---|---|---|
| MEDCs | North America | 7 | 32 680 |
| | Australasia | 1 | 25 124 |
| | Western Europe | 80 | 14 910 |
| LEDCs | Latin America | 50 | 2076 |
| | E & SE Asia (excl. China) | 1100 | 473 |
| | Africa | 170 | 406 |

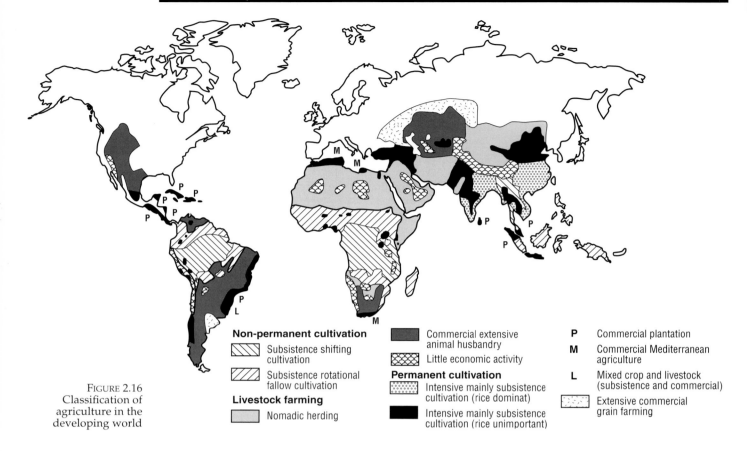

FIGURE 2.16
Classification of
agriculture in the
developing world

**Non-permanent cultivation**

⬜ Subsistence shifting
cultivation

⬜ Subsistence rotational
fallow cultivation

**Livestock farming**

⬜ Nomadic herding

⬜ Commercial extensive
animal husbandry

⬜ Little economic activity

**Permanent cultivation**

⬜ Intensive mainly subsistence
cultivation (rice dominat)

⬛ Intensive mainly subsistence
cultivation (rice unimportant)

**P** Commercial plantation

**M** Commercial Mediterranean
agriculture

**L** Mixed crop and livestock
(subsistence and commercial)

⬜ Extensive commercial
grain farming

## LEDC farming – changes and issues

FIGURE 2.17 Changes and
issues in developing
countries

| Input changes | Processes changes | Output changes |
|---|---|---|
| – higher levels of investment<br>– the Green revolution<br>– water control and conservation | – appropriate technology<br>– Integrated Rural<br>Development Planning | – role of agriculture<br>and national economies<br>– food policies |

| Input issues | Process issues | Output issues |
|---|---|---|
| –desertification<br>– salinisation<br>– other environmental issues | – labour surpluses<br>in rural areas<br>– TNC interests | – food & population growth<br>– governments & agriculture<br>– food shortages |

## Input changes

*Higher levels of investment* – for example capital
spent on:

- improved inputs
  e.g. fertiliser/pesticides
  use of new hybrid seeds;
- water control and conservation;
- improvements in animal husbandry
  e.g. inoculation against pests
  selective breeding.

*The Green revolution* – this is the most important
movement for change, which began in the 1960s as
an attempt to close the gap between population
growth and food output. Research and
development of **high yielding varieties** (HYVs) of
wheat (bred in North Mexico) and rice (IRs bred in
the Philippines), was financed by US (Ford &
Rockefeller) foundations. This successful
technology has been transferred to other LEDCs
with similar environmental conditions. Globally
rice, wheat and maize yields rose initially by 3–4
per cent, but in the 1990s the rate is below 1 per
cent. The revolution has become a process of
evolution, encompassing many other types of
change, for example land reform.

FIGURE 2.18
Characteristics of
desertification

| Environment impacts | Linked causes | Remedial measures |
|---|---|---|
| reduction of vegetation | collection of firewood | afforestation |
| overgrazing | increased surface run-off | paddocks/contour ridging |
| fall in water-table | gulleying and erosion | soil conservation e.g. mulching |
| salinisation | poorly managed irrigation | education/motivation |
| spread of sand | marked deterioration of soil | shelter-belts |

**Conservation usually involves remedial measures to remove negative environmental impacts**

*Water control and conservation* – irrigation has been used to extend cultivated areas, notably in marginal and arid lands, experiencing seasonal or perennial drought, for example, much of Pakistan and central India. The main use of irrigation is however to intensify land-use by increasing yields of improved quality while also countering climatic unreliability.

*Salinisation* – irrigation followed by a lengthy hot dry phase can result in a substantial upward movement (capillary action) of groundwater. This can cause formation of a salt pan, a toxic layer which kills agricultural crops. Large-scale government irrigation schemes such as the Rajastan canal (India) and the Aswan dam (Egypt) have been affected by this problem.

## Input issues

*Desertification* – is a process by which the productivity of the land is so reduced, that desert-like conditions come to prevail in environments previously regarded as only semi-arid. Characteristics of the desertification process are shown in Fig 2.18.

Although there is some evidence for climate shift as a cause, in the Sahel human mismanagement is largely responsible for creating the imbalance between environmental systems and human production systems.

### Integrated rural development planning - communal lands in Zimbabwe (see also fig 2.33)

**Model C: Development model in natural regions IV & V for communal areas**

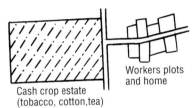

Estate is owned and managed by government. Workers get their plot and also work on the estate. e.g. Chisumbaiwe, Middle Save, Tsovane, Sanyati, Ngwezi.

Cash crop estate (tobacco, cotton, tea)

Workers plots and home

**Model A: Intensive resettlement**

Intensive individual settlement, 500 families in 15 villages linked by roads with clinic primary schools and extension officers.

| | |
|---|---|
| ☐ Residential stand | ▪ House |
| ▨ 5hcs arable/family | ● Borehole |
| ⌄ Communal grazing 5 livestock units / family in region | ◆ Diptank |

**Model D: Central estate farm and individual settlement**

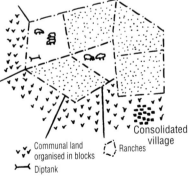

Cattle ranches used in rotation grazing areas vacated in the season to allow growth of grass. Each community uses ranch once every two years allowing surrounding communal land to recover during the west season.
Eg in Gwanda district on the Tuli and Moneburn ranches 19500hcs divided into 6 grazing units. Fenced and provided with water.

Consolidated village

⌄ Communal land organised in blocks   ⌁ Ranches

⊢ Diptank

**Model B: Cooperative resettlement - Pamberi Ne Kubatawa**

Converted commercial farm purchased and owned jointly by members 50=200 management and production planned by a committee.

S  Store built by members
G  Grinding mill built by members
D  Communal dinning hall
C  Creche built by members
H  Housing - individual or shared

P  Piggery
SH Sheds
T  Tractor shed
O  Cooperative office
F  Fields

**Model E: Group ranching model on former commercial ranch**

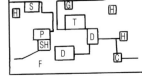

Group management of ranching and irrigation.
Irrigation used on pastures and to grow fodder crops.

Game animals

Livestock ranch

▣ Residential stand on 1hcs and 6hcs irrigated vegetables
⤬ Game fence
⊢ Cattle fence

*Other environmental issues* – have arisen from a combination of population pressure, extensification into new areas and intensification in production. Negative impacts include:

- erosion of fragile soils by:
  interrupting the nutrient cycle e.g. in rainforests
  extending the cultivated area on to slopes
  overloading soils by monoculture, overcropping and overgrazing;
- pollution of:
  streams and lakes by overuse of fertilisers leading to eutrophication
  the atmosphere by burning the rainforest.

## Process changes

### Appropriate (or intermediate) technology
Production changes in LEDCs tended at first to copy those developed in MEDCs. For example Brazil has invested heavily in MEDC style large-scale water resource schemes such as the Itaipu dam. These are seen as the surest way to hasten national development. As a strategy it calls for massive amounts of foreign capital (with the risk of international debt) as well as technology transfer and foreign expertise.

Appropriate technology encourages local labour to regulate river channels by small earth dams which are easy to repair, require little or no capital and only simple tools.

Experience has shown the need for differing approaches. LEDCs need straightforward, low-cost and labour-intensive projects, as opposed to capital-intensive high technology approaches. Intermediate technology uses techniques and equipment suited to the needs of an LEDC. For example ox-drawn reapers and planters made of local materials, may be more useful than tractors and combines, which are expensive to run and difficult to maintain using expensive imported fuel.

### Integrated Rural Development Planning
– IRDP is a form of rural development which stresses the interdependence of all aspects of the region. Projects promote planning of agriculture, water supply, roads and education to be interdependent. This is a **bottom-up approach** characterised by local planning which contrasts sharply with the top-down approach of the CAP (see Fig 2.19).

## Process issues

### Labour surpluses in rural areas
– changes in agricultural production can result in fewer people employed in agriculture. This important 'push' factor, causing migration particularly of economically active young males, leads to destabilising effects on production in rural donor areas because it leaves an ageing remnant workforce. Urban reception areas accumulate a surplus of unskilled labour, leading to the growth of an informal economy and attendant social problems.

### TNC interests
– The interests of transnational companies (TNCs) may conflict with national social and economic goals. Many of these companies are involved in the production of industrial raw materials (e.g. cotton, palm oil, jute and sisal), 'drink' crops (e.g. coffee, tea, cacao), and even flowers for sale or further processing in MEDCs. Profits from these agribusinesses may be 'leaked' back to shareholders in MEDCs reducing their value to the LEDC producing country. Much of the foreign currency gained is then spent on importing basic foodstuffs for rapidly growing cities, and to make up for the reduction in home produced food supplies.

## Output changes

### The role of agriculture and national economies
– varies considerably within the developing world, and is influenced by both physical and economic factors. The physical environment affects farm inputs e.g. soil quality. The level of economic development affects the relative and absolute importance of farming itself, as an economy moves from agriculture/primary commodity export to manufacturing/services.

Some idea of the variation may be gained from Figure 2.20.

The need to change and reform is self-evident but it is difficult to switch established food production systems:

- from the **economic goals** of profit-maximisation in the markets of the MEDCs;
- to the **social goal** of affordable foodstuffs for low-paid labour of the LEDCs;
- while paying due regard to the global goal of **environmental conservation**.

For example commercial farmers in Kenya find it profitable to produce fresh vegetables (beans, mange-tout) for European markets. Production is intensive, using irrigation systems fed by abstracting water from local rivers. This is turn reduces supplies for local subsistence pastoralists whose livestock and survival is threatened. Natural habitats and wildlife also suffer and in some cases are permanently affected as certain species cannot survive. The large European retail food outlets make a profit, the European consumer is satisfied, the large Kenyan commercial farmer is successful, but the local environment and domestic food production are diminished.

The Green Revolution is the best known strategy for improving domestic food output. Other strategies have focused on:

- increasing exports e.g. palm oil in Malaysia, cotton in the Sudan;
- investing in rural infrastructure e.g. by building roads to make markets accessible and so encourage a shift from subsistence to commercial production;
- land reform to remove absentee landlords and by various means enabling hitherto landless rural labourers entry into an exchange economy, as attempted in Cuba, Peru, and Tanzania.

Unfortunately development is viewed as the

FIGURE 2.20 Economic indicators for developing countries

| | export earnings as % G.N.P. | G.N.P. per Capita 1994 $ | % share of primary and manufactured commodities in total exports | | | |
| --- | --- | --- | --- | --- | --- | --- |
| | | | fuels/ minerals/ metals | agricultural commodities | machines/ transport equipment | other manufacturing (including textiles) |
| Hong Kong | 49 | 21 650 | 2 | 3 | 24 | 71 |
| Togo | 43 | 320 | 45 | 44 | 1 | 10 |
| Saudi Arabia | 38 | 7050 | 99 | 0 | 1 | 0 |
| Venezuela | 36 | 2760 | 86 | 3 | 1 | 10 |
| Jamaica | 34 | 1540 | 18 | 27 | 0 | 55 |
| Sri Lanka | 27 | 640 | 1 | 27 | 2 | 70 |
| Kenya | 14 | 250 | 16 | 55 | 10 | 19 |
| Mexico | 11 | 4180 | 35 | 10 | 33 | 22 |
| Brazil | 7.5 | 2970 | 13 | 29 | 21 | 37 |

maximisation of income rather than the improvement of the quality of life. This approach arose in the colonial era bequeathing:

■ export based economies;
■ an uneven pattern of regional development;
■ an 'inside-out' transport network focusing on communications with the rest of the world through a primate city, usually a port.

*Output issues*

*Food supplies and population growth* – The central issue is the carrying capacity of a given environment. **Carrying capacity** can be defined as the maximum sustainable population in an area, which can be supported at a given standard of living. Views on this relationship are often polarised. To this discussion should be added concern over what is meant by carrying capacity. Environmentalists tend to the gloomier Malthusian determinist perspective that continued population growth = not only famine but ecological disaster i.e. carrying capacity overload.
Technologists embrace the alternative possibilist outlook that since necessity is the mother of invention, mankind will come up with solutions to these pressing problems. This will allow the earth to feed more than twice the current population.

Nineteenth century-Malthus view (Determinism)
■ Population grows faster than food
■ So numbers will overshoot capacity
■ Starvation + fewer births = new balance

Twentieth century-Boserup view (Possibilism)
■ Not necessarily, more people, more demand
■ Capacity increased by new technologies
■ Increased production + fewer births = new balance

*Governments and agriculture* – Agriculture is a favoured sector of most countries. Most countries have some sort of agricultural policy or guidelines, since:
■ governments want to keep food prices as low as possible to promote the health and welfare of their populations;
■ rural regions make up the bulk of national territories and so the support of agriculture prevents their decline;
■ self-sufficiency in basic foodstuffs brings a degree of national 'peace-of-mind' or security.

*Food shortages* – Many MEDCs have problems of surplus, while LEDCs have problems of shortage. These food shortages are not the result of a total global failure in production, but the ineffectiveness of current trading mechanisms in securing food supplies for LEDC populations. Food security rather than food availability is the key to understanding famine and hunger. Correcting this problem is usually approached:

■ either by food aid a short term solution, which may have adverse effects on traditional agriculture in receiving countries e.g. leading to dependence on imported food which does not necessarily go to the most needy for political reasons;

■ or by technological change, longer term solutions like the Green Revolution, enabling individual countries to develop their own food production potential and increase their carrying capacity. Biotechnology has enormous potential to increase world food production, as the manipulation of genes is applied to food, crops and livestock.

# Land-use theories

**Von Thunen's discovery – The Concept of Zones –** Although writing in 1826 long before the industrial period, this landowner's research helps us to understand present day land-use patterns. His main finding was that concentric agricultural land-use zones could be detected around a market town. This discovery was important because it showed that whatever farmers decide to do with their properties is the result **not only** of physical factors (climate, weather, slopes and soils) **but also** of economic variables (market prices and especially transport costs).

In response to criticism Von Thunen developed a second revised model showing the effects of a river and small market town on land-use patterns, to add a touch of realism. Clearly he was well aware of the limitations of a simplistic approach.
**Von Thunen's legacy –** Later writers and fieldworkers have explored this finding in a number of ways. Geographical enquiries have confirmed the existence of zones around other central places, for example encircling villages in Africa and Italy, and even at a continental scale across Europe from a core region in Benelux. See Fig 2.21.

FIGURE 2.21
Development models

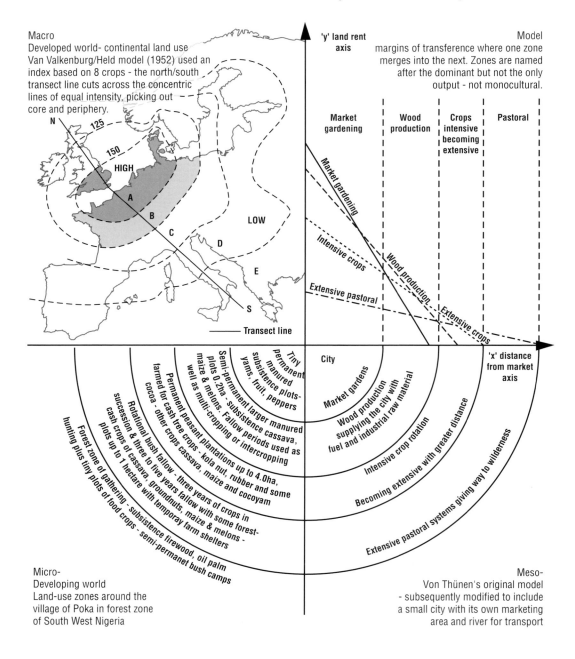

Macro
Developed world- continental land use
Van Valkenburg/Held model (1952) used an
index based on 8 crops - the north/south
transect line cuts across the concentric
lines of equal intensity, picking out
core and periphery.

Micro-
Developing world
Land-use zones around the
village of Poka in forest zone
of South West Nigeria

Meso-
Von Thünen's original model
- subsequently modified to include
a small city with its own marketing
area and river for transport

■ Von Thunen's work was seminal because it stimulated other geographers to take up the concept of zones and investigate its relevance in other locations and at differing scales.

■ These confirm the importance of cost-distance from central places even if costs increase with distance.

■ *For example Sinclair's model* – This investigation in the American mid-West revealed an inversion of the usual cost-distance findings. The value of land in rurban fringes was found to be lower than in more distant areas. The explanation given for this land-use pattern is:

efficient transport enables intensive land-uses to locate further away from markets;
low land values on city margins are created by the speculative holding of land, bought by developers from farmers, in anticipation of development as the city grows.

■ Other variables affecting land-use are recognised and now include less precise social and psychological influences – for example personality attributes affecting motivation.

Whatever the fieldwork details of the patterns, the spatial sorting of land-use into recognisable concentric zones confirms that rural landscapes are cultural mixtures of people, production and the environment.

# Rural environments and the role of agriculture – contrasting case-studies

Within many landscapes there is a mixture of production systems, reflecting the physical factors of the environment, accessibility, general levels of development, and individual choices. We can get some idea of this complexity by examining one type of production system, farming, in the context of samples of rural regions.

**MEDC located studies – in England**
mid-latitude temperate environments
*Dartmoor* – Western upland

*East Anglia & the Fens* – Eastern lowland
both regions highly accessible within the E.U. and affected by C.A.P. policies
**LEDC located studies – in Zimbabwe**
tropical environments – varied altitude
Eastern upland – *High veld/Region 2\**
Western lowland – *Low veld/Region 4\**
both landlocked in Southern Africa
*notation\* used by African geographers*

## CASE STUDY

## MEDC – temperate upland – Dartmoor

Dartmoor may be conveniently if not precisely defined by the National Park boundary. A relatively small park of 945 km$^2$ (cf. Lake District 2243 km$^2$). It is the largest area of marginal land in Southern England, and is made up of two plateaux, divided by the West branch of the Dart river. The Northern plateau is larger and higher.

Dartmoor is one of a series of compact granite uplands, making up the backbone of the South West peninsula. Each is a distinct igneous intrusion of granite into sedimentary Carboniferous rocks (known locally as killas).

The upland environments stand in sharp contrast to those of the valleys and coastal plains, and the potential for farming differs as a consequence, see Figs 2.24 and 2..25.

This marginal land is owned by a variety of bodies, such as the Ministry of Defence, Water Companies, National Trust, Forestry Commission, but by far the largest single land-owner is the Duchy of Cornwall estate, farmed by tenants e.g. Brimpts Farm.
*Land use* is related to height, slope and aspect. Over the whole moor the percentages are:

Open country 52%
Enclosed farmland 35%
Commercial Forestry 4.5%
Deciduous woodland 4.5%
Priorities differ with owners – best appreciated on OS map extract – see Fig 2.24

This sample of SW upland shows a variety of past and present land-uses related to geology, relief (height, slopes and aspect) and drainage. The map extract lies wholly inside the National Park – 35 km$^2$ of upland marginal fringe.

FIGURE 2.22 A comparison of uplands and lowlands

| | |
|---|---|
| Igneous uplands | Sedimentary lowlands |
| cold wet regime | warm wet regime |
| blanket peat soils and peaty gleyed podsols* | deeper colluvial soils* |
| difficult to drain and impossible to plough | high water table promotes seeded pasture |
| shorter growing season (perhaps 6 weeks) | longer growing season – fewer fodder purchases |
| exposed – high wind speeds/chill factor | sheltered and warmer – less risk of damage |
| unattractive to investment in farming | more options therefore more attractive |

*Note: *The potential for farming high elevation bogs is quite different from that in alkaline eutrophic (nutrient-rich) environments such as the East Anglian Fens. High elevation bogs are poor in nutrients and usually acidic (pH 3.4–5.0) because high rainfall and winter cold prevent the decomposition of organic matter.*

### Mining and quarrying
- show direct disused connections quarrying for building and road stone and mining for tin
- there were many such small-scale tin workings, often developed by wealthier farmers. The ore was dug from shallow workings along the line of the lode. Tin content being low the cassiterite (tin oxide) would be crushed locally by water-driven mills, prior to refining (remains of 'blowing houses')

### Water resources
- Venford Reservoir completes the list of primary production systems. The demand and potential for water is high throughout the SW region.

FIGURE 2.23 Demand and potential for water in the South West region

| Potential | Demand |
|---|---|
| high constant rainfall input | expanding major tourist region |
| impermeable rock structures | domestic demand rising with increasing GDP |
| gravity feed to lowland settlements | growth of 'footloose' industries |

### Farming
- Open moorland country exceeds enclosed farmland – the OS map clearly shows the difference and distribution.
- Open country occupies the higher, more exposed areas and, although in production, does not attract the investment of effort that goes with the creation of farmscape field-systems. The landscape is one of smooth slopes broken by tors – e.g. Yar Tor – around which there is evidence of earlier settlement and farming.
- The lack of enclosure does not mean the landscape is natural in the sense of lacking the touch of production. The major system is livestock farming. The grazing of sheep since medieval times has ensured the persistence of rough pasture at the expense of trees.
- Enclosed land is in lower areas, notably in the valley of the West Dart. There is also an association with aspect. Compare the land-use
  - West and East of the river Dart
  - West and East of the East Dart river
- Diversification of function is an alternative view of the role of farms. The focus may shift from conventional to specialised production or from farming to other ways of using the land profitably.
- On Dartmoor investment in leisure and tourism is the main change

### Forestry
- Deciduous stands dominate the steep lower slopes of the valley sides of the Dart below Dartmeet. The incision of the East and West Dart rivers above Dartmeet on the upland plateau proper is less marked. Their valley cross-profiles, especially the West Dart, are less steep and so although the land is higher, enclosed farming takes priority.
- Conifer plantations occupy higher ground, functioning as land-use and shelter belts, for example to the West and North of Brimpts Farm. They are also used to slow surface run-off around Venford Reservoir (6864).

### Leisure and Tourism
- The map shows clear evidence of facilities: parking places for motorists – for example along the road leading to Dartmeet; facilities for the more active – for example pony trekking and camping barn.
- Marginal regions such as Dartmoor do not attract investments in agriculture. The costs of overcoming environmental constraints are too high. In such regions farmers have to look for alternative ways of making a living, for example, Brimpts Farm is now a conference centre for regional and national business meetings.

---

**STUDENT ACTIVITY**

For the area of the whole map extract
1 Describe the distribution and location of the farms.
2 Suggest reasons for the diversity of economic activity.
3 Locate places where there are likely to be conflicts between locals and visitors. Give reasons for your choices.

FIGURE 2.24  Climate details for South West England

**Average Monthly Rainfall 1941-70**

**Location**
- Exeter
- Plymouth
- Dartmoor

Warm saturated air from the SW is the dominant air movement

*Exmoor*
*Old Red Sandstone*

Upland temperatures reduced by height increased cloud cover and relief rain much shorter growing season on poorer soils

■ **Exeter**

*Bodmin Moor*

Transect line 42 miles/ 72 kms approx

■ **Plymouth**

*Hensbarrow*

Deep-seated granitic ridge forming batholithic intrusion

Tees/Exe line

Coastal temperatures raised by effects of lower height and warming effect of sutropical heat transferred by North Atlantic Drift

*Land's End*

*Cammenellis*

*Scilly Islands*

**Transect line from Plymouth to Exeter**
Sedimentary - metamorphic - igneous - metamorphic - sedimentary
lowlands     aureole      granite     aureole       lowlands
                          massif
**This pattern repeats for each granite upland massif**

FIGURE 2.25  OS Map, Dartmoor

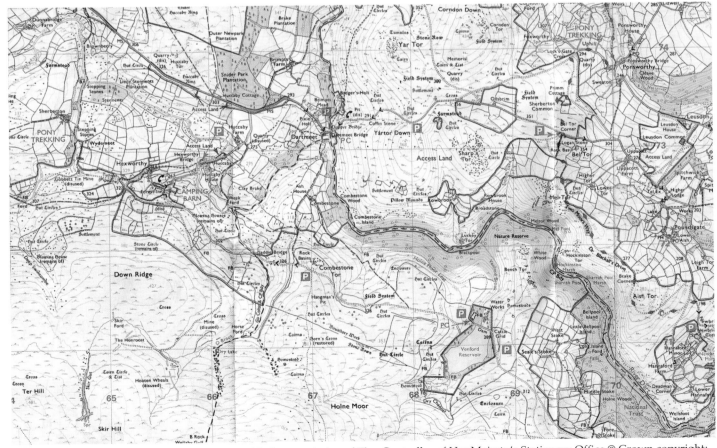

## CASE STUDY

### MEDC – temperate lowland – East Anglia and the Fens

FIGURE 2.26 The landscape of East Anglia

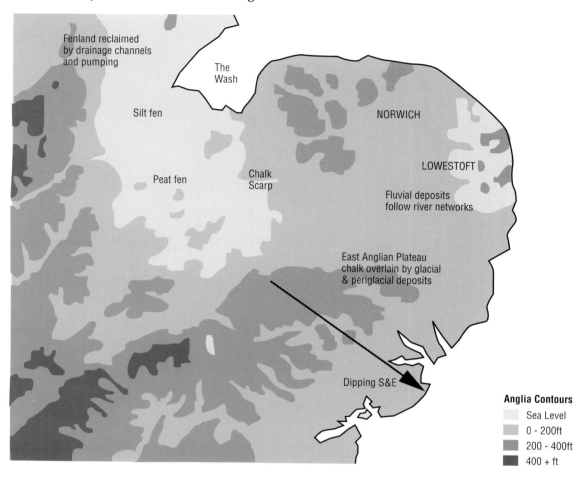

FIGURE 2.27 The importance of soil types in East Anglia

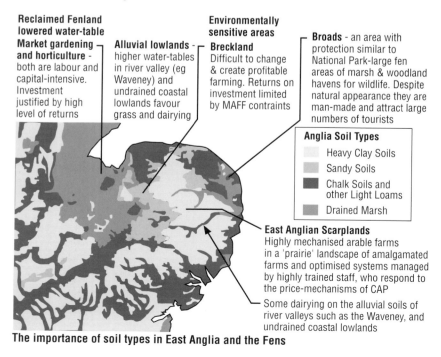

**Reclaimed Fenland lowered water-table**
Market gardening and horticulture - both are labour and capital-intensive. Investment justified by high level of returns

**Alluvial lowlands** - higher water-tables in river valley (eg Waveney) and undrained coastal lowlands favour grass and dairying

**Environmentally sensitive areas**
**Breckland**
Difficult to change & create profitable farming. Returns on investment limited by MAFF contraints

**Broads** - an area with protection similar to National Park-large fen areas of marsh & woodland havens for wildlife. Despite natural appearance they are man-made and attract large numbers of tourists

**Anglia Soil Types**

| | |
|---|---|
| | Heavy Clay Soils |
| | Sandy Soils |
| | Chalk Soils and other Light Loams |
| | Drained Marsh |

**East Anglian Scarplands**
Highly mechanised arable farms in a 'prairie' landscape of amalgamated farms and optimised systems managed by highly trained staff, who respond to the price-mechanisms of CAP

Some dairying on the alluvial soils of river valleys such as the Waveney, and undrained coastal lowlands

**The importance of soil types in East Anglia and the Fens**

Frequently referred to as an 'isotropic plain' in the context of locational analysis, the farmscape of East Anglia is far from uniform. Environmental variations in surface geology (Fig 2.26) condition rural land-uses (Fig 2.27). In addition the regional landscape is an historical document, because the details show a succession of human impacts. This process of change continues today.

*The East Anglian plateau* – in this area modern British arable farming developed. Historically this change is linked to the transformation of the UK economy in the period 1750–1914. As the Northern coalfields were the 'hearth' of industrial change, Norfolk was the 'hearth' of agriculture change. The 'new' English techniques improved the soils by draining and marling. This technique involved bringing up the deeper solid chalk and working it into the superficial glacial clay. The soil structure was altered and production consequently improved. This and other innovations, such as crop rotation, were aimed at increasing production by overcoming physical limitations.

*The Fens* – where soils are naturally fertile, drainage has been one of the most successful ways of increasing agricultural productivity. Attempts to drain the Fens date from Roman times, but large-scale success had to await the arrival of the steam engine in the nineteenth century. This farmscape is distinctly rectangular and has few settlements of any size. Constant pumping allows the permanent lowering of the water-table which has enabled the conversion of the area from watery summer pasture to intensive arable farming, especially the field cropping of vegetables – peas, beans, carrots. This engineered comparative advantage has created stiff competition for the older areas of production in the rurban fringes of city-regions.

*The coastal towns* – and their traditional links with North Sea fishing have made an indirect important contribution to contemporary agriculture. In the traditional North Sea fishing ports such as Great Yarmouth and Lowestoft, companies such as Birds Eye developed modern techniques of handling and preserving fish. These processes have been modified to include the handling, freezing, and canning of fruit and vegetables. This food-technology allied to the distribution systems of supermarket chains have made possible rapid movements of fresh farm produce.

*Modern market forces* – in common with other favoured farming regions, agricultural industrialisation has come into East Anglia and the Fens from outside, largely in the twentieth century.

Many traditional farms and estates have been transformed into large-scale, capital-intensive production systems where outputs are determined by contracts with food-processing businesses. Features of such systems include:

■ mechanisation and the removal of hedgerows;
■ increased use of fertilisers, herbicides and pesticides associated with the pollution of rivers and groundwater;
■ selective breeding and genetic engineering of plants and livestock.
■ Innovations are increasing as agribusiness try to develop vertical linkages and so control all stages of food production.

Two smaller **Environmentally Sensitive Areas** (ESA) contrast with these economically efficient sub-regions of East Anglia. They are:

■ *the Norfolk Broads* – originally thought to be natural periglacial depressions, fieldwork studies linked to documentary research strongly suggest that they result from peat cuttings, prior to AD1300. Today they form the basis of an important tourist attraction, and nature reserve.
■ *the Breckland* – shows that influences external to the region are not solely those of market forces, modified by CAP quotas and subsidies. Here within an ESA farmers follow guidelines aimed at conservation – for example planting conifer shelter belts to prevent soil erosion and they receive payments for maintaining dry grassland and heath, thus preserving important wildlife habitats. Alternative sustainable production is the goal.

## LEDC – Zimbabwe Region 2

This favoured region (Fig 2.28) is dominated by croplands farming. Most of the farms are large, often over 2000 ha and vital to the Zimbabwean economy. For example tobacco, one of the largest exports, is grown almost entirely on white-owned commercial land, although 70 per cent of this land may be unused at any one time. Population densities are only half the national average (9/km²). There are a number of resettlement areas but very little state land. Commercial farmers have good access to credit, markets, extension services and infrastructure. In contrast, the small farmer in a resettlement area or on communal land has few of these benefits and is likely to be short of labour and machines or draught power (oxen). He lacks capital investment, the key to increased productivity.

So in this region agriculture may be economically successful but not everyone has enough to eat. Hungry people with no land become hostile to fields of cotton and tobacco, grown primarily for export. Many will leave for the towns and cities, unless alternative opportunities are provided.

FIGURE 2.28 Cross-section of Zimbabwe

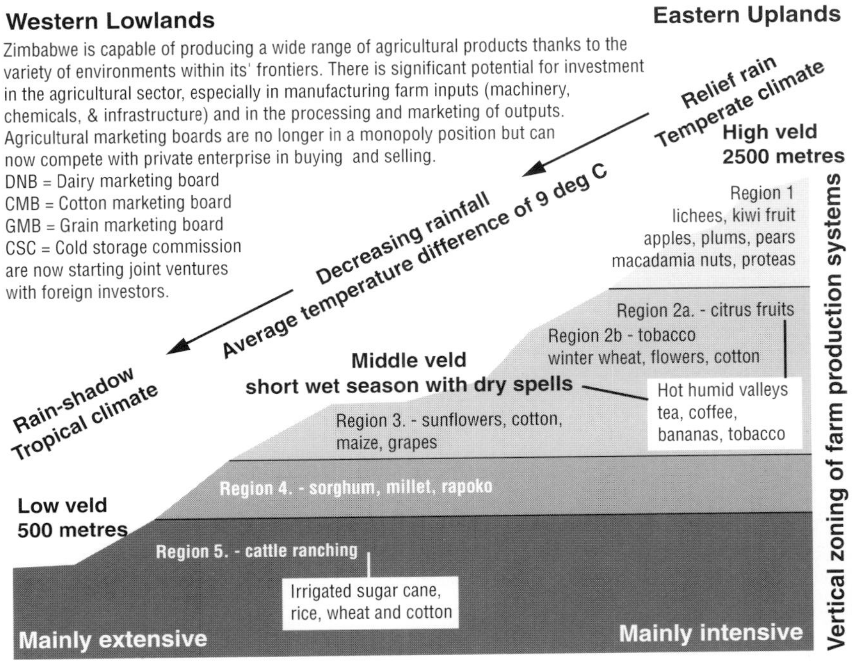

**Western Lowlands**

Zimbabwe is capable of producing a wide range of agricultural products thanks to the variety of environments within its' frontiers. There is significant potential for investment in the agricultural sector, especially in manufacturing farm inputs (machinery, chemicals, & infrastructure) and in the processing and marketing of outputs. Agricultural marketing boards are no longer in a monopoly position but can now compete with private enterprise in buying  and selling.
DNB = Dairy marketing board
CMB = Cotton marketing board
GMB = Grain marketing board
CSC = Cold storage commission
are now starting joint ventures
with foreign investors.

**Eastern Uplands**

Relief rain
Temperate climate
**High veld**
**2500 metres**

Region 1
lichees, kiwi fruit
apples, plums, pears
macadamia nuts, proteas

Decreasing rainfall
Average temperature difference of 9 deg C

Region 2a. - citrus fruits
Region 2b - tobacco
winter wheat, flowers, cotton

Hot humid valleys
tea, coffee,
bananas, tobacco

**Middle veld**
**short wet season with dry spells**

Region 3. - sunflowers, cotton,
maize, grapes

Rain-shadow
Tropical climate

Region 4. - sorghum, millet, rapoko

**Low veld**
**500 metres**

Region 5. - cattle ranching

Irrigated sugar cane,
rice, wheat and cotton

**Mainly extensive**

**Mainly intensive**

Vertical zoning of farm production systems

Drought is a serious hazard in Southern Africa - for example in 1991/2 Zimbabwe lost some 50% of production, and became an importer rather than an exporter of grain (critically maize). This had notable effect on the balance of payments. 1993 saw a notable recovery but the region lost a higher proportion of its' crops than Ethiopia and Sudan in the highly publicised ( Bob Geldorf) drought of 1985. Many poor rural communities slaughter their main assets cattle and livestock. Farm regions 1-5 see Fig 2.29

*Agricultural Development Authority estates* – This government agency operates under the Ministry of Lands, Agriculture and Rural Resettlement. Its overall aim is to promote Zimbabwe's food security through the development of agricultural resources on a commercial basis. The ADA operates in all regions but the potential for success is greater in Region 2 thanks to its more favourable physical and economic environment. There are several objectives:

■ to promote projects with smallholders in the communal lands – for example:
    small-scale dairy production at Rusitu in the wetter area of the East
    fruit and vegetable production in Mashonaland East, the immediate catchment area of Harare;
■ to develop a large number of estates producing both cash and food crops – for example:
    cotton production has greatly increased since independence and most of this has been due to the involvement of farmers on communal land and ADA estates

irrigated sugar cane production in the drier South East;
■ to generate employment on these estates both in farming and related agro-industries;
■ to provide services to local farmers;
■ and to provided educational, recreational and medical facilities to both estate workers and other local farmers.

Such economic and social investments are expensive and impossible without government intervention in the economy. Not least important is the transfer of successful methods and technology from the large established commercial farm enterprises.

*Dual economy and rural land-use in Zimbabwe* – this is evident in the contrast between regions 4 and 2 – see Fig 2.30.

The table illustrates the regional contrast between two cultures. Their relative importance in each region is evident in the proportion of communal to commercial land (see Fig 2.31).

FIGURE 2.29 Farming in Zimbabwe

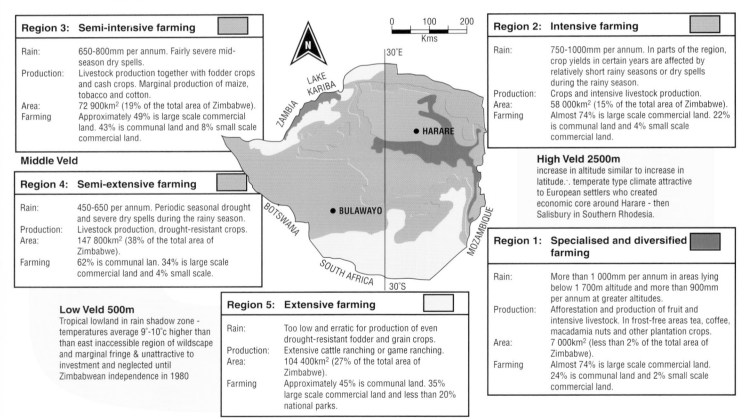

FIGURE 2.30 Regional contrast between two cultures

| | Farming region 4 – outer periphery | | Farming region 2 – inner periphery |
|---|---|---|---|
| Comparative disadvantages | in SW focused on provincial Bulawayo<br>low veld in rain-shadow<br>high temperatures and frequent droughts<br>dominated by communal land<br>isolated, marginal land and wildscape<br>traditional land-uses strongly entrenched<br>essentially indigenous and African | Comparative disadvantages | in the NE centred around the capital, Harare<br>high veld-height reduces temperatures<br>relief triggers regular rainfall<br>dominated by commercial land<br>accessible and largely farmscape<br>attractive to investment and innovation<br>external (mainly European) development |

| Region | Farming | % Commercial | % Communal | State owned | Resettlement areas |
|---|---|---|---|---|---|
| I | specialised and diversified | 24 | 74 | 8.2 forest plant | 0.4 |
| 2 | INTENSIVE FARMING | 74 | 22 | 1.3 | 18.0 |
| 3 | semi-intensive farming | 49 | 43 | 18.1 | 46.9 |
| 4 | SEMI-EXTENSIVE | 34 | 62 | 28.7 Nat Parks and | 30.9 |
| 5 | extensive farming | 35 | 45 | 43.7 game reserves | 3.8 |

The state also has lands. These 5 million ha are protected areas such as national parks and safari areas. They are largely in areas of low agricultural potential, tsetse infested and low in population density for example the Southern shores of Lake Kariba. The main purpose of these lands is to preserve wildlife, conserve biodiversity and maintain a potential for tourism. The government also operates resettlement schemes and these tend to be in these less developed areas.

## LEDC – tropical lowland – Zimbabwe Region 4

Region 4 has high proportions of National Parks and game reserves, and land allocated for resettlement. The communal lands (see Fig 2.32) are dominated by subsistence crop systems and ranchland. Both types are affected by land degradation.

*Subsistence systems* – Before the impact of white settlement, traditional systems of farming were sustainable. Land-use systems maintained soil fertility by:

■ long fallow periods. For example shifting cultivation (Chitemene system) had a fallow period of 22–25 years;
■ intercropping – a number of crops including fruit trees are planted in permanent fields
the crops grow to different heights and some species provide shade for others
no modern fertilisers are required because the crops use nutrients in different ways and some are leguminous. Pesticides are needed less because a variety of plants reduces the rapid spread of disease seen in monocultures.

The present-day pressure to produce has reduced fallow periods (from 20 to as few as nine years in some cases) and soil erosion has occurred. In some areas shifting cultivation has given way to rotational bush fallowing. In this system the village remains in one place and different kinds of land-use develop around it. Land is allocated by chiefs or village councils but grazing and woodland resources are exploited communally. Farming is largely subsistence but incomes are likely to be supplemented by young adult males sending remittances from commercial farms, mines or urban centres. The number of adult males remaining on the land is low.

*Ranchland* – Only about one-third of the country (High veld) gets enough rain for crop cultivation. Much of the land, especially in the West is suitable only for extensive livestock farming of cattle. It is the dominant land-use in Region 4. Extensive farming means low inputs of capital and labour and low outputs per hectare. It is only in irrigated areas that farming can be intensified, and such areas are very limited. Elsewhere massive increases in livestock, associated with expanding population numbers, have resulted in land degradation as desirable stocking ratios are exceeded, and trees are felled to clear marginal land for pasture and firewood.

FIGURE 2.31 Resettlement schemes

FIGURE 2.32 Principal urban settlements in Zimbabwe

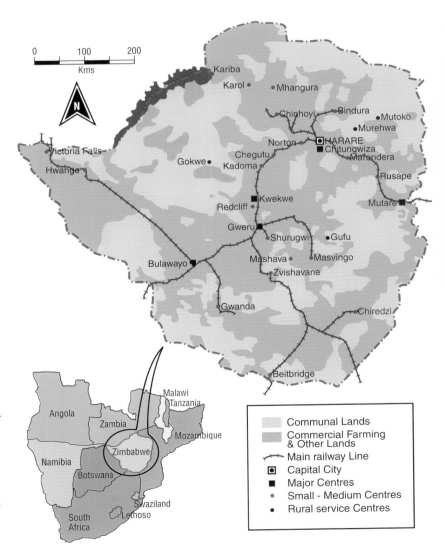

FIGURE 2.33 The influence of cattle on vegetation

| Sandy areas | Clay areas |
|---|---|
| cattle remove vegetation results in: | cattle compact soil results in: |
| less vegetation cover = depleted A horizon | gulleying and erosion remove A horizon |
| plus effects of deeper water table | water table drops |
| vegetation takes longer to recover | vegetation takes longer to recover |
| soil structure under threat | soil structure under threat |

The influence of cattle on vegetation varies, see Fig 2.33.
Land degradation – reasons for the decline of productivity.

1. population increase (often over 3% p.a.)
2. increase of cultivated area in marginal areas
3. grazing & woodland depleted
4. yields decline with reduced periods of fallow
5. grazing shortages/overstocking
6. loss of vegetation on pastureland
7. abandonment of farmland
8. acute poverty & hunger
9. migration for survival
10. aging population structure

---

**STUDENT ACTIVITY**

Study the table below, Fig 2.34 which shows the contrasting perceptions of the soil erosion problem across the political spectrum in the developing world. Answer the following questions

1  In what ways do farm systems damage soils?
2  How may farm systems become sustainable?
3  Why is it possible for environmentalists and economists to have differing perceptions of the causes of soil erosion?

---

FIGURE 2.34 Different perceptions of the soil erosion problem

| Values motivated by the structure of society and the distribution of power | Values motivated by the management of resources and the production and consumption of goods |
|---|---|
| Soil erosion is a symptom of an unjust society. Rich people own most of the land, which forces poorer people to farm intensively on the remaining land. They cannot afford to pay for anti-erosion measures. Economic development is in the interests of wealthy urban elites. They are powerful and have little concern for peasant farmers and land degradation. Thus resources, including aid, are not directed to rural areas. When they are, they most often reach larger commercial farmers whose attitude to farming is often exploitative and damaging. Soil erosion will only be tackled by taking away land from wealthy land-owners and sharing it out fairly. | Soil erosion is largely caused by poor farming methods and overpopulation. Too many people create a demand for food when the available land cannot supply on a sustainable basis. So measures must be taken to help farmers and reduce population growth. People need laws and financial penalties to encourage them to combat soil erosion Grazing must be banned in vulnerable areas people should be required to build terraces and conservation works; soil conservation education should be introduced to counter ignorance and demonstrate new techniques Aid must be tied to making farmers conserve soil and adopt new technologies which allow greater sustainable food production. Soil erosion will only be tackled by making the farmers follow strict directives and encourage them in conservation |

# *Summary*

Rural environments are, like urban environments, home to a complex mixture of economic systems which create distinctive landscapes. Rural environments in both the MEDCs and the LEDCs provide a livelihood for the rural population but also provide resources and markets for urban economic systems and comparative advantages for national development. Increasing modernisation and changes to farming systems have brought a range of new challenges for rural populations. In the MEDCs there may be surpluses of production and a necessity to take land out of production. In the LEDCs, the focus is invariably a need to provide more food. Within countries at all stages of development there are tensions caused by the inter relationships between urban and rural economic systems. Rural-urban migration within LEDCs, and counterurbanisation in MEDCs provide evidence of the continuing and ever changing interdependence of rural and urban economic systems. The globalisation of food supplies and rural resource development has resulted in a complex web of social, economic and environmental impacts on the world's rural regions.

## *Key Ideas*

- Major primary production systems exist in rural regions
- The characteristics of farming systems depend on the type of inputs, processes and outputs
- The spatial patterns of primary production can be explained by the principle of comparative advantage
- The economic systems of rural areas cannot be separated from those in urban areas
- Rural economic systems have impacts on the environment

# 3
# INDUSTRIAL LOCATION AND MANUFACTURING SYSTEMS

In 1900 the United Kingdom was the richest country in the world. It was known as the workshop of the world. Look around you. What is made in Britain today? Your car could have been assembled in Britain but the company is probably a foreign one. It could well have been made abroad and imported to Britain. What about the computer you use? or the TV? or the Walkman? It was probably made in Japan or Taiwan or 'Somewhere in the East'.

Today industrial production processes are very different from those of 1900. Terms such as **Globalisation** and **Deindustrialisation** are commonly used. Countries which even 50 years ago had no industrial production now produce more manufactured products than the United Kingdom. Within the United Kingdom areas such as South Wales which had produced 90 per cent of the total tin plate production of the United Kingdom have declined.

## *The economic process – Manufacturing matters*

FIGURE 3.1 The economic process

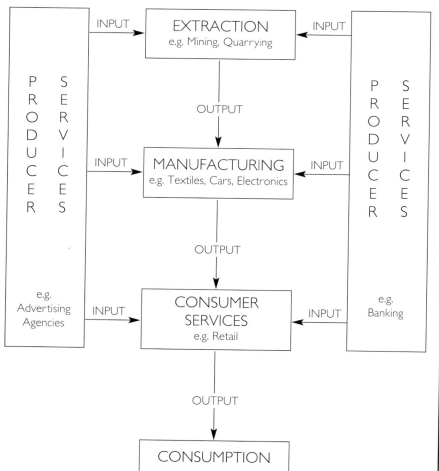

Manufacturing is just one stage in the economic process (Fig 3.1). Although the recent changes to the relative importance of manufacturing and services in some countries has been seen as signs of a post-industrial society, manufacturing industries still matter. It is important to remember that the wealth of a country depends upon it being able to trade manufactured goods or services with other countries. It was manufacturing industries that provided the wealth that caused economic development in what are now termed **Newly Industrialised Countries**. In addition, many service industries, particularly producer services rely upon manufacturing industries. Some studies have even shown that up to half the number of service sector jobs are reliant on manufacturing industries.

---

### STUDENT ACTIVITY

**1** Study Fig 3.2
Rank the six countries in order of wealth in 1965, 1980 and 1995. Using graph paper plot the relative change between nations over this period.
a. What patterns can you see?
b. Which country has made the biggest increase in rank?
c. Which has made the biggest fall?
**2** Now rank the same six countries in the share of manufacturing in their economies during the same period. Similarly to the wealth of these countries, plot out the relative changes over time.
**3** Does this support the view that we have a post-industrial society, or does manufacturing still create wealth?

|  | 1965 | | 1980 | | 1995 | |
|---|---|---|---|---|---|---|
|  | GDP$ | % MANU | GDP$ | % MANU | GDP$ | % MANU |
| France | 99 300 | 27 | 664 595 | 24 | 1 536 089 | 19 |
| Germany | 114 790 | 40 | 1 678 340 | 37 | 2 415 764 | 28 |
| Italy | 66 880 | 28 | 452 648 | 28 | 1 086 932 | 21 |
| Japan | 91 290 | 34 | 1 059 257 | 29 | 5 108 540 | 24 |
| UK | 100 690 | 34 | 537 383 | 27 | 1 105 822 | 21 |
| US | 701 380 | 27 | 2 708 147 | 22 | 6 952 020 | 18 |

FIGURE 3.2
Manufacturing and wealth

(*Source: World Bank*)

# *Creating comparative advantage*

The location of an industry is the place where production occurs. It is the commitment of a firm to that particular location. All firms have various requirements and a location that has certain attributes which can satisfy a firm's requirements will be more likely to attract that firm than locations which do not. The attributes of locations which encourage production to occur are called factors. These factors are then said to create a comparative advantage over locations which do not encourage production to occur (Fig 3.3).

The characteristics of manufacturing industry are a commitment of a firm to a particular process of manufacturing (Fig 3.3), which then develops the location's comparative advantage.

Factors and processes are not independent of each other and therefore the creation and development of a location's comparative advantage is a result of a two way interaction between factors that affect manufacturing and the processes of manufacturing (Fig 3.3). This creation and development of a location's comparative advantage then determines the pattern and characteristics of manufacturing.

FIGURE 3.3 Factors and processes affecting comparative advantage

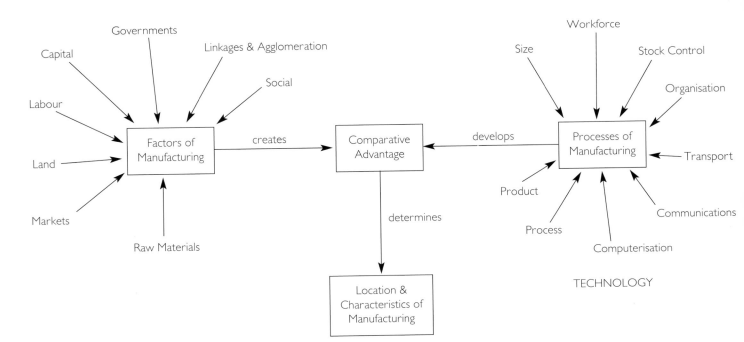

# Factors affecting the location of manufacturing industry

There are a variety of both physical and human factors which affect the location and characteristics of manufacturing industries (Fig 3.3). The relative importance of each factor will vary between industries as different industries have different requirements. The relative importance of factors will also vary over time with changes in the processes of manufacturing.

FIGURE 3.4
Manufacturing adds value

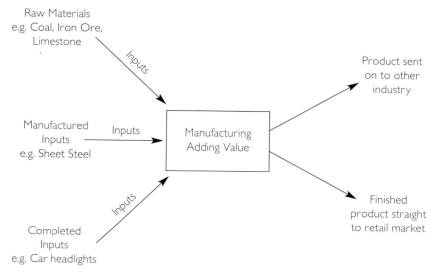

Raw Materials
e.g. Coal, Iron Ore, Limestone

Manufactured Inputs
e.g. Sheet Steel

Completed Inputs
e.g. Car headlights

Inputs

Inputs

Inputs

Manufacturing Adding Value

Product sent on to other industry

Finished product straight to retail market

## Raw materials and markets

Manufacturing is the processing of inputs into a product which adds value to that input (Fig 3.4). This product then has to be sold in a market. The locations of both the inputs required by a firm, and the market where the firm hopes to sell the product are therefore of great importance in determining the comparative advantage of different manufacturing locations.

The manufacture of steel requires large amounts of iron ore, limestone and coal which are bulky and difficult to transport. In addition, much of the weight of the iron ore, coal and limestone is lost. Steel industries such as in Sheffield and Corby developed close to the source of their raw materials.

In contrast the brewing industry requires raw materials that are either easy to transport (hops) or were found in abundance everywhere (water). It is the product that is difficult to transport and so brewing industries locate close to the site of their markets which are in large urban areas.

It was the importance of the location of raw materials and markets in creating a location's comparative advantage that led authors such as Weber, Losch and Smith to develop 'classical' **industrial location models** (Fig 3.5) which were used to explain the pattern of industrial location.

FIGURE 3.5  (a) Classical industrial location models; (b) Industrial location by maximum revenue; (c) Industrial location by mutual interdependence

(a)

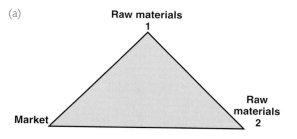

**Raw materials**
1

**Raw materials**
2

**Market**

**Least cost - weber**
Assume £1per unit of raw material per length of triangle
Weight gaining industry ie brewing
Requires 1 unit $RM_1$ = 1 unit $RM_2$ to create 2 unit product
∴ At M : cost $RM_1$        = £1      Total cost = £2
        cost $RM_2$        = £1
        cost to market  = £0

At $RM_1$ or : cost $RM_{1/2}$  = £1      Total cost = £3
  $RM_2$      cost to market = £2

**Weight losing industry ie steel**
Requires 3 unit $RM_1$ + 1 unit $RM_2$ to create 1 unit product
∴ At $RM_1$ : cost $RM_1$        = £0
            cost $RM_2$        = £1      Total cost = £2
            cost to market  = £1

At $RM_2$/M : cost $RM_1$        = £3
  $RM_2$      cost $RM_1$/M    = £1      Total cost = £4

(b)

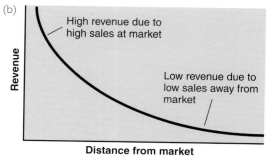

High revenue due to high sales at market

Low revenue due to low sales away from market

**Revenue**

**Distance from market**

(c)

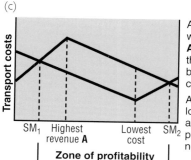

**Transport costs**

$SM_1$    Highest revenue **A**    Lowest cost    $SM_2$

**Zone of profitability**

An **Optimiser** would locate at **A** as in this case the profit (difference between revenue & costs) is greatest.

An **Satisfier** would locate between SM1 and SM2 there a profit is made but is not as great as at **A**

The location of raw materials and the location of markets are still important factors in determining the location and characteristics of manufacturing industries. The movement of integrated steel works from inland sites to coastal locations in the UK was due, in part, to the need continue to be near the site of raw materials (deep water ore terminals), as the home produced iron ore which they had relied upon had become exhausted. Similarly, the decision to site a Honda factory in northern France instead of the UK was explained by the fact that the product of the factory was aimed at the European rather than the British market.

It is however undeniable that the site of raw materials and markets are now not as important as they once were. The use of electricity rather than coal for power allows firms to locate away from coalfield site. Developments in transport technology and costs have reduced the cost of transport and allowed firms greater flexibility in their choice of location.

## Land, labour and capital

These terms have long been used by economists to describe what they term 'factors of production'. As with all factors the importance of land, labour and capital vary between industries and their relative importance has changed over time.

### Land

The attributes of land that create a comparative advantage of a location are its characteristics, cost and availability. Firms will be attracted to areas that have good public services and good access to transport networks, markets and a workforce. The cost of the land is also important. Urban areas are more expensive than rural areas and this factor was used to explain the movement of industries from inner urban areas to suburban and greenfield sites from the 1920s onwards. It was also the lack of available land for expansion adjacent to the factory site that encouraged this movement. Manufacturing firms were not only taking advantage of a change in transport technology (from rail to road) but this movement also reflected the desire of firms to expand and develop new technologies. Cheap, purpose built factories on greenfield sites therefore had a greater comparative advantage than constrained inner city brownfield site locations.

The land must also be suitable for the construction of large manufacturing plants and not suffer from contamination. It was highly polluted land of the Lower Swansea Valley that was one of the reasons for the reluctance of new firms to locate in the area [see Fig 3.6].

### Labour

Labour is increasingly an important factor in determining the comparative advantage of a location, through cost, flexibility, skills, militancy and type.

Labour costs vary within countries and between countries (Fig 3.7). As we shall see later on it was certainly an important factor in attracting firms to locate in low wage economies such as Taiwan and Malaysia.

Labour costs are not simply the wage that the workforce costs. The true cost of labour is the wages as well as costs of benefits paid to the workforce in the form of pensions, company cars etc. It also includes payments that the firm may have to pay such as National Insurance which vary between countries. Productivity will also effect the true cost of labour as higher waged workers such as the German auto industry are more productive than lower waged British workers and therefore the overall cost per unit is cheaper in Germany than in the UK.

The skill level of the workforce will create a location's comparative advantage. The success of the Cambridge Science park in attracting industries was due to the proximity of the skilled research workers available from Cambridge University.

The flexibility of the workforce is also important in affecting the comparative advantage of locations. Flexibility refers to the ability of a workforce to adapt to new technologies and working practices. Nissan located an assembly plant in Smyrna in Tennessee in the US as it was able to hire workers who were not members of the United Auto Workers union. These non-members were said to be more receptive to Japanese style work practices as opposed to workers in the Detroit area – the traditional centre for automobile production in the US.

The militancy of the workforce in terms of industrial action organised by trade unions is also an important factor. Although some authors have accused industry of 'running away' from trade unions, there is little evidence to substantiate this. Indeed areas with a long history of militancy still attract firms. Ford has committed itself to produce Jaguar cars at the Halewood site in Merseyside despite a long history of industrial disputes at the site.

### Capital

All firms need both fixed capital which is plant, machinery etc. as well as financial or monetary capital to produce goods. Whilst fixed capital is said to be immobile financial/monetary capital is said to be mobile. This means that fixed capital can attract new businesses to or force companies to stay in a location. When it is uneconomic to move locations due to the loss of fixed capital industrial inertia is said to have occurred. In the Lower Swansea valley, the presence of fixed capital in the form of large copper smelting factories encouraged the conversion of these factories to the smelting of zinc. Similarly the low start up costs (i.e. monetary capital) of developing tin plate factories in the Lower Swansea valley also contributed to the rapid development of that industry in the area.

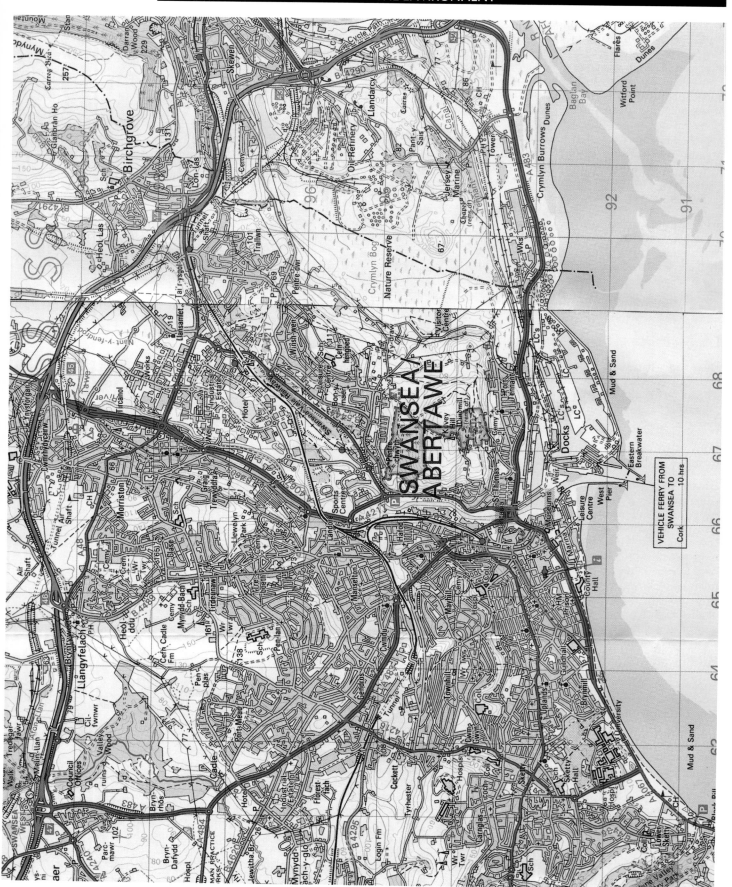

FIGURE 3.6  OS map, Swansea (Reproduced from Ordnance Survey mapping with the permission of The Controller of Her Majesty's Stationery Office © Crown copyright; Licence No: 399450)

FIGURE 3.7 (a)  Average weekly earnings (pounds sterling) in manufacturing; (b) Labour wage costs within the UK and the world

| Region | Male | Female |
| --- | --- | --- |
| North | 254.60 | 146.60 |
| Yorkshire & Humberside | 245.10 | 141.70 |
| East Midlands | 246.00 | 141.70 |
| East Anglia | 263.00 | 158.80 |
| South East | 303.60 | 189.80 |
| South West | 260.50 | 156.60 |
| West Midlands | 246.70 | 143.10 |
| North West | 253.10 | 150.10 |
| England | 266.80 | 160.70 |
| Wales | 246.10 | 155.10 |
| Scotland | 249.30 | 145.50 |
| Northern Ireland | 211.50 | 134.00 |
| Great Britain | 264.50 | 159.10 |

Financial/Monetary capital is mobile and therefore the cost and availability of monetary capital can affect the location of manufacturing. Large companies have little difficulty in obtaining monetary capital from financial markets. Small firms, particularly those concerned with the development of new technology, however, are dependent upon **venture capital** to fund research, development and expansion. Specialist firms inject capital into small firms and at the same time take a stake in the firm. These venture capital firms hope to realise a profit in the future when the company expands and is successful. As the availability of venture capital is not equal, small firms are likely to choose areas where there is greater availability of venture capital. In the United Kingdom, 60 per cent of all venture capital investment has been within the South East. It is the effect of venture capital that has been partly responsible for the development of small firms specialising in technological developments along the M4 corridor between London and Bristol.

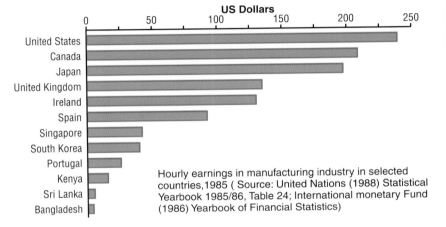

Hourly earnings in manufacturing industry in selected countries,1985 ( Source: United Nations (1988) Statistical Yearbook 1985/86, Table 24; International monetary Fund (1986) Yearbook of Financial Statistics)

FIGURE 3.8  Export processing zones

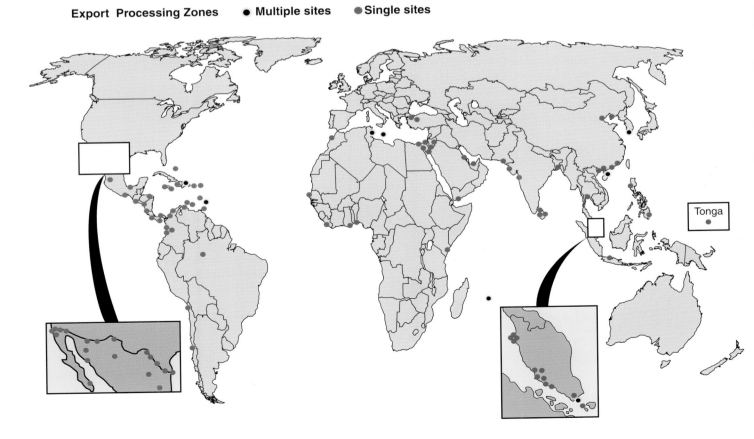

## Governments

Governments create a location's comparative advantage (for instance through the granting of special tax incentives) or lessen a location's comparative advantage (through increases in tax) at a range of scales, international, national and local.

### International government action

The comparative advantages of both countries and locations can be affected by international government action. This is either through the adoption of trade policies through the GATT (Global Agreement on Trade and Tariff) or now the WTO (World Trade Organisation), or through the development of regional trading blocks such as the EU (European Union) or NAFTA (North American Free Trade Association). With the development of NAFTA, Mexico received much new investment at the expense of Canada from US owned TNCs as a result of the lifting of restrictions.

Similarly, the large expansion of Japanese firms into the UK has been seen in part as a response to trade policies in Europe. Initially, investment in Europe was to overcome the 'voluntary' quota of imported Japanese cars. As the cars are made in the UK they count as a European firm and therefore do not count as an import. Subsequently, the development of the EU further encouraged Japanese car firms to locate in Europe. Indeed the whole of Europe is benefiting from the development of the EU. In 1985 the EU only accounted for 38 per cent of total inward investment from Multi National Companies but by 1990 with the rise of the single market this had risen to 45 per cent.

In addition, the EU has also long supported problem regions in Europe. Grants and loans are available and have been used in areas such as the Lower Swansea Valley and the Rhonda Valley to improve housing and the economic infrastructure. It is hoped by improving the infrastructure the comparative advantage of these areas would be increased and therefore industries would be attracted to locate here.

### National government intervention

The type of government that controls a country is the most important factor affecting government intervention. The 'political dimension' is vital in determining the extent to which a country allows foreign penetration by TNCs as well as the working practices adopted by the TNC. Some countries such as the UK and the US have few if any controls on the level of penetration by foreign TNCs whilst others such as China have very restrictive legislation. The level of government intervention, therefore, varies both over time as even democratic countries such as the UK will have changes in political orientation, and in different industries, as different governments will support different industries. The Newly Industrialised Countries, in particular, have had some the biggest government interventions in recent years.

Most National governments have two principal objectives for their policies which affect industries. Firstly they will try to attract industries to the country by increasing the comparative advantages of locations within the country. One such approach is through the development of **Export Processing Zones** (EPZs) (Fig 3.8). These are locations where foreign firms can import raw materials and produce finished products for export without the payment of any tax. They are therefore of great importance for TNCs who can employ cheap labour in areas such as South Korea or Mexico and not pay taxes on the finished products. The impact of both supra and national government action in creating comparative advantages for locations is clearly shown in the development of the US/Mexico border Maquiladora centres which are not only EPZs but have also been developed by the creation of NAFTA (Fig 3.9).

Another approach is through grants to attract industries to locate in their countries such as the £125 million given to Nissan to locate in Sunderland.

Secondly, National governments try to reduce regional differences in economic development (such as the North/South gap in the UK). National governments have tried to reduce regional differences in two main ways – indirect and direct. Indirect policies are those carried out by the government where although they are not deliberately designed to effect specific locations, the effect of them is to increase some location's comparative advantage at the expense of others. In countries such as the UK, procurement is one such indirect policy. All governments need to purchase or procure both goods and services. Governments can therefore stimulate local economies by procuring these goods and services from specific locations.

Direct policies are where a government through a variety of policies changes the comparative advantages of areas either to attract firms or to discourage firms (Fig 3.10).

FIGURE 3.9 Employment in Mexican Maquiladora centres

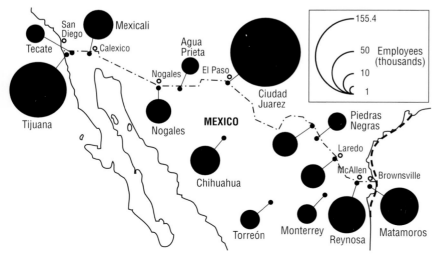

| National Policies Regional Assistance | In the 1960s and 1970s the Government gave grants and tax incentives to encourage firms to move to these depressed areas. Assisted areas are large areas such as S. Wales which have been targeted by the Government for improvement. Between 1961–1981, 600 000 jobs have been created in AA. This has cost vast amounts – £700 million in 1983. Costs have been slashed with a strict £10 000 per limit. Firms were attracted to such areas by few restraints on planning permission, low rents and rates, and funds for relocation. There were also tax incentives. |
|---|---|
| Enterprise Zones | Such as in Docklands and in Swansea were set up. Although they were initially different from the AA, they ended up having very similar effects. They were usually for only ten years duration and unlike the AA they were often heavily advertised. Some were successful such as Swansea, Corby and Docklands and others not such as Clydeside and Belfast. |
| Urban Development Corporations | These were set up by the government to combine public and private investment to regenerate run down areas. Tyneside, Teeside, Bristol/Manchester, Leeds, Sheffield, Cardiff and Stoke on Trent. |
| Capital programme | Road building linking peripheral areas to the rest of the UK. The Head of the Vallies road (Merthyr Tydfyll to Swansea) was completed in 1967 and later the M4 was extended from Bristol to Swansea. This encouraged firms such as Ford, Sony and Hoover to located in Bridgend in Wales. |
| Development agencies | Such as the WDA which promoted private investment in a region. These advertised extensively, particularly overseas to attract foreign companies to locate in their regions. |
| **Local Governments** | |
| Enterprise Boards | Such as West Yorkshire Enterprise Board and Lancashire Enterprise Limited. The exact nature of the board reflected their area. In London, long term jobs particularly for Women and EM were the priority, whilst in WY the priority was creating any jobs and arresting industrial decline. |

FIGURE 3.10 Direct government policy in the UK

FIGURE 3.11 Linkages and agglomeration

## Linkages and agglomerations

Linkages are the relationships that firms have with their suppliers and their markets (Fig 3.11). There are two types of linkages – material flows such as car parts etc. and information flows such as knowledge of potential customers etc. These linkages can also be either **upstream linkages** where firms obtain the materials/information required to manufacture a product, whilst **downstream linkages** are where the firm produces a component in another firms production process. Firms can also outsource or externalise some of their production and as explained in Figure 3.1 all manufacturing firms will need some form of producer services.

**Agglomeration** factors are the benefits that firms gain by locating in close proximity to other firms which in turn develops the comparative advantage of the area (Fig 3.12). Linkages and agglomeration factors rely on existing manufacturing industries being present in an area and therefore do not actually create an area's comparative advantage. Instead they develop the comparative advantage. This process is also known as the **multiplier effect** or **cumulative causation** (Fig 3.13).

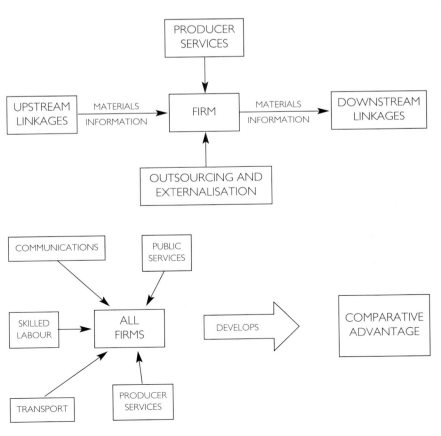

FIGURE 3.12 Agglomeration economies

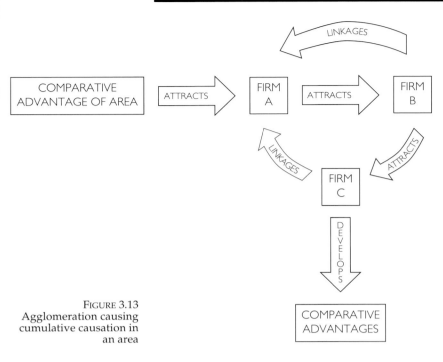

FIGURE 3.13
Agglomeration causing
cumulative causation in
an area

During the 1970s and 80s productivity was much higher in Japan and Germany than in the UK, which was a result of the different attitudes to work found in these countries. Similarly, the adoption of flexible working practices by the UK and the US during the 1990s compared to the slower adoption of these practices by France and Germany has been identified as a factor in explaining the faster growth experienced in the UK and the US from 1992 onwards.

## Conclusion on factors affecting manufacturing industries

Factors therefore greatly affect a location's comparative advantage. Different industries have different requirements and therefore locations with different comparative advantages will attract different industries. These differences in comparative advantage can therefore be used to explain the location of industry.

### Social factors

Social factors (the interactions of class, gender, race etc.) are part of a two way interaction between industry and people. Industries shape social factors whilst social factors can affect the location of industry.

---

**STUDENT ACTIVITY**

1   Find out which manufacturing industries are located in your area. Draw their locations on a map and try to establish what factors might have led them to locate in your area.
2   Which do you think was the most important factor in effecting the comparative advantage of your area?

---

# Processes of manufacturing

There are a variety of both technological and organisational processes that develop a location's comparative advantage (Fig 3.3). Changes in the processes of manufacturing will increase the comparative advantage of some locations while diminishing others.

## Technology

There are various forms of technology that affect the processes of manufacturing (Fig 3.3), and it is a combination of these forms of technology that ultimately affects the location and characteristics of manufacturing.

### Product technologies

The **Product Life Cycle** shows how the development of a product affects the location of manufacturing industries (Fig 3.14). In Stage I, the product requires a high degree of technically skilled labour. This is then reflected in the price which is high. The demand is therefore low. In Stage II as the product starts to gain widespread acceptance

demand increases and the scale of production therefore increases. Skilled labour is still required but it is not as technical as in Stage I. The increased scale of production reduces the price which further increases demand. In Stage III, the product and process of manufacture is no longer new. Competition further reduces the price and demand peaks. Firms will seek to maintain profits by reducing the cost of their labour. By Stage IV demand is falling and firms seek to reduce costs further by the use of large scale standardised production techniques which allows them to utilise semi-skilled labour.

As the life cycle of a product develops there is a transfer of comparative advantage from locations that satisfy the firm's requirements in Stage I to those that can satisfy a firm's requirements in Stage II. This transfer then also occurs between Stage III and Stage IV. Wealthy locations with a highly skilled labour will therefore be where Stage I of the PLC will develop. In the UK locations such as the Cambridge Science Park and Uxbridge Science Park fit these requirements. The Cambridge Science Park is now the centre of the UK's Biotechnology

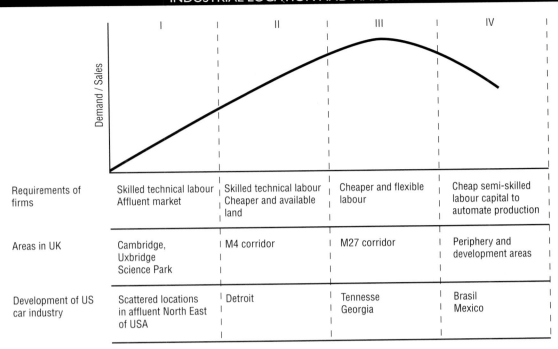

FIGURE 3.14 Product life cycle

| | I | II | III | IV |
|---|---|---|---|---|
| Requirements of firms | Skilled technical labour Affluent market | Skilled technical labour Cheaper and available land | Cheaper and flexible labour | Cheap semi-skilled labour capital to automate production |
| Areas in UK | Cambridge, Uxbridge Science Park | M4 corridor | M27 corridor | Periphery and development areas |
| Development of US car industry | Scattered locations in affluent North East of USA | Detroit | Tennesse Georgia | Brasil Mexico |

industry and is also where Microsoft located their development plant. In Stage II there is still a need for skilled labour but more land is needed and so expansion occurs away from the small clusters of research firms such as the Cambridge Science Park to locations where land is cheaper and more available such as the M4 corridor. As demand increases and the need for skilled labour reduces, firms seek to locate in locations where labour is cheaper such as the M27 corridor. Finally in Stage IV, large scale production techniques are used and semi-skilled labour is required so production is switched to lower cost locations such as South Wales.

The product life cycle has also been used to explain changes in the global locations of various manufacturing industries.

Cars were initially hand built, expensive and built and sold in small quantities close to the site of their development (Stage I). In the United States this was scattered locations in the affluent North East. As wealth increased there was more demand and so production increased in scale. The introduction of assembly line techniques reduced the time taken to build a car and hence the cost was also reduced. This further increased demand (Stage II). Production was now centred in Detroit. Detroit had several comparative advantages that other locations in the US lacked. It had a skilled workforce, sufficient capital available and it was a break of bulk location for iron and coal from the Great Lakes and the railroads. With growing competition firms sought to increase their markets by expanding production to other sites (Stage III). Ford and General Motors expanded into Europe during the 1930s and production moved away from the Great Lakes area to more southern locations such as Tennessee and Georgia. Eventually, the rate of

demand decreased and intense competition from Japanese and European producers encouraged Ford and General Motors to close US plants and relocate in Mexico and Brazil (Stage IV) (Fig 3.14).

*Process technologies*

Process technologies refers to the type of technologies that are being used by manufacturing industries in the process of manufacturing. There have been several key technological developments that have affected the ways in which products are manufactured. These developments have been termed 'Long Waves of the Economy' and are known as **Kondratieff long waves** after the economist who first drew attention to them (Fig 3.15). Each Long Wave is associated with a development in new technologies. As new processes of technology are developed it changes the requirements of industries. This means that if a location no longer has a comparative advantage in the factors that the new process of technology requires, that location will decline and other locations which do have a comparative advantage will attract these new industries. As can be seen from Fig 3.15 locations such as Shropshire and the Black Country (Wave I), South Wales (Wave II), and the West Midlands (Wave III) have in turn suffered economic decline while locations associated with Wave IV and V (M4 corridor) have undergone economic growth.

'Long Waves' have also been applied to countries on a global scale (Fig 3.15). It is interesting to note that whilst the United States seems to have been involved in the last four Kondratieff waves, this was in different locations. Wave II locations in the US surrounding the Great Lakes have suffered just as much as similar locations in the UK and have been termed the 'Rustbelt'.

FIGURE 3.15 Long waves in the economy

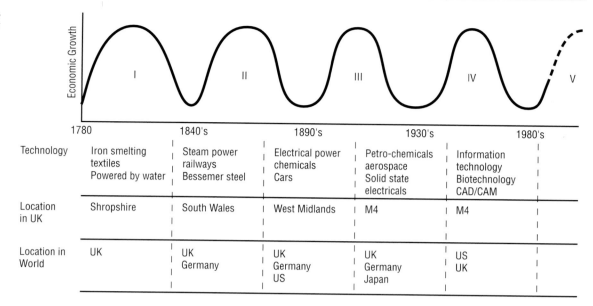

FIGURE 3.16 Production at the Dagenham factory 1931–95

| Technology | Iron smelting textiles Powered by water | Steam power railways Bessemer steel | Electrical power chemicals Cars | Petro-chemicals aerospace Solid state electricals | Information technology Biotechnology CAD/CAM |
|---|---|---|---|---|---|
| Location in UK | Shropshire | South Wales | West Midlands | M4 | M4 |
| Location in World | UK | UK Germany | UK Germany US | UK Germany Japan | US UK |

## Total vehicle production

| | | | | |
|---|---|---|---|---|
| Dagenham factory produces first vehicle at 1.15 pm on October 1st – a 30 cwt Model A Truck | → 1931 | 4547 | New Tractor Plant at Basildon | → 1964 681 753 |
| | 1935 | 75 746 | | 1965 670 444 |
| Second World War – factory converts to military production | → 1940 | 60 045 | Swansea and Belfast plants opened New Dagenham Engine Plant | 1966 655 895 |
| | 1945 | 46 671 | | 1970 653 146 |
| New truck assembly plant opens at Langley, Buckinghamshire | → 1949 | 151 793 | | 1975 535 773 |
| | 1950 | 185 124 | The millionth Transit is built → | 1976 600 426 |
| | 1955 | 355 772 | Halewood produces its 3-millionth vehicle | → 1978 474 873 |
| Southampton begins production | → 1958 | 417 084 | Bridgend Engine Plant opens → | 1980 513 993 |
| | 1960 | 575 417 | Introduction of Ford Sierra | → 1982 453 219 |
| | | | | 1985 455 147 |
| Halewood Body & Assembly Plant opens | → 1962 | 529 127 | Dagenham converts to single-car production of the Fiesta range of cars and vans | → 1990 480 541 |
| | | | | 1995 419 985 |

### Computerisation

This refers to the use of computers in the process of automation in the manufacturing process. Early automation started with the development of the water powered loom in the eighteenth century but still required many operators. During the 1960s, Computer Numerical Control machines were developed, so that a series of operations could be controlled by just one central computer. This was termed Direct Numeric Control (DNC). The power of these computers was further enhanced by the invention of the microchip and the development of fully computerised production systems (Computer Assisted Manufacture, CAM). Computers were also used in the design of new products (Computer Assisted Design, CAD).

CAD/CAM has been extensively used in automobile production. The design of cars was always very expensive – the Ford Escort reputedly cost $3 billion in research and development costs. This was one of the reasons why production runs had to be so large – to recoup the high design costs.

## Ford Manufacturing Facilities in the UK

*Assembly*
Dagenham: Ford Fiesta cars and vans and the Courier van. Also Mazda 121 model.
Halewood: Ford Escort cars and vans.
Southampton: Ford Transit vans.
*Engine Production*
Bridgend: 1.6L and 1.8L Zetec and 1.4L PTE.
Dagenham: 2.5L, 1.8L diesel and DOHC.
*Transmission/Steering*
Halewood: B5 and MT75 transmissions.
Swansea: Axles, hubs, brake discs and drums, rotors, knuckles, spindles, crankshafts, camshafts, differentials, halfshafts, carriers and flanges.

*Casting/Forging*
Leamington Foundry: Engine and transmission components, brake discs, drums, flywheels, exhaust manifold and bearing cups.
*Stamping*
Croydon: small metal stampings.
*Climate Control*
Basildon: Aluminium radiators, air conditioning, refrigerant hoses, condensers and intercoolers.
*Electronics*
Enfield: Instrument clusters, fuel and temperature gauges, fuel pump senders and plastic subassemblies
*Electrical and Fuel Handling*
Belfast: Oil and water pumps, fuel injection assemblies and throttle modulators.

---

**STUDENT ACTIVITY**

1  Study Fig 3.16
2  Plot out the total production of Cars made by Ford UK over time. Try to fit stages II, III and IV of the PLC onto this graph.
Now study the location of Ford plants and the date which they were opened. Does the history of Ford UK fit the PLC? If not try to give reasons.
3  Look again at the production of vehicles from the Ford Factory at Dagenham. CAD/CAM was steadily introduced into the Plant from 1989 onwards. Does the introduction of this technology partly explain why the manufacture of vehicles does not fit the product life cycle?

The use of CAD has substantially reduced this cost and has led to car manufacturers to be able to produce far smaller production runs of vehicles profitably.

In addition the development of Computer Assisted Manufacture (CAM) has greatly reduced the labour required by automobile production. At the Ford Dagenham works in London the development of CAD/CAM led to the loss of over 60 per cent of the workforce. In the US General Motors have built new plants that have utilised this new technology. The $5 billion plant in Smyrna was the first to use Manufacturing Automation Protocol (MAP).

The adoption of CAD/CAM also gives companies what has been termed Economies of Scope. These are savings the company makes when it uses CAD/CAM to make different products at the same time rather than separately, one after the other.

### Communication technology

Communication technology allows firms that are flexible in their choice of location to take advantage of locations that would otherwise not have a comparative advantage. Without failsafe international telephone communications Gateway would not have chosen Ireland as its base for customer enquiries and production of its computers. Ireland has several comparative advantages – a skilled and educated and relatively cheap workforce with a supportive government and low land costs. These advantages were therefore magnified by the fact that telecommunications allowed Gateway to set up here and incur no more costs than setting up anywhere else in Europe.

### Transport technologies

Transport technologies have 'shrunk the world' and led to industries 'being freed from the tyranny of transport costs' (Fig 3.17). These developments have been enabled by parallel developments in communications technologies. Modern aeroplanes are dependent upon satellite communication links for navigation across oceans and continents.

These developments in transport and communication technologies are essentially enabling technologies. Their vital influence on the comparative advantages of locations is to reduce the importance of the location of the market and the source of raw materials and at the same time to magnify the influence of other factors. In the UK the movement of integrated steel works to deep water coastal locations was influenced by the development of the super ore carriers in the 1960s. Similarly the reduction in transport costs brought about by the developments in the transport technologies allowed TNCs to spread production to NICs, whilst NICs themselves utilised the developments in transport technologies to develop their own industries and export their products to MEDC markets.

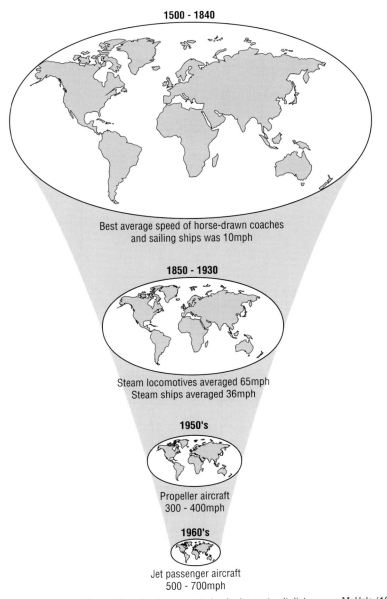

Global shrinkage the effect of changing transport technologies on 'real' distance on McHale (1969).

FIGURE 3.17  Shrinking the world

## Organisation

Organisation refers to not only the size and geographical spread of manufacturing companies but also the use of the workforce as well as the way in which how the actual process of manufacturing is organised.

### Size and spatial scale of firms

The size and the geographical spread of firms have become greater. These large firms known as Trans National Companies (TNCs) are vast with turnover's far larger than the GDP of many industrialised and wealthy countries (Fig 3.18).

Indeed TNCs now account for 25 per cent of total world production. They also dominate trade with 50 per cent of the US trade being through TNCs and 80 per cent of the UK's trade.

FIGURE 3.18 The size of
the largest TNCs in
manufacturing
compared with the GDP
of selected countries

| | |
|---|---|
| UK | 729 |
| Mexico | 142 |
| General Motors | 127 |
| Austria | 117 |
| Ford | 97 |
| Denmark | 93 |
| Norway | 83 |
| Argentina | 79 |
| IBM | 63 |
| Toyota | 60 |
| General Electric | 55 |
| Thailand | 54 |
| Hitachi | 51 |
| Greece | 48 |
| Matsushita | 43 |
| Daimler-Benz | 41 |
| Philip Morris | 39 |

FIGURE 3.18 The size of the largest TNCs in manufacturing compared with the GDP of selected countries

It is also true that only a few TNCs control vast amounts of the world trade – 12.5 per cent of total world production is in the hands of only 74 firms and the amount of production that these control is growing by the day. Companies become multinational through what is termed Foreign Direct Investment (FDI). Although it is commonly thought that TNC invest primarily in LEDC, in fact 75 per cent of all FDI is in Japan, the US and the EU.

Multinationals will therefore effect the location and characteristics of manufacturing as they have different requirements than other firms which operate only in one country. TNCs still select a location based on that location's comparative advantage. It is simply that the first comparative advantage that a TNC seeks is based on international rather than domestic considerations. Furthermore, a TNC will not necessarily choose a location within a country which appears to have the best comparative advantage. It will instead be

influenced by international rather than domestic factors.

There are many different theories as to why TNCs have proliferated and grown so powerful over the last 50 years. An important factor in encouraging firms to become TNCs was the drop in average profits from 17 per cent to 11 per cent between 1960 and 1980. Firms therefore became TNCs to either expand their markets and hence their sales or to reduce costs in the production process. Attention has therefore focused on how TNCs can out complete local domestic firms in terms of market penetration as well as how TNCs can reduce costs by locating abroad (Fig 3.19).

The growth and influence of TNCs has caused concern to both MEDCs and LEDCs. Their huge size and control of world trade has led to many of the problems of areas being put at the feet of TNCs. The turmoil that engulfed the NICs in 1997 was blamed by Heads of States on the malign influence of TNCs. The presence of multinationals can bring both positive and negative aspects to the country in which they operate.

### Labour processes

Labour processes are the way in which the labour employed in a firm is organised, controlled and used in the production process. The adoption of a particular process then develops the comparative advantage of that location. There have been four developments in the use of labour in the production process (Fig 3.20).

### Processes of production

As well as the process of labour adopted, the overall economic process of production can develop a location's comparative advantage. **Fordism** was the name given to the large scale mass production and mass consumption production systems developed in the 1930s and in operation until the 1970s, coupled with an aim of full employment and the development of a welfare state. The large scale assembly line techniques used, encouraged industry to locate near to large scale markets and labour pools. In the UK this was centred around the two largest populations, London and the West Midlands. Thus these locations developed their comparative advantages whilst other peripheral locations which were not so well suited to such a production process were therefore at a disadvantage.

As well as these large scale immobile plants, Fordism was also synonymous with state intervention in the economy and the development of the welfare state. Government policy in assisting periphery locations was therefore a consequence of this system of production, as was the subsequent subsidising of loss making industries such as British Steel and British Leyland in the 1970s and keeping inefficient plants such as Ravenscraig Steel plant in Scotland open.

FIGURE 3.19 Factors that have allowed companies to internationalise, and why TNC will then be able to outcompete domestic firms

| Companies have been allowed to become TNC by: | TNC outcompete local firms by: | | |
|---|---|---|---|
| | **Ownership** | **Internalisation** | **Location** |
| ■ similar infrastructure and marketing | ■ size | ■ no disruptions in supply | ■ size of market |
| ■ similar markets | ■ access to capital | ■ transfer pricing | ■ variations in demand |
| ■ mobile capital | ■ brand name | | ■ variations in land and labour costs |
| ■ free trade agreements | ■ production technique | | ■ variations in government regulation |
| ■ increases in transport technology | | | |
| ■ increases in communication technology | | | |
| ■ increases in product technology | | | |

The change from this system of production to a smaller and more flexible system is one of the biggest changes that has occurred in the production process in recent years.

### Organisation of stock control

Under the Fordist regime of production firms had traditionally held large inventories of parts required in the manufacturing processes. This system was termed '**just in case**' (JIC) stock control. This was expensive in not only the land required to warehouse this stock but also in the labour required to monitor the stock and the interest charged on the purchased stock. The Japanese developed the Kanban system or '**just in time**' stock control (JIT). Instead of having large numbers of stock, the parts required are delivered on a weekly or even daily basis. In addition the number of different components were reduced. This has made the production process far more efficient and is thought to reduce costs by up to 25 per cent. It has been estimated that JIT can give Nissan in Sunderland a cost advantage of £250 per car.

In conjunction with JIT, there has been the increased use of inventory control using Electronic Data Interchange (EDI). This allows all the components required by a factory to be labelled with an electronic identity which can then be checked by the factory and sent to where it is required. This, along with the requirement to give multiple daily deliveries, has prompted some authors to suggest that JIT will encourage agglomerations of suppliers around the factory.

The decreased use of components, the use of JIT and Electronic Data Interchange has been termed 'lean production' techniques and has been a major factor in explaining the globalisation of Japanese industries in particular.

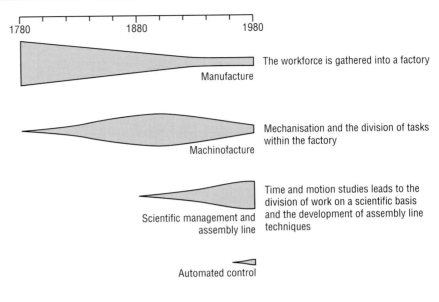

The workforce is gathered into a factory

Manufacture

Mechanisation and the division of tasks within the factory

Machinofacture

Time and motion studies leads to the division of work on a scientific basis and the development of assembly line techniques

Scientific management and assembly line

Automated control

Strategic Alliances, where large TNC combine with other large TNC, are becoming more important. BP have an alliance with Mobil in Europe, whilst they have an alliance with Amoco in the US in what is – at present – the largest ever corporate deal in history. Daimler-Benz are also in alliance with Chrysler in the US. This consolidation is expected to spread to other sectors of the economy such as transport (the proposed British Airways/America Airlines alliance) and even in banking.

FIGURE 3.20
Developments in the use of labour in the production process

## Organisation of firms

As well as the development of JIT, the way in which the suppliers to the firm are organised will affect a location's comparative advantage. Firms have always subcontracted out parts of the production process, but this process of sub-contracting has accelerated in recent years. Firms have changed from organising production to be rather the organiser of firms. This system of one large TNC organising and collaborating with many other suppliers through sub-contracting, alliances and mutual ownership is known as **Keiretsu**. One firm (e.g. NEC) will have links with and organise all aspects of its supplies such as telecommunications parts and components and information processing (Fig 3.21).

Not all firms will operate a Keiretsu form of organisation but those that do will have important impacts on developing a location's comparative advantage.

FIGURE 3.21 Keiretsu

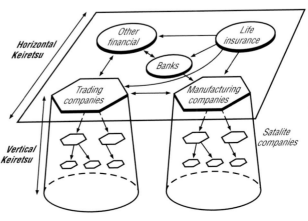

*Horizontal keiretsu* are highly diversified industrial groups organised around two key institutions: a core bank and a general trading company *(sogo shosha)*. Three of the horizontal *keiretsu* groups (Mitsubishi, Mitsui, Sumitomo) are the successors of the prewar family-led zaibatsu groups which were abolished after 1945. The others are primarily bank controlled. *Vertical keiretsu* are organised around a large parent company in a specific industry (for example, Toshiba, Toyota, Sony).

# Outcomes in Manufacturing

Outcomes (Fig 3.22) are caused by changes in the relative influence of factors and processes and are of great interest to geographers. Outcomes range from changes in the characteristics of manufacturing industries (such as the development of flexible manufacturing systems) to changes in the location of manufacturing industries (such as the development of NICs). Often these outcomes reflect both changes in characteristics and locations of manufacturing (such as the development of new industrial spaces).

## Changing manufacturing characteristics – How are things made now?

The most important change in the characteristic of manufacturing has been the development of flexible forms of manufacturing. Essentially, flexible manufacturing is an amalgamation of new technologies and organisational processes that are distinct from the Fordist system of production (Fig 3.24). This new form of manufacturing has been termed **Flexible Accumulation**.

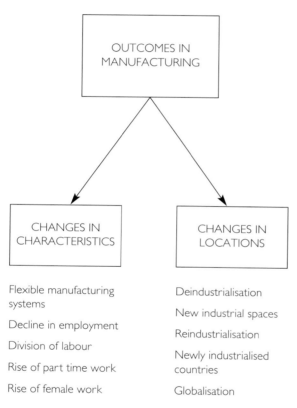

FIGURE 3.22 Outcomes in manufacturing

Flexible Machines where one machine which can be used to make more than one similar product

Flexible Manufacturing Systems, where these machines are linked together and controlled by one computer

Flexible stock control, specifically the adoption of Just in Time stock control

Flexible customerisation where firms can respond to changing market demands in type and amount rapidly

Flexible integration where production occurs at different sites but can be seamlessly integrated when required

Flexible labour where amount of labour required is constantly changed as well as the fact that the workforce can adapt more quickly and carry out a range of tasks

Flexible outsourcing where firms externalise production to firms and are flexible in who they sub contract work out to

FIGURE 3.24 Flexible manufacturing systems

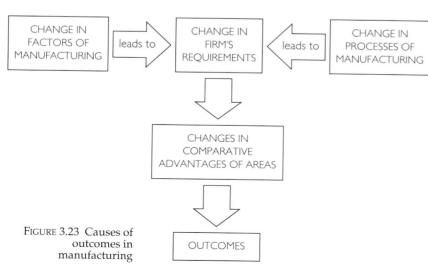

FIGURE 3.23 Causes of outcomes in manufacturing

A good example of how the flexible production system works is the Mercedes Benz factory in Stuttgart, Germany. Mercedes Benz introduced CAD/CAM in 1985 and now implement a JIT stock control system. The manufacture of Mercedes Benz is now far more flexible in terms of the customers needs – the C180 for instance comes in four different models, Classic, Esprit, Elegance and Sports. Each model appeals to a different niche in the already niche luxury car market. In doing so it has operated so called economies of scope. Making all four models at the same time to a customer's order is cheaper than making a batch of Classics followed by a batch of Sports. In line with other car manufacturers they now have a supplier site adjacent to their factory in Stuttgart where their suppliers can locate and there are even plans to invite the supplies in to fit the components rather than use Mercedes Benz personnel.

There is doubt, however, about the actual extent of adoption of flexible manufacturing. Whilst many firms do employ flexible production techniques, not all firms do and it is often essential for there to be large Fordist plants working and subcontracting work for the flexible systems of production to operate.

Flexible manufacturing systems incorporate flexibility in supplier relationships, flexibility in products, flexibility in the labour requirements and how they are used, flexibility in the amount of production sub-contracted and above all flexibility in the way the product is manufactured.

## *Changing labour requirements*

One of the most noticeable outcomes has been in the changes in the numbers employed in manufacturing in MEDCs. This has been caused by a variety of factors.

Changes in the availability of raw materials had consequent effects on industries which utilised these raw materials. Inland steel plants in the UK such as Corby were closed down and production was moved to coastal locations. This movement was also effected by the development of large super ore carriers in the 1960s and 1970s which allowed the importation of cheap foreign ore.

Changes in the processes of manufacturing particularly the increasing use of information technology in the production process has also resulted in large job losses in the manufacturing sector. In addition, automation and the development of CAD/CAM in the manufacture of automobiles has reduced the numbers of jobs. Ford's largest assembly plant at Dagenham in East London has seen production reduced by 10 per cent while the workforce has been reduced by 66 per cent. Similarly, the development of large integrated steel works coupled with continuous casting techniques in steel production resulted in the loss of over 200 000 jobs in British Steel in 20 years from 1967.

Competition in the market place due to the rise of Japan and other NICs forced many MEDC manufacturing firms to go out of business leading to massive job losses. As a result many forms were forced to change their processes of manufacturing by intensifying their production to increase productivity and reduce labour to remain competitive with this new competition. This competition was also blamed for TNCs running from high cost militant workforces in the MEDC to cheaper union free locations in NICs. In actual fact whilst there was some investment in NICs the majority of investments still occurred in MEDCs (Fig 3.25).

Rationalisation, particularly with the abandonment of active state subsidies for loss making state industries. The Steel Industry in the UK had too many small inefficient plants which were loss making. These were rationalised so that production was contained within a few key sites

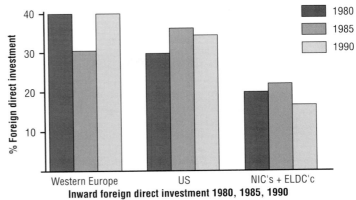

**Inward foreign direct investment 1980, 1985, 1990**

Foreign Direct Investment is the process whereby TNC become internationalised. This can be through aquistion of domestic firms, mergiges with domestic firms, or the setting up either sale outlets or production facilities.

increasing profitability but reducing employment. This led to the loss of hundreds of thousands of jobs. Governments, particularly in the US and the UK no longer believed in massive state intervention and instead developed a much freer unrestrained market philosophy. Loss making firms would not be supported and so went out of business.

The net result of these processes culminated in the dramatic decline of manufacturing employment when one million jobs in the manufacturing sector of the UK were lost between 1979 and 1981.

### *Spatial divisions of labour*

There have also been changes in the type of labour employed. There appears to be a segmented or dual labour market with primary or core workers and secondary or periphery workers.

Core workers are highly desired by the company. They have high salaries, a clear career and high job security. They are moved from plant to plant and often from country to country so that they do not become too attached to one locality. They are given considerable help with relocation expenses and are given large amounts of fringe benefits such as cars, pensions and health care. In part their location on new, edge of town housing estates has given impetus to the development of out of town shopping centres.

Periphery workers are less valued by the company. They consist of three main groups. The semi-skilled worker performs routine tasks for less pay than a core worker. They have less job security and lower fringe benefits. Immense pride in the workplace is encouraged and they are exhorted to work harder so that the factory can achieve the best group records. There are also part-time and temporary workers, particularly women who have even fewer rights than the semi-skilled worker. Finally there are self-employed workers who are contracted by the firm to perform specific tasks at random intervals.

This division of labour has led to concentration of primary workers in core locations such as the M4 and secondary workers in periphery locations such as South Wales. This has been termed a **Spatial**

FIGURE 3.25 Changes in FDI 1980–90

**Division of Labour (SDL)**. It is not just the type of primary and secondary labour that appears to show a spatial pattern. Many large firms now also separate their workforce. Plants employing mainly primary workers are found in the prosperous core locations such as M4, whilst those employing secondary workers are found mainly in poorer periphery locations. This has also been termed a Social Division of Labour.

This dual labour market has also been applied to the world with what has been termed a **New International Division of Labour (NIDL)**, with routine secondary jobs in the NIC and primary jobs in the MEDC.

### Structure of the workforce

The reduction in the manufacturing workforce and the development of a spatial division of labour has also helped changed the structure of the workforce particularly in the UK. During the 1980s there was a dramatic rise in the number of self-employed workers – to about 10 per cent of the workforce or some two million people in the UK. In addition there has also been a rise in part-time work.

Another change has been the substantial increases of women employed in manufacturing. This has been the result of changes brought about by the product life cycle with firms relocating production to take advantage of cheaper female labour, as well as firms utilising processes that no longer require the strength advantage that men have over women.

The age of the workforce has also changed. Men over the age of 45 who were made redundant found it difficult to gain meaningful work. These workers are often given few opportunities to retrain for the newer manufacturing jobs, and in many cases these jobs are not available in the areas where they live. House price differentials caused by the high unemployment where they live and the high employment in the areas where manufacturing is still occurring makes migration for work difficult.

The workforce that remains in manufacturing is therefore younger and more likely to accept new flexible working practices such as one union or no union representation.

## Changing manufacturing locations – Where are things made now?

Changes in the location of manufacturing industries have occurred on a regional scale, national scale and an international scale (Fig 3.26).

FIGURE 3.26  Manufacturing around the world

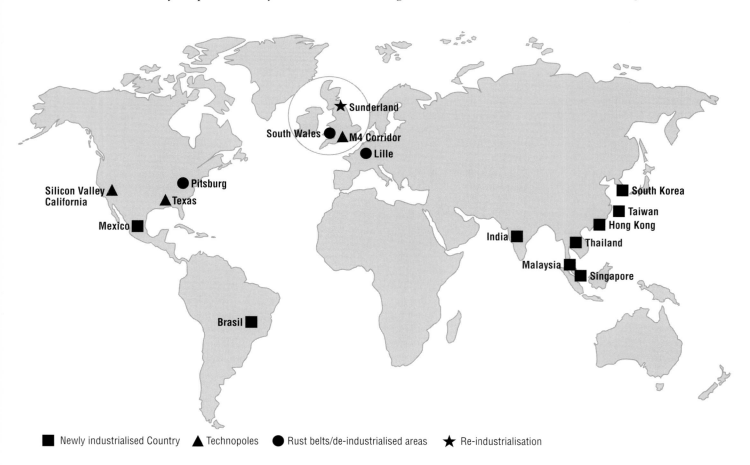

■ Newly industrialised Country　▲ Technopoles　● Rust belts/de-industrialised areas　★ Re-industrialisation

## Deindustrialisation – 'Rustbelts'

One of the most controversial outcomes has been the loss of manufacturing and employment in many traditional manufacturing locations in MEDCs. This process has been termed **deindustrialisation**. There is however debate on the precise meaning of the term. Some see deindustrialisation as a decline in employment in manufacturing. This is misleading as a decline in manufacturing employment in many MEDCs has been occurring for many decades and does not necessarily mean a drop in industrial production. Others see deindustrialisation as the inability of a country to compete internationally in the production and export of manufactured goods both for the domestic and foreign markets. It effectively means that the country or region no longer has a comparative advantage in manufacturing and therefore the drop in employment in manufacturing is a consequence of deindustrialisation.

If this latter definition of deindustrialisation is adopted it is clear that deindustrialisation occurs on three scales; within urban areas, within countries and on an international scale.

Urban deindustrialisation, where manufacturing moved from inner city locations to suburban and then periphery sites occurred during the 1920s and was caused by the change in transport from train to truck, the cheaper costs of land and labour in suburban and periphery locations and the lack of available and suitable land in inner city locations.

Regional deindustrialisation has on the other hand been attributed to the exhaustion of resources. Undoubtedly the initial decline of the Lower Swansea Valley was caused by the exhaustion of Cornish copper ore and the LSV was also dealt a death blow with the exhaustion of the coal.

Areas can remain competitive even in mature products such as steel if they can reduce costs. In the Lower Swansea Valley they could not do this as raw materials had to be imported and so it became a casualty of DI. It has also been attributed to changes in the use of technology with areas based on Wave II and III of the Kondratieff Long Waves losing out to areas in Wave IV. The Lower Swansea valley also suffered from this when the use of tin plate declined during the twentieth century.

International deindustrialisation has been attributed to globalisation. As the world economy grew and the growth in significance of TNCs meant that production could be more easily switched from MEDC to NIC locations. MEDCs therefore became deindustrialised as NICs became industrialised. In addition new investment into NICs meant that many areas did not receive investment that would have allowed them to compete with NICs. Plants that Lower Swansea Valley might have hoped to attract instead were set up in low wage areas such as Taiwan.

As well as the switch of investment from MEDCs to NICs there also appears to be a lack of investment by MEDC firms in advanced technology to achieve productivity gains. Firms, particularly in the US and UK reduced investment and paid higher dividends to shareholders and to the workforce. These two countries have suffered particularly badly in terms of deindustrialisation. Countries such as Japan, Italy and Germany invested heavily in technology and as a consequence have not suffered so much through deindustrialisation.

Finally, the growth of international competition inevitably meant that some countries would benefit and others lose out. The US and the UK were systematically outcompeted by cheaper and better products from Germany, Japan and then the NICs.

It is interesting to note that the US does not seem to be making the same mistake. In the late 1990s the US has regained is position as not only the largest economy in the world (a position which it never lost) but also the strongest in terms of sustained growth. As Japan has stagnated and the NICs, particularly in the Pacific Rim have faced currency crises, the US has powered on. Many people attribute this success to the massive adoption of computers in all aspects of the economy. The US has by far the greatest use of computers anywhere in the world.

Of course not all industrial production has been lost from MEDCs. Manufacturing is still a significant component of MEDCs economy and without manufacturing many service jobs would not exist. There even appears to be a distinct re-emergence of manufacturing in MEDCs. This is not only associated with the development of Wave V industries such as Biotechnology and Information technology in new locations termed New Industrial Spaces, but also the reindustrialisation of areas such as Ravenscraig in Scotland and South Wales with the building of new plants owned by foreign multinational companies.

FIGURE 3.27 Flexible manufacturing, sub-contracting and the development of new industrial spaces

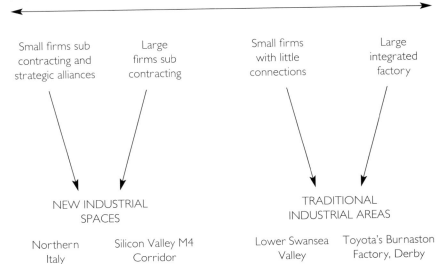

HIGH DEGREE OF SUB-CONTRACTING    LOW DEGREE OF SUB-CONTRACTING

Small firms sub contracting and strategic alliances

Large firms sub contracting

Small firms with little connections

Large integrated factory

NEW INDUSTRIAL SPACES

TRADITIONAL INDUSTRIAL AREAS

Northern Italy

Silicon Valley M4 Corridor

Lower Swansea Valley

Toyota's Burnaston Factory, Derby

## Market
The M4 corridor is close to the market of London – A World City – and hence there are many Manufacturing and Service MNC for producer service firms to serve. In addition the SE is the most affluent part of the UK and London alone has 7 million potential customers.

## Land
Land costs are far cheaper than in the congested City of London and in many cases far more available. The greenfield sites are also more attractive to modern High Technology firms than the polluted areas such as the Lower Swansea Valley.

## Labour
Labour costs are lower than in the City of London and there was a large pool of female labour. Near London the Universities and the Government Research Establishments provided skilled core workers, whilst further from London and particularly in Wales, secondary workers in both services and manufacturing were available. Over the entire length of the M4 corridor the work force is flexible.

## Capital
The initial stimulus of the M4 corridor for manufacturing was the large number of specialist producer service and high tech companies. These were all relatively small and needed venture capital to expand. Once developed, they were taken over by other larger companies coming into the area.

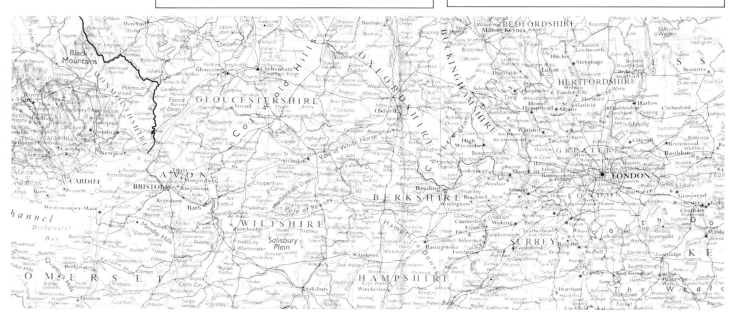

FIGURE 3.28  The M4 corridor

## Government
Initially during the 1960's, grants were available to relocate along the M4 and the Location of Office Bureau encouraged development in the area. The Welsh Development Agency and local authorities have recently been instrumental in persuading firms such as Lucky Goldstar and TSB to locate in Wales.

## Transport Technology
A key 'enabling' factor in the development of the M4 corridor is the good transport links. Heathrow with Five terminals is an essential prerequisite to attract MNC and allow UK firms to globalise. The good motorway network allows the efficient transport or raw materials in and the finished products out. It also allows for the easy access for workers and facilitates the face to face contacts needed for linkages to occur. The importance of the western end of the corridor is seen by the building of a second bridge over the River Severn and the development of two airports on Bristol and the upgrading of Cardiff airport.

## Industries along the M4 corridor

**Type of industry** – Firm – Location

**Electrical Manufacture** – Sony and Hoover at Bridgend

**Defence** – British Aerospace at Bristol

**Computer manufacture** – Intel at Swindon

**Software** – Logica at Swindon

**Computer design** – IBM at Hounslow; Digital and Oracle at Reading

**Technological Development** – AEA at Abingdon

**Biotechnolgy** – GlaxoWelcome in Uxbridge

**HQ's MNC** – Honda at Swindon; Panasonic at Farnborough

**Financial Services** – Nationwide and Allied Dunbar at Swindon

**Tourism** – First Choice at Reading

### New industrial spaces – Growth zones

New Industrial Spaces are areas of economic growth where flexible manufacturing systems are often used. There is a high degree of sub-contracting and often these areas are at the forefront of technological research. Not all growth zones, however, use such flexible production techniques. There is instead a broad continuum between large scale mass production and small scale flexible production (Fig 3.27).

The M4 corridor is a well known example of a new industrial space and is examined in Fig 3.28.

### Reindustrialisation – New life in old areas

Reindustrialisation is the re-emergence of industry in regions or countries which have suffered from deindustrialisation. In the UK, reindustrialisation has brought many new jobs in areas of high unemployment as a result of government incentives. Direct action has attracted manufacturing firms to the UK (such as the £125 million paid to Nissan to locate in Sunderland) or to encourage existing firms to stay (such as the £40 million Ford was paid to keep production in the Halewood factory on Merseyside). It is also a result of foreign firms desire to locate within the EU. Toyota located in Burnaston not as a result of government aid but rather to be able to build cars which can then be sold in the whole of the EU. As they are built in the UK they are classified as EU made and therefore do not attract taxes nor are they subject to import restrictions.

As much of this reindustrialisation uses routine poorly paid work some authors have seen it as part of a Newer International Division of Labour – where TNC are relocating in such areas to take advantage of low cost and flexible labour. The one union deal struck in the Nissan factory in Sunderland is an example of this Newer International Division of Labour.

## Newly Industrialised Countries (NICs)

Newly Industrialised Countries have gained a significant percentage of world trade and are now home to some of the largest companies in the world (Fig 3.30).

Despite some attempts to industrialise through import substitution – the development of indigenous industries in developing countries to meet home demand for manufactured goods – it has been the development of export led economic growth that has been the most spectacular in recent years.

The development of an NIC is unique to each country but there do appear to be some common characteristics.
- A low wage and educated workforce
- Cooperative governments with an aim to increase industrialisation
- Foreign economic assistance and investment
- High rates of savings and investments
- Development of an export based industry focused upon Export Processing Zones

Most of these are shown in South Korea which achieved among the highest sustained rates of growth since the 1960s (See Fig 3.29).

## Global shift

This growth in the importance of NICs in world manufacturing production coupled with the growing interdependence of economies has been termed global shift. This global shift has been caused by three major factors: development of technology and communications, growth in importance of TNCs and government action.

Although globalisation of the economy has occurred, this does not mean that production is the same throughout the world, nor that local areas are unimportant. Instead it is recognised that the world economy consists of a mosaic of interlinked and interdependent areas, all with unique social and geographical characteristics. This concept of unique local areas interbedded with a global economy has been termed **Glocalisation**. This concept refers to global companies which produce country specific products using the flexible manufacturing systems as well as through sub-contracting and externalisation. The alliances that subcontracting brings allows firms to deal with rapidly changing local conditions over the whole world.

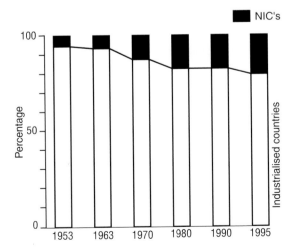

FIGURE 3.29 The growth of NICs

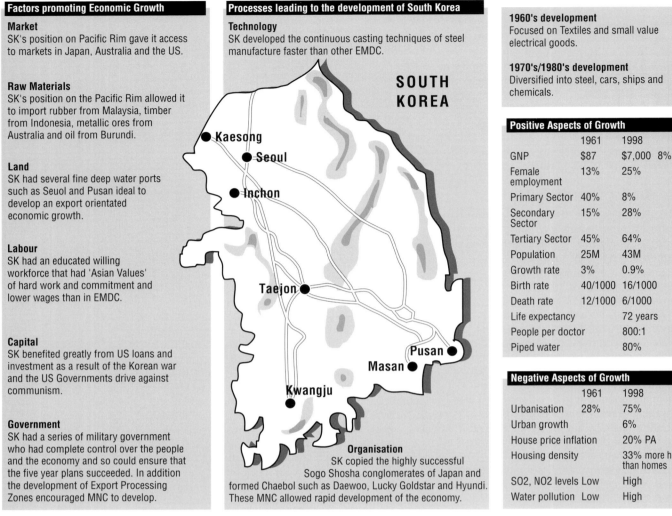

**Factors promoting Economic Growth**

**Market**
SK's position on Pacific Rim gave it access to markets in Japan, Australia and the US.

**Raw Materials**
SK's position on the Pacific Rim allowed it to import rubber from Malaysia, timber from Indonesia, metallic ores from Australia and oil from Burundi.

**Land**
SK had several fine deep water ports such as Seuol and Pusan ideal to develop an export orientated economic growth.

**Labour**
SK had an educated willing workforce that had 'Asian Values' of hard work and commitment and lower wages than in EMDC.

**Capital**
SK benefited greatly from US loans and investment as a result of the Korean war and the US Governments drive against communism.

**Government**
SK had a series of military government who had complete control over the people and the economy and so could ensure that the five year plans succeeded. In addition the development of Export Processing Zones encouraged MNC to develop.

**Processes leading to the development of South Korea**

**Technology**
SK developed the continuous casting techniques of steel manufacture faster than other EMDC.

SOUTH KOREA

Kaesong
Seoul
Inchon
Taejon
Masan
Pusan
Kwangju

**Organisation**
SK copied the highly successful Sogo Shosha conglomerates of Japan and formed Chaebol such as Daewoo, Lucky Goldstar and Hyundi. These MNC allowed rapid development of the economy.

**1960's development**
Focused on Textiles and small value electrical goods.

**1970's/1980's development**
Diversified into steel, cars, ships and chemicals.

**Positive Aspects of Growth**

|  | 1961 | 1998 |  |
|---|---|---|---|
| GNP | $87 | $7,000 | 8% PA growth |
| Female employment | 13% | 25% |  |
| Primary Sector | 40% | 8% |  |
| Secondary Sector | 15% | 28% |  |
| Tertiary Sector | 45% | 64% |  |
| Population | 25M | 43M |  |
| Growth rate | 3% | 0.9% |  |
| Birth rate | 40/1000 | 16/1000 |  |
| Death rate | 12/1000 | 6/1000 |  |
| Life expectancy |  | 72 years |  |
| People per doctor |  | 800:1 |  |
| Piped water |  | 80% |  |

**Negative Aspects of Growth**

|  | 1961 | 1998 |
|---|---|---|
| Urbanisation | 28% | 75% |
| Urban growth |  | 6% |
| House price inflation |  | 20% PA |
| Housing density |  | 33% more households than homes |
| SO2, NO2 levels | Low | High |
| Water pollution | Low | High |

FIGURE 3.30 The development of S Korea as an NIC

# Where do we go from here?

Manufacturing industries are not static, they are in a constant state of flux. What appears as outcomes when this book was written will merely be characteristics and locations of Kondratieff Wave V long waves. What will not change is the fact that future outcomes will continue to be the result of interactions between factors affecting manufacturing and the processes of manufacturing.

# Key Ideas

■ Manufacturing industries will seek locations that have a comparative advantage over other locations.
■ The physical and human factors that create a location's comparative advantage are raw materials, markets, land, labour, capital, governments, linkages and agglomeration and social factors.
■ The technological and organisational processes develop a location's comparative advantage.

■ The main outcome in the characteristic of manufacturing has been the development of a Flexible Manufacturing System and changes in the workforce.
■ The main outcome in the location of manufacturing industries has been deindustrialisation, New Industrial Spaces, Reindustrialisation, NICs and globalisation.

# 4
# SERVICE INDUSTRIES

There has been an increase not only in the number of people employed in services but also the importance of the service industry to the economies of MEDCs. Those of you who have acted as baby-sitters or had a paper round will already have been part of this sector! Indeed this change has been termed the Second Industrial Revolution.

As with manufacturing industries, the service sector has outcomes. World Cities such as London and New York have developed business where currency speculators trade £trillions every day in what is now a truly global money merry-go-round. Yet in both cities you can obtain a far more humble

global service – a McDonalds! You also now possibly shop in a superstore situated in an out of town location and on the way could have passed suburban offices.

This chapter will start by trying to define what the service sector is, and explain why this sector has grown in importance over the last 50 years. It will then seek to identify the factors and the processes that give locations a comparative advantage in attracting service industries. Similarly, it will explain that it is changes in these factors and processes that explain the outcomes in the location and characteristics of service industries.

# *What are services?*

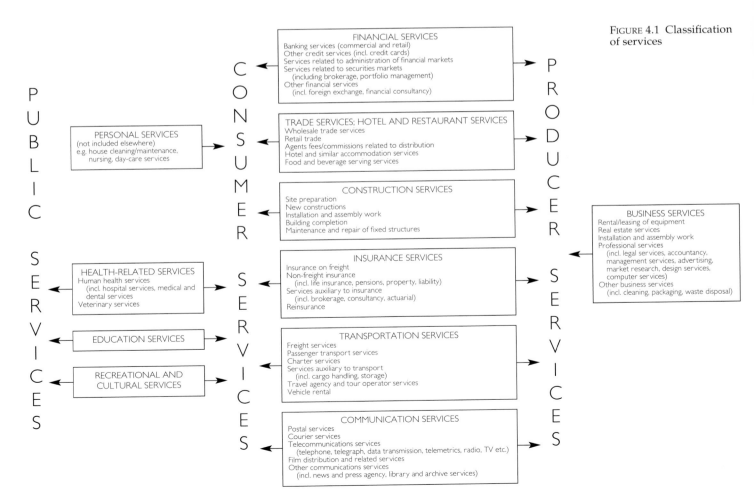

FIGURE 4.1 Classification of services

Services encompass a wide range of activities (Fig 4.1) which can be subdivided into **producer services**, which provide services to other firms rather than people, and **consumer services** which provide services for people, though these two types of services are not mutually exclusive. Many firms involved in producer services such as banks will also offer consumer services (Fig 4.1). There are also two main types of consumer service – private services such as retail outlets and public services such as hospitals and schools. These two types of service also overlap with private services offering private schools and hospitals and public services such as hospitals offering services such as private maternity wards (Fig 4.1).

It is also vital to remember that services and manufacturing are inextricably interlinked. Manufacturing requires both producer services and consumer services. Yet if there was not manufacturing many producer services and consumer services would not exist.

Finally, many people are proposing that we should take a service informed view of work. Instead of seeing a car as a manufactured product and therefore those people involved in building the car as part of the manufacturing workforce, we should view a car as a means of transport and in competition with other forms of transport such as buses etc. A car could therefore be viewed as a service and the distinction between manufacturing and service work become meaningless.

# Causes of service growth

A commonly held misconception is that the growth of services is all part of a 'natural' progression of an economy as it develops. The Clark and Fischer Sector Model appears to show that the growth of the service sector is inevitable and that it is part of a 'post industrial society' and the development of an 'information economy'. These 'stage' theories are, however, descriptive and do not explain why services have grown.

Another misconception is that the growth of services has been at the expense of manufacturing and is a cause of deindustrialisation. Locations which experience an increase in services can also experience an increase in the level of manufacturing such as the M4 corridor. Similarly, as areas such as the North West of the UK have lost their industrial base, they have also recorded below average increases in service sector work.

In addition not all service industries have grown over the last thirty years. Some such as personal services have steadily declined, whilst public services in many countries first increased and have now decreased. Even financial services which have seen some of the largest increases over the last 30 years are also now contracting.

Given the complex nature of services and commonly held misconceptions it is unsurprising that there are many theories as to the causes of the growth in services. It is therefore an example where there are multiple explanations.

## Increases in affluence – *more money means more services*

Traditional economic theory suggests that as income rises, so does the demand for services. Indeed, over the last thirty years, as both individuals and governments in MEDCs have steadily become more affluent, there has been a greater demand for both consumer and public services. People now have more disposable incomes to spend on holidays and eating out, and therefore it is unsurprising that the tourism industry, reputedly the largest industry in the world, has shown such a massive increase in the last 30 years. In the wealthiest countries such as the US, the

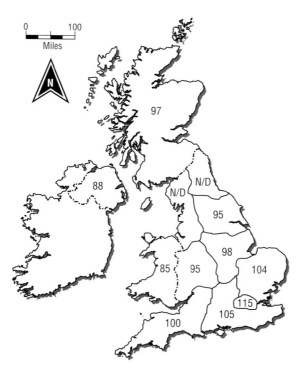
FIGURE 4.2 Variations in incomes

increased individual affluence has also increased the demand for private health care and education.

This affluence is not however always evenly distributed throughout the populations of MEDCs (Fig 4.2). There is still a gap between rich and poor, particularly between primary (core) and secondary (periphery) workers. In the UK even within the wealthiest region, London, there are great differences in affluence with three boroughs, Hackney, Tower Hamlets and Newham having the greater proportions of their population on income support than any other borough in the United Kingdom. This difference in the distribution of affluence in MEDCs has also been used to explain the growth in services. As primary workers increase their disposable incomes they can afford more services, particularly if the cost of services is becoming relatively cheaper. The demand for services therefore rises, particularly in those services which employ a high percentage of low paid, secondary workers. Such industries include the tourist, leisure and catering industries, all of which have recorded some of the largest increases in service work over the last 30 years.

This link between service growth and affluence is not, however, as simple as is often suggested. Much of the increased affluence has been spent on manufactured goods, particularly in those used in the 'self service' economy such as washing machines and vacuum cleaners.

## Changes in the form of economic production – making money in different ways

The growth in services can also be explained by the changes in the form of economic production. It is thought that the increase in the importance of the service sector is a direct result of the change from a Fordist system of accumulating wealth to a different form of producing wealth called Flexible Accumulation.

This move from mass production to a more flexible form of production has made the production process more complex and firms now require more service workers to be able to add value in the manufacturing process. This therefore requires more highly skilled producer service workers. Flexible production has also increased sub-contracting of many parts of the production process and this has further increased the demand for specialist producer service workers from small firms. In fact the greatest percentage growth in the service sector appears to be related to producer services.

Services have also grown as manufacturing TNCs have diversified away from manufacturing. USX, the largest steel producer in the US, and once the largest manufacturing firm in the world, has diversified into real estate, whilst BAT, a tobacco firm, has bought Eagle Star, an insurance firm.

There have also been changes in the way in which some countries organise their public services, with some public services being privatised and others being subcontracted. This privatisation and subcontracting has reduced the numbers of people employed by governments and therefore explains how public services are no longer increasing in many MEDCs.

## Globalisation – You can't dominate the world on your own

As globalisation has occurred in manufacturing, firms have a greater need to employ 'service experts' to allow them to continue to accumulate wealth. 'Experts' are needed for a variety of tasks. As TNCs seek to increase their profits from an ever increasing world market, the skills required to maintain communication links and compete with other firms increases.

Many services have now become internationally tradable. This has meant that service firms are now serving larger markets and therefore need more workers and so the level of services increases. These internationally tradable services have also diversified, particularly in financial services, and new products such as Eurodollars, Eurobonds and junkbonds have been developed. These sophisticated financial products all require service experts to be able to trade and deal in them.

Globalisation has also exposed many firms to a wide variety of different tax regimes. As different countries have different tax laws, firms employ service experts to minimise their tax bills.

## New Technology – someone has to use computers

There is one final cause of the growth in services. The development of computers and telecommunications has given rise to new jobs such as computer programming. It has also increased the influence of services in the economy, particularly in MEDCs where the development of this technology

---

**STUDENT ACTIVITY**

1  Draw a family tree for both sides of your family.
2  Find out what firms your relatives work for and classify their jobs into Primary, Secondary and Tertiary. Now group your relatives into generations (i.e. brothers/sisters/cousins; Parents/Uncles/Aunts; Grandparents/Great Uncles etc.).
3  a  Is there a change in the types of jobs that your relatives have carried out?
b.  Does it fit in with the descriptive 'stage' models outlined above?
4  Now reclassify their jobs by occupation i.e. what they actually did.
Does this help you understand the difference in classifying people by the firm they work for or the job (occupation) they actually did?

# Location of service industries

has occurred – one of the richest men in the US is Bill Gates, the owner of Microsoft.

As with manufacturing industries, service industries will locate where there is a comparative advantage over other locations. These comparative advantages will still be the result of the factors and processes identified in chapter three.

## Raw materials

Service industries do not have the same raw material requirements as manufacturing industries. Raw materials in a conventional sense do not therefore affect the location of most service industries. Some service industries such as tourism do require 'raw materials' which create comparative advantages. Climate, relief, landscape and the environment are all comparative advantages that have been vital in establishing areas such as Blackpool, the Lake District and Barbados as areas where tourism plays a vital role in the local, regional or national economy. Similarly, 'raw materials' in the form of human environments have led to some cities having a comparative advantage in the concentration of art galleries, architecture etc. This has encouraged the growth of cultural tourism in cities such as Venice, Bath and towns such as Stratford-Upon-Avon.

## Market

The majority of service work still requires direct interaction between supplier and purchaser (such as a haircut) and, therefore, the production and consumption of many services happens almost simultaneously. These types of services are called fixed services (in contrast to mobile or tradable services) and have traditionally located at fixed points where the comparative advantage of offering a service is greatest – at the market.

Early service studies in Geography such as Christaller's Central Place Theory have concentrated upon this aspect of service work location and stated that the pattern of service work, particularly consumer services, reflect the pattern of demand. High order functions producer service industries, such as TNC accountancy firms, will locate their HQs where the demand for their services is highest – in financial centres such as London. Similarly, high order consumer services will also locate where demand for their goods is highest in areas of high populations or high levels of affluence. Low order producer or consumer services (such as a local solicitor or a newsagent) will correspondingly, locate in areas of lower populations or lower levels of affluence.

## Land

Although service industries do not require as much land as manufacturing industries, it will still affect the comparative advantage of one location rather than another. The movement of many office based producer and consumer services to locations on the edge of urban areas or even semi rural areas is due primarily to save rental and rate costs.

The availability of office space has also caused changes in a location's comparative advantage. During the 1960s the availability of office space in London declined, mainly due to government action, and so secondary, suburban areas, such as Croydon developed as alternative sites where office space was available.

The suitability of sites also determines the comparative advantages of various service work locations. The movement of consumer services to out of town locations has been encouraged by the building of purpose built retail parks. Similarly, the movement of producer services away from traditional locations such as the City of London and Wall Street was due to the availability of trading desks equipped with all the latest electronic technology needed to trade on the world markets.

## Capital

The location of capital also effects the location of service industries. It was the presence of large amounts of fixed capital in the form of purpose built large office suites in Docklands that attracted many financial service firms to relocate from the City of London. Monetary capital is also important. Micromuse were a UK based firm that provided computer consultancy. They found it impossible to raise venture capital in the UK and have therefore relocated to California where there was more capital available.

## Labour

Labour has different effects on the location of consumer and producer services. Producer services have traditionally required a highly skilled labour force and therefore producer services are attracted to locations which have such a workforce – large urban areas.

Consumer services, however, usually require less skills and if firms are flexible in their choice of location, consumer services will locate where the cost of labour is less. Nevertheless, the availability of labour is also becoming more important in creating comparative advantages for consumer service work. Increasingly, women are being used in service work and so locations where there is a large unused female labour force such as old heavy industrial areas (such as the Lower Swansea Valley) and rural areas such as East Anglia and the South West have attracted service work companies.

## Government policy

Governments play an increasingly important role in determining the comparative advantages of locations and therefore the location of services. At a national scale there was little internal government policy regarding the location of service industries until relatively recently. The first direct action to affect the comparative advantages of locations in the United Kingdom was the introduction of Office Development Permits in London in 1965. These, in conjunction with the Location of Offices Bureau, were designed to stop the rapid growth of offices in London and encourage firms to seek other locations. The UK government also developed the Office and Service Industry Scheme (OSIS) in 1973, but by the early 1980s both the ODP scheme and the OSIS were not thought to be working and were abandoned.

Local governments can also have an impact on the comparative advantages of locations particularly through planning permission and other restrictions. The development of out of town super stores would not have been possible without planning permission.

Governments have also affected the location of public services. Traditionally public services such as hospitals, benefit offices and tax offices located in large urban areas where there was demand. There are however many public service jobs that have been located by successive governments to provide employment in unemployment blackspots and to take advantage of cheaper rents and rates (Fig 4.3).

Governments have also affected services through procurement – the process whereby governments buy services from outside contractors. Military installations such as the Royal Aircraft Establishment (RAE) were an important factor in the initial development of specialised software companies around Farnborough in the M4 corridor. Similarly, the development of the M27 corridor was also aided by procurement contracts from the Royal Navy in Portsmouth. EDS, a large US computer firm has located in Swansea, partly as a result of a contract with the DVLA in Moriston.

## Agglomerations and linkages

The effect of agglomerations and linkages in determining the location of service industries is becoming increasingly important. As firms are increasingly outsourcing and subcontracting their service requirements, firms providing these services need to be near to their clients. Producer services

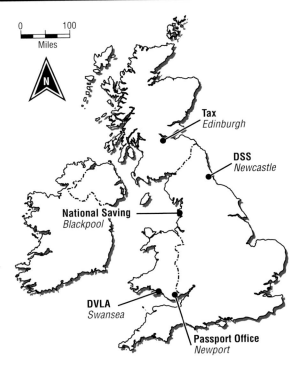

FIGURE 4.3 Location of some public services

will therefore locate where there are existing agglomerations of manufacturing industries which are utilising flexible forms of production called **New Industrial Spaces (NIS)**. Indeed NIS such as the M4 corridor have been the focus of growth in the location of producer services. In fact it has been suggested that it was the location of producer services in the M4 corridor, often as a result of government procurement, that created the location's comparative advantage to flexible manufacturing firms.

Linkages also increase the comparative advantages in large urban areas in terms of service work. Despite advances in technology, face to face meetings are still vital in many producer service industries. The merger of BP and Amoco was carried out in New York as the producer service firms used by both oil companies were US based.

---

### STUDENT ACTIVITY

**1** Study Fig 4.4.
Draw up a list of factors that account for the continued presence of producer services in London's Square Mile.
**2** What factors might encourage producer services to leave the Square Mile?
**3** Explain why this is unlikely to happen.

# Processes of services

As with manufacturing there are processes that have developed a location's comparative advantage.

## Technology

Technology is one of the most important processes in explaining not only the growth of service work but also its importance to national economies. As the 'raw material' of much service work is information, developments in Information and Communications Technology (ICT) has increased the role that services can play.

ICT has allowed new techniques of speedily recording, transmitting and storing data. Crucially, ICT costs have been reduced by 95 per cent since

Figure 4.4 The lure of London's Square Mile

1964. ICT has allowed firms to increase productivity, to develop linkages and to increase the speed at which service work can occur.

These developments in ICT have affected all types of service work. It has been responsible for allowing producer services to relocate away from expensive metropolitan locations to cheaper sites. ICT has also allowed the development of a major new service activity 'call centres' – telephone enquiry offices (Fig 4.5). In 1997 call centres employed 200 000 people or 1 per cent of the total working population. In contrast 50 000 are employed in the British car industry and 60 000 in the British steel industry. Indeed, the largest private service employer in the Lower Swansea Valley is a Midland Bank Call Centre.

# High technology fails to weaken the lure of London's Square Mile

A decade ago, at the time of the City of London's Big Bang, derivatives were an alarming innovation which people needed a PhD to understand. To many people, they are no less alarming and no easier to comprehend now, but they are part of the landscape. And they do make it clear that the financial service industry is on the frontier of the information revolution in economics.

For Big Bang in London and similar changes in other financial centres were defined as much by the huge investment in information technology and telecommunications as by regulatory change.

This investment, the need to stay on the technological wild west, remains the hallmark of the financial markets – the first and biggest cyberindustry. William Mitchell of the Media Lab at the Massachusetts Institute of Technology calls derivatives 'pure creations of cyberspace'.*

The economic engine of the financial services industry is the production, transformation, distribution and consumption of digital information. It is in the front line of the shift towards what I call the weightless world.

This name reflects the fact that the economy physically weighs about the same now as it did a century ago, partly because most goods are smaller and lighter, partly because the things that increasingly have the greatest economic value are software and services.

This shift raises some interesting questions. Digital industry can take place anywhere, so why do financial services continue to be focused on the City? And would a UK decision not to join the European single currency threaten the City?

It is a paradox that, as its activity has dematerialised, the City as a place has become ever more important. Obviously, some things that were done in London have moved, thanks to high technology.

This includes back offices, registrars – any functions where the information can be put on a production line. But the high value

added functions remain and are becoming increasingly concentrated in the Square Mile as more foreign banks move in.

There are certainly cost pressures to move out, or Canary Wharf would not exist and thrive. Rents and taxes are high in the City, the burden of commuting is heavy, deliveries and logistics are difficult, and there is even the threat of terrorism.

With the cost of telecoms falling and quality rising steadily, acting as a powerful decentralising force, there must be some strong glue.

So what explains the paradox? A lot of the standard explanations for London's appeal seem pretty weak. There is a pool of skilled labour, the English language, the time zone – but this is just as true of Luton as of London. And a lot of City workers probably live closer to Luton than to London.

Another standard explanation is that processing and exchange of information is essentially social. That you're not in the know if you're not in the bar. That rumours, gossip, sensitive conversations and spin doctoring don't work on the phone.

There may be something in this. But frankly, anyone who says you can't gossip down the line hasn't listened to a teenager recently.

It is the weightless economics that explain London's magic. One key is the existing infrastructure, representing enormous fixed investment – in expensive equipment, in the initial concentration of information, as well as the ease of connecting with other people. History matters in economics, like path-dependence in science – just think of the enormous cost of laying cable and installing screens in other locations.

A related element is the 'oasis' effect of access to high bandwidth cable connections, the fibres whose capacity to transmit digital bits is effectively infinite. The cost of using these channels increases enough with distance that users cluster together.

But just as important is the fact that tele-

coms allow concentration as well as decentralisation, to exploit economies of scale. It means that trading operations for international banks are increasingly centred on London. Deutsche Bank's decision to base its trading in the City is emblematic.

In economic geography, the key to the location of economic activity is concentration. The obvious manifestation of this is that most people live in urban areas.

US economist Robert Hall puts this in extreme form when he says a city and a boom are essentially the same thing, one in space and one in time. In addition, most urban areas are very specialised because of the economies of scale. Hollywood does movies, Seattle does aircraft, Paris does couture.

London does financial services. It embodies the circularity of economic geography that companies want to be where the market is biggest and the market is biggest where the companies are.

This happens where there are big enough economies of scale and low enough transport costs. The economies of scale are clear in something like trading in the financial markets although they probably do not exist to as great a degree in sales. Falling transport costs, which comprise telecoms costs as far as the City is concerned, have therefore probably helped reinforce the concentration of some types of financial services in London.

Last but not least among the economic explanations is the fact that the financial services industry is growing rapidly, and a lot of the growth is going to take place where it is already located.

The advantage of infrastructure and economies of scale and growth will not be overturned until there is technical obsolescence on at least the scale of Big Bang, 10 years ago, and perhaps not even then. It is similarly implausible to suggest that UK membership or non-membership of the single European currency would make all that much difference.

Could these economic buttresses of the City's preeminence ever crumble? New technologies will almost certainly change the economic calculations significantly.

Techno-authors such as Nicholas Negroponte describe the possibilities eloquently, from clothes that form part of your computer such as batteries in the belt buckle and antennae in the frames of your glasses, to holograms of software agents sitting in front of your computer screen, waiting for verbal instructions.

This still seems the stuff of science fiction but one thing that is already clear is that modern technology and communications mean the link binding work to workplace is crumbling.

Not too long ago a fine building in the Square Mile would correspond one-to-one with a fine old institution. It rendered the institution visible and concrete. This is no longer true. It is people, not places, who define the institution these days, and a shifting group of people at that. It is at least as true of financial services as of advertising that it is a people business.

Equally, work is making greater claims over people. Work follows most of us everywhere, thanks to the phone, fax, pager, mobile and laptop. We could be seeing the start of a reversal of the trend towards the divorce of home and workplace identified by the historian Lewis Mumford in his 1934 classic, *Technics and Civilisation*. In financial services, as in many other professional or white-collar jobs, work attaches itself to the person, not the place.

These shifts will continue to work against London's primacy as a place, a three-dimensional city in geographical space. But if it can survive the plague and the Great Fire, industrialisation and the automobile, it can probably also beat off the challenge of cyberspace.

* 'City of Bits', William Mitchell, MIT Press 1996.

## Organisation

Services have experienced large changes in the size of firms and have become globalised. This has been particularly important in the Financial Service Industry and the Tourist Industry. Indeed in most MEDCs the greatest amount of Foreign Direct Investment (FDI) is now in service industries rather than in manufacturing industries (Fig 4.5). As with manufacturing TNCs there are multiple explanations as to the cause of growth of service TNCs (Fig 4.6). There is, however, criticism of the impacts on LEDCs of TNCs, particularly tourist TNCs (Fig 4.7).

There is also a high degree of networking or linkage in services which has been termed **Gurupu**. It is the financial side to the flexible form of production noted in Chapter Three – **Keiretsu**.

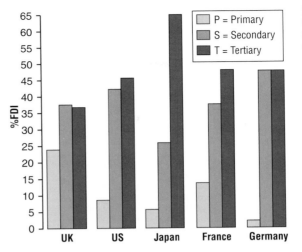

FIGURE 4.5 Percentage of total foreign direct investment in selected countries, 1990

FIGURE 4.6 Causes for the growth of service TNCs.

| Why go global? | Advantages of being global |
|---|---|
| Uncertainty over home markets | Ownership of techniques for service provision |
| Opportunities in new markets | Reduction of costs through selection of location |
| Global presence required to keep existing global clients | Coordinating advantages where international risks can be spread globally |

FIGURE 4.7 Advantages and disadvantages of International Tourism

| Economic environment | |
|---|---|
| **Advantages** | **Disadvantages** |
| Increases Balance of payments investment in capital equipment | Leakages through importation of food and drink, profit retention by MNC |
| Can compete in a global economy without unfair trade and tariffs | Seasonal |
| Diversifies Economy | Mostly Female workers |
| Value of primary products are more if consumed by tourists rather than exported | Part time |
| Creates Jobs | Low status |
| Requires less capital per job created than other industries | Leakage also occurs at a regional level |
| Higher rates of pay in ELDC than in other industries | Competes with other development projects such as agricultural projects |
| Provides jobs where potential for other employment is low | Increase in money increases inflation in food and housing |
| Helps in regional development | |
| Creates the multiplier effect | |
| Taxes increase | |
| Distribution of benefits and hence wealth uneven through the country | |

# Phone factories – Britain's new boom industry

They are the new white-collar factories. The disembodied voice you hear on the end of the telephone is being monitored every minute of their working day and when they finish with your call, 10 seconds later they are expected to be dealing with someone else.

On the walls of the vast open-plan offices are Orwellian exhortations to maximum effort. Conversations with colleagues are frowned upon.

By some estimates there are now some 200,000 people involved in such 'call centres' – easily outstripping the number employed in steel, coal and in vehicle manufacture. In fact there are now more call-centre staff than coal miners.

The so-called 'computer telephonists' are the fastest growing occupational group in Britain today, providing customer services, and sales information. There can be few businesses which do not require such facilities and there are few senior managers who cannot see advantages in farming out such activities to call centres.

Further evidence of the boom in call centres came yesterday when Sitel UK, an American-owned company which already operates six centres announced that it was planning to create 10,000 jobs over the next five years.

Sue Fernie, of the Centre for Economic Performance at the London School of Economics, estimates there are now 7,000 such 'factories' which employ 1.1 per cent of the British workforce. Academics calculate that the proportion will double to 2.2 per cent by 2001.

There are strong similarities between the 'dark satanic mills' of the nineteenth century and the new production lines of the 21st century – except they are safe, well-lit and there is sometimes a veneer of worker participation.

There is, however, little opportunity to stand and stare. The number of calls waiting is often displayed on a monitor above the 'shop floor'. Visits to the lavatory are timed.

In most such factories, operators are expected to take a maximum 10-second break between each call. Employees can be routinely dismissed for not meeting their production target without 'reasonable' excuse.

In some call centres, turnover in staff can be as high as 30 per cent a year, although the larger companies are beginning to see the advantage of hanging on to experienced staff.

Appropriately, one popular software package used by management in call centres is marketed as 'Total Control Made Easy'. These white-collar factories often require articulate and adaptable people and some centres attract graduates who are still searching for a permanent career. One such employee – a 26-year-old graduate currently working at First Direct in Leeds – said he worked a nine-hour shift with half an hour for lunch. 'It is noticed if you take 32 minutes rather than 30,' he said.

'You are monitored by supervisors all the time and they sit next to you if there is a particular problem. You are given scores from one to five each month and you have a one-to-one interview with your supervisor if you fail below target.'

He earns a basic £11,800 a year which can reach £13,000 with a bonus, but finds the regime 'oppressive'. He works non-stop and processes some 100 calls a day. 'It's all right as long as you're doing well,' he said.

The call companies reject criticism of their treatment of employees. Ann Gunter, head of telephony at NatWest, says staff at the bank's Harrogate call centre are 'very very proud of what they do' and apart from the odd niggle 'have an awful lot of fun'.

Their view is supported by Alastair Hatchett, of research group Incomes Data Services, who says that while the work environment is 'very pressured', a lot of younger people enjoy it and 'seem to respond to the team-working environment'.

Staff at Norwich Union Direct centres recently received pay rises of up to 18 per cent depending on productivity. 'Good performers' received 8 per cent while small numbers got the top pay rises and the company's pay bill rose by around 10 per cent.

Employees, especially in areas of high unemployment, clearly appreciate the higher rates of pay they can earn, and quickly become acclimatised by the higher levels of monitoring they receive.

Nevertheless Ms Fernie identifies a problem of 'burn out' which is often associated with the need to repeat endlessly the same basic script many times a day. 'Eighteen months is usually about as much as a computer telephonist can cope with,' she said.

Many centres increasingly rely on bonuses to motivate staff. Twenty-four hour operation also means that staff receive an increasing range of overtime and shift premium payments hitherto unknown in the traditional office.

Many of the big centres are located outside London to take advantage of plentiful relatively skilled staff and lower wages. London Electricity's billing operation, for instance, is now carried out in Sunderland. The whole process in Britain was pioneered in Britain by Direct Line insurance and by First Direct banking, but has since been adopted by companies in virtually every industrial sector.

FIGURE 4.8 Phone factories

**Britain's biggest call centres** showing numbers employed

Tesco Customer Centre 340
Sky Subscribe 3,099
London Electricity 585
Royal Bank of Scotland (direct banking) 519
Barclaycall 415
Littlewoods Home Shopping 519
Halifax Direct 500
First Direct 2,930
Freemans Services 1,001
CO-OP Bank personal customer services (also Skeimersdale 754)
Alliance + Leicester Personal Fin. 390
Barclaycall 415
Virgin Direct 350
Sitel 771
NatWest Primeline 405
Prudential retail customer services 268
Guardian Direct 426

Dundee, Livingston, Doxford, Sunderland, Leeds, Salford, Stockport, Manchester, Sheffield, Leicester, Norwich, Coventry, Stratford, Colchester, Theale, Reading

---

## STUDENT ACTIVITY

Study Fig 4.8.

**1** Study the map of the location of the largest call centres closely. Choose four call centres and explain what has allowed these firms to set up in those locations and try to put forward arguments as to why they have chosen those particular locations.

**2** For your chosen four locations try to identify and explain their traditional economic base

# Outcomes – What happened in services?

There have been a variety of outcomes (Fig 4.9) in the characteristics and location of services.

## Changing characteristics of services

There have been significant increases in female service work which is often part-time (Fig 4.10). This has been attributed to service firms wanting to exploit a pliant, non-unionised dependent workforce that is flexible.

It is also due to tradition with many service sector jobs being gender divided such as in hotel and catering. As these sectors grew, there was an increase in demand for female labour (Fig 4.10).

As well as the growth of producer services, there has also been a growth in tourist service industries. People now have far more time available such as eight Bank Holidays and up to 21 days paid holiday. This allows them to not only have weekend breaks and maybe two holidays a year but also it allows them to travel further. In addition the level of car ownership has risen and the number of international airports capable of dealing with wide bodied Jumbo jets has increased. The increase in affluence already discussed has also been a vital factor in increasing the tourist industry and publicity in the form of advertisements on the radio, papers and TV have increased the awareness of the attractions of distant places. Tourist Information Centres (TIC) are found in most UK cities and most countries have a national tourist board that promotes its own country. Even George Bush, a president of the United States, has appeared in an advert encouraging people to come to the US. All these factors have increased the need for tourist service industries not just in MEDCs but in an ever increasing number of LEDCs.

## Changing locations of consumer services

Changes in the location of service industries have occurred on local, national and international scales.

### Local changes in consumer services

Consumer services have moved from the centre of urban locations to the rural urban fringe. These are known as 'Out of Town' shopping centres. The first true out of town shopping scheme was Brent Cross in London in 1976. Since then there has been rapid growth of such centres (Fig 4.11) and now there are massive developments such as that at Lakeside on the M25 in Essex which now boasts a cinema, and a whole floor devoted to over 20 types of restaurants.

These centres have developed because, as with relocations of manufacturing industries, changes in the importance of factors and processes affecting consumer services have reduced the comparative advantages of city centre locations and increased

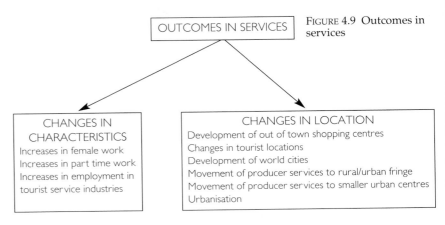

FIGURE 4.9 Outcomes in services

OUTCOMES IN SERVICES

CHANGES IN CHARACTERISTICS
Increases in female work
Increases in part time work
Increases in employment in tourist service industries

CHANGES IN LOCATION
Development of out of town shopping centres
Changes in tourist locations
Development of world cities
Movement of producer services to rural/urban fringe
Movement of producer services to smaller urban centres
Urbanisation

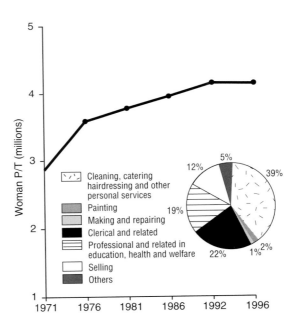

FIGURE 4.10 (a) Increases in female part-time employment; (b) Percentage of employees that are women, according to industry

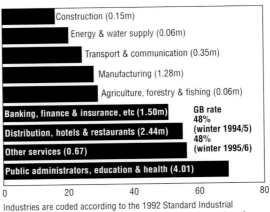

Industries are coded according to the 1992 Standard Industrial Classification. ( ) The figures shown in brackets are the number of women employees in each occupation and industry.

FIGURE 4.11 Location of large out of town shopping centres and factory outlets

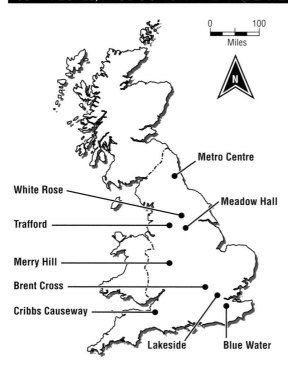

the comparative advantage of rural urban fringe locations.

The comparative advantages of the city centres have been lost as there was an increase in rates and rents, lack of room for expansion, congestion, parking problems, security problems, planning permission problems. The rural urban fringe, however, had gained a comparative advantage as it provides parking areas nearer to where the retail park customers live (due to suburbanisation) and are situated on ring roads or motorways for easy access to those people who have left the city (due to Counter urbanisation). They also provide weather free and usually crime free shopping and a larger range of goods and services. These goods and services are often cheaper than those found in the CBD. The labour costs are also less at these locations and the stores benefit from economies of scale.

The most obvious impact is that on the natural environment. The building of the stores is visually and aurally intrusive. Wildlife is disturbed and scared away and habitats are lost. The hydrological cycle is modified with more tarmac and impermeable surfaces being created which leads to a greater danger of flooding. The increased cars in the area cause more air and noise pollution and accidents.

The houses in the immediate vicinity lose some of their value, but there are local jobs provided. Congestion in the area increases but there are large shops close by offering a wide range of shops and services.

There have even been changes in the location of retail services on an international basis. The development of the EU and the Channel Tunnel has seen an increase in the number of superstores and out of town shopping centres situated in Northern France. The Cité D'Europe is a large out of town shopping centre situated at the mouth of the Channel Tunnel.

## National and international changes in consumer services

As well as changes in retail consumer services there have also been changes in the location of tourism both nationally and internationally (Fig 4.12).

FIGURE 4.12 (a) Domestic (UK) development; (b) International development

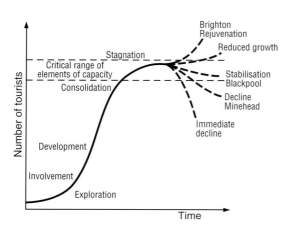

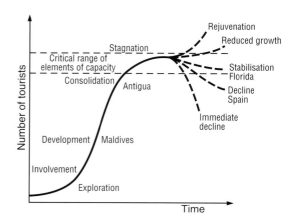

As can be seen, the first development of tourism in the United Kingdom was for rich people in fashionable resorts such as Brighton, Bognor Regis and the Isle of Wight which all attracted the wealthy due to their royal connections. With the rise of the middle classes, Butlins became popular and areas such as Minehead grew in importance in the 1930s. The 1950s saw a mass revolution of tourism in United Kingdom, with areas such as Blackpool becoming very popular especially for industrial workers of the North West. The growth of package holidays in the 1960s and 1970s led to the decline of traditional seaside holidays such as Shanklin on the Isle of Wight due to the allure of foreign places and the poor climate of the United Kingdom. Recently, speciality areas such as Cornwall and activity areas such as the Lake District and Peak District, have grown in importance.

As can be seen from the international model (Fig 4.12) the same principles apply. Areas such as Pengwar are on the discovery trail. They have few hotels and do not cater for mass tourism. The Maldives are now at take off. The economy is booming but the traditional values are already being lost as alcohol is now served all day in a Muslim state which used to allow only a small glass of wine at the meal. Antigua is now at the apex of the model and could shortly go going into decline. Its culture and economy is now geared for tourism

and the island is developing rapidly. Florida is on the decline. There are numerous resorts and the numbers of people going are declining. Spain too has been oversaturated and has a declining tourist base. This means that it either has to change and win back new tourists or it will eventually have to reduce capacity.

## Changing producer service locations

The growth of producer services has created 'World' or 'Global' cities while at the same time this growth has also resulted in the relocation of producer service work away from major urban areas to smaller areas and in some cases to other countries.

### World Cities

Producer services have always been attracted to central urban locations for a variety of reasons (Fig 4.13). The comparative advantages of large urban areas have however been magnified in the context of three cities in the world – London, New York and Tokyo (Fig 4.14). These cities have been termed World Cities as they have producer services which primarily operate between other world cities and countries rather than in the countries within which they are placed.

FIGURE 4.13 Comparative advantages of large urban areas for producer services

Raw materials: urban environment of leisure

Technology: good communications, both physical and electronic

Agglomerations and Linkages: accessibility and proximity to other offices

Land: availability of office accommodation

Labour: competitive market assuring high quality skilled labour and clerical labour

### Location of banks and traders in foreign exchange, 1985

| Location | No. of banks | No. of traders |
|---|---|---|
| *Asia and Middle East* | | |
| Tokyo | 30 | 169 |
| Singapore | 69 | 293 |
| Hong Kong | 52 | 306 |
| Bahrain | 38 | 176 |
| Total | 189 | 941 |
| *North America* | | |
| New York | 108 | 793 |
| Toronto | 18 | 120 |
| Chicago | 14 | 81 |
| Los Angeles | 11 | 46 |
| Total | 158 | 1083 |
| *Western Europe* | | |
| London | 258 | 1603 |
| Luxembourg | 74 | 353 |
| Paris | 75 | 459 |
| Zurich | 35 | 245 |
| Frankfurt | 48 | 334 |
| Milan | 37 | 191 |
| Brussels | 33 | 201 |
| Total | 560 | 3386 |

*Source: extracted from Levich and Walter, 1989, 68, table 4.9*

### Top twelve banking centres in the world,[a] 1986

| City | No. of firms | Income ($m) | Assets[c] ($b) | Net income/asset ratio[d] (%) |
|---|---|---|---|---|
| | | | Ranked by:[b] | |
| Tokyo | 22 | 6424 (1) | 1801.4 (1) | 0.357 (10) |
| New York | 16 | 5673 (2) | 904.8 (2) | 0.627 (2) |
| London | 5 | 2934 (3) | 390.3 (5) | 0.752 (1) |
| Paris | 6 | 1712 (4) | 659.3 (3) | 0.260 (12) |
| Osaka | 4 | 1261 (5) | 557.6 (4) | — |
| Frankfurt | 3 | 1003 (6) | 306.8 (6) | 0.327 (11) |
| Zurich | 2 | 826 (7) | — | 0.524 (4) |
| Amsterdam | 3 | 739 (8) | 193.4 (7) | 0.382 (9) |
| Basel | 1 | 415 (9) | — | 0.489 (7) |
| Hong Kong | 1 | 392 (10) | 90.8 (12) | 0.432 (8) |
| Los Angeles | 1 | 386 (11) | — | 0.617 (3) |
| Montreal | 1 | 354 (12) | — | 0.520 (6) |

*[a] Data for top 50 commercial banks, top 25 securities firms.*  *[b] Rank in brackets.*
*[c] Other cities are: Munich (8), Nagoya (9), San Francisco (10), Kobe (11).*  *[d] Other city: Toronto (4).*
*Source: extracted from Noyelle, 1989, 101, table 5.5*

### Location of international organisations[a] by city, 1987 and 1988

| Rank | City | No. of international organisations | Rank | City | No. of international organisations |
|---|---|---|---|---|---|
| 1 | Paris | 866 | 11 | Strasbourg | 93 |
| 2 | Brussels | 862 | 12 | Zurich | 89 |
| 3 | London | 493 | 13 | Oslo | 88 |
| 4 | Rome | 445 | 14 | Bangkok | 82 |
| 5 | Geneva | 397 | 15 | Helsinki | 75 |
| 6 | New York | 232 | 16 | Nairobi | 75 |
| 7 | Washington DC | 180 | 17 | Mexico City | 69 |
| 8 | Stockholm | 128 | 18 | Caracas | 68 |
| 9 | Vienna | 115 | 19 | The Hague | 67 |
| 10 | Copenhagen | 114 | 20 | Tokyo | 65 |

*[a] Number of headquarters and regional secretariats.*
*Source: extracted from Knight and Gappert, 1989, table 1.2*

FIGURE 4.14 Growth of three world cities

There are a variety of reasons why these three cities have become global cities, general reasons applicable to all three cities (Fig 4.15) and specific reasons for each city. These reasons are often self-reinforcing (i.e. cumulative causation) and therefore agglomeration economies have tended to increase the dominance of these cities. The development of London as a World City is examined in Fig 4.15.

---

**STUDENT ACTIVITY**

Study Activity material 4.3.
1  Which borough has suffered the most from deindustrialisation?
2  To what extent is London's role as a 'World City' benefiting all the people of London?
3  What type of jobs might people living in Richmond have?
4  What types of jobs might people living in Hackney have?
5  To what extent has the growth of the service sector in London and the development of London as a World City made up for the loss of 300 000 manufacturing jobs?

---

*Movement of producer services away from central urban areas*

Producer services have also moved from the centre of large urban areas to the rural urban fringe. This outcome was also a result of changing factors and processes increasing the comparative advantage of the rural urban fringe.

The availability and cost of land was a vital factor in increasing the comparative advantage of rural/urban locations. In the UK, the desire of offices to be near one another lead to a chronic lack of space in city centre locations and in particular, the development of London as a World City, caused office space in London to become increasingly expensive. This drove companies to slim down their operations in large urban areas and to relocate their routine operations in cheaper locations.

Changes in the comparative advantage of labour were also important. Although high level producer services need an extremely educated workforce, not all the jobs in producer service firms requires face to face meetings. These jobs, often known as 'back office' operations could therefore be moved out of city centre locations and could be relocated in locations where the demand for skilled office staff and the wages for such staff were lower.

Rural/urban locations also had a comparative advantage as they suffered less from congestion than city centre sites. Service industries have to have people who can serve and therefore if they are

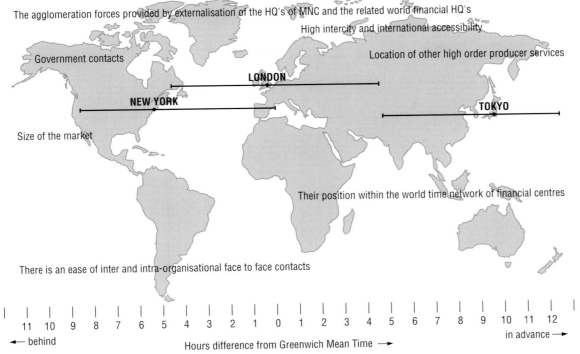

The agglomeration forces provided by externalisation of the HQ's of MNC and the related world financial HQ's

High intercity and international accessibility

Government contacts

Location of other high order producer services

**LONDON**

**NEW YORK**

**TOKYO**

Size of the market

Their position within the world time network of financial centres

There is an ease of inter and intra-organisational face to face contacts

| 11 | 10 | 9 | 8 | 7 | 6 | 5 | 4 | 3 | 2 | 1 | 0 | 1 | 2 | 3 | 4 | 5 | 6 | 7 | 8 | 9 | 10 | 11 | 12 |

← behind                in advance →

Hours difference from Greenwich Mean Time →

Banking must be compatible with other areas e.g. 6 am in Europe is close of business in Tokyo

FIGURE 4.15
Development of London,
New York and Tokyo as
World Cities

late service industries lose money. In large cities such as London, the average speed of vehicles is now as low as 6 mph. With over 1.5 million people also commuting to London the overstretched transport systems could not cope and therefore delays were (and are!!!) common.

The net result was that in many large urban areas, offices relocated to rural/urban fringe locations, often in purpose built office parks. In London between 1964 and 1979, 30 000 office jobs relocated to Croydon. These were however routine and middle management jobs.

The decision makers stayed in London due to the need for those vital face to face meetings.

### Movement to other smaller urban centres

The same factors propelled more office jobs to other smaller urban centres where the costs were even cheaper than in Croydon. Firms such as IBM went to Portsmouth, BP to Harlow, Eagle Star to Cheltenham, NatWest to Bristol and Chase Manhattan to Bournemouth.

An important factor in this relocation was the advances in communication technology such as faxes, telephones and e-mail. This allowed firms to keep in constant communications with its branches and therefore enabled these firms to move their back office operations even further from large urban areas.

It was also important that these new centres were close to London so that people could still get back to London for meetings and not have to pay large sums in travelling. It has been estimated that

over a distance of 130km the cost benefits of moving from large urban areas is outweighed by the increased transport costs visiting these offices.

### Movement to periphery areas

Offices also relocated from London to periphery locations such as Cardiff. AXA, an insurance firm, TSB and Lloyds are just a few of the companies which have relocated their offices in Cardiff. The comparative advantages of Cardiff for these producer services are the same as for all movements from large urban areas but in Cardiff's case there were also financial incentives such as grants from the government and a highly motivated workforce. It is also only two hours from London by train.

It is clear from this decision that, as in manufacturing, there appears to be a spatial division of labour in producer services. Highly specialised jobs are still to be found in the large urban areas, but routine 'back office' jobs are now found in more periphery areas. They have particularly located in areas where there is an available female workforce which will be flexible.

### Movement of producer services to inner city redevelopment areas

Urban deindustrialisation (Chapter Three) left many inner city areas derelict and decayed. As a result many were redeveloped with the principal aim of regenerating the area through the attraction of producer services. The Docklands area in London was one such area and is examined in the following case study.

## CASE STUDY

### *Docklands*

**Loss of comparative advantages leading to Decline**
**Changes in Transport technology**
The introduction of containers benefited ports such as Tilbury where there was greater areas to store the containers, the transport network was better, and the river deeper.

**Changes in Land**
The congested and cramped western Docks could not compete nor able to invest in machinery to handle these new containers.

**Changes in Capital**
The Eastern docks did not have enough new investment to make it compete with newer docks in Tilbury etc.

**Changes in the Market**
The loss of 375,000 manufacturing jobs left London for greenfield or periphery sites meant that Docklands lost its market. In addition the change of market from the Empire to Europe meant that other ports, notably in East Anglia and Kent were better placed to take advantage of this rather than London.

**Changes in Labour**
Labour costs were high due to the well organised structure of labour but it is more likely it was the higher degree of mechanisation of other Ports that kept their labour costs lower. Finally there was intense competition from other ports, and with the increase in trade with Europe, as opposed to the Empire.

**Outcomes of Decline**
From 1961 to 1985, all the docks closed, starting with the Western docks in 1967 through to the closure of all the Royal docks by 1985. During this period direct employment in the docks fell from 50,000 to 3000. This was accompanied by the loss of 200,000 jobs lost from Docklands Boroughs. Unemployment stood at 24%.
Land and buildings had become derelict, with haulage and scrap operators taking up large areas of land paying little in rent and employing few people.
The area was polluted, derelict and appeared to have little economic potential.

**Factors and processes leading to Dockland's regeneration**
**Land**
The cost per square foot was far lower than in the 'Square Mile' of London . In financial services, the use of networked computers is essential. The new offices developed in Docklands came ready equipped with the infrastructure to link computers. Finally, there was little new office development allowed in the city. This then forced firms seeking to expand in the world city to look to Docklands for extra space.

**Government Policy**
The Isle of Dogs in Docklands was set up as an Enterprise Zone and therefore firms who relocated here gained tax advantages. It also created the London's Docklands Development Corporation which created a unified approach to all aspects of redevelopment over several boroughs. Although the effectiveness of the LDDC has been challenged it is undeniable that it developed the Docklands area more quickly and rapidly than the other multi-borough organisations. £8 billion has been spent – far more than one other EZ such as the Lower Swansea Valley (£116 million).

**Transport technology**
New roads such as the Limehouse Link and new railways such as the Docklands Light Railway and the Jubilee line extension were critical in persuading firms to relocate in Docklands. In addition an airport, the City Airport was constructed in what had been the Royal docks and this also increased the desirability of the site, particularly as it is 'the wrong' side of London for Heathrow airport, the main business airport of London.

FIGURE 4.16 (b)  Docklands, after regeneration

FIGURE 4.16 (a) Docklands, before regeneration

## GOVERNMENT

London is the centre of government despite some relocation of administration to other centres. All decisions on funding and all policy is made in London. Recently, the rumours that the UK would join the EMU which sent shares up over £billions originated in London. Since 1979, the Conservative government had a 'hands off' approach to regulating the financial market and so in contrast to Paris, where regulation was tighter, foreign firms located in London.

## MARKET

London is also the largest most affluent market in the UK amd therefore the top international retailers locate in London to take advantage of this market (Ferrari, Chanel etc.).

## OUTCOMES

London has adapted its traditional world trading role that was supplied by Docklands to one of a financial world trading centre.
The United Kingdom is home to 12 of the largest 100 TNC and 45 of the 500 largest companies. Only the United States and Japan have more TNC and larger companies.
271 from 500 UK TNC HQ's locate in London.
118 of Europe's top 500 companies are located in London all of which require producer services.
A further 125 TNC have their HQ's in the South East of the UK whilst 90% of all producer services in the UK are located in the SE.
35% of all producer service jobs in the UK are located in London which exceeds the entire population of Frankfurt.
This workforce is also highly educated, with 23% having a degree, compared with a UK average of only 14%.
London produces 15% of the total GDP of the UK - more than the bottom 100 ELDC countries. It has a bigger GDP than Ireland, Norway, Greece ,Saudi Arabia or Malaysia.

## AGGLOMERATION

It has many business services such as KPMG (management consultants), EY (accountants) Wilde Sapte (lawyers) and Saatchi and Saatchi (Advertising). This means that other firms are attracted to London because if they locate in other centres in Europe the range of such international services would not be available. This is of course cumulative causation.

## LINKAGES

The 'square mile' of the City of London is a dense highly concentrated area of offices. It would be easier and cheaper to have offices outside of London but vital face to face meetings are still necessary for all business deals. The compactness of the City of London make this ideal.

## GLOBAL POSITION

London has also become the international financial centre for the European time zone. This is because Big Bang in 1986 removed restrictive practices that were still present in other European centres such as Frankfurt and Paris. There were also skilled workers in world wide banking and Independent corporate accounting. In addition the scale of managed funds and experienced managerial staff in takeovers etc meant that firms specialising in financial trading on a world scale would pick London to be the European time zone centre.

## TECHNOLOGY

London is at the hub of domestic transport routes. It has an orbital motorway (M25) and a series of M-ways linking it with the other major centres in the UK: (M1 Leeds, M4 Bristol, M2 Dover etc). It is also the focus of the rail network with 7 major rail termini (Waterloo, Paddington etc.). It has 5 international airports and the business airport of Heathrow has four terminals. It is also the site of the Eurostar.

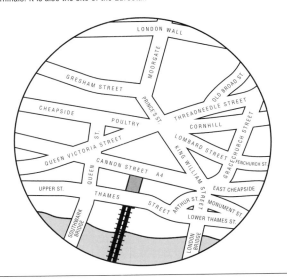

FIGURE 4.17 London as a World City

## Outcomes of regeneration

The population of the area has increased by 29,000 people from 39,500 to 68,000.
64% of the population is working and only 12% is unemployed (from 24% in 1981). This is still above the National average of 8.4 and the London average of 9.9%.
50% of all the jobs were in the Isle of Dogs, with only 14% of the jobs in the Royal docks where some 30% of Docklands population lives.
There are now 11,000 manufacturing jobs and only 4000 transport related jobs.
40,000 new service sector jobs were created in Docklands, mainly in financial services (20,500 new jobs) and Publishing/Media (7,750 new jobs). Hotel and Catering has 9,400 jobs, 42,000 of the 68,000 jobs are taken by commuters not by people living in Docklands.

Examples of firms which have moved to Docklands include News International (Wapping – P/M) and Coutts and Co. and Nomura (both Banks).
24.4 million sq. feet of development has occurred as well as 19,000 new houses mainly in the Isle of Dogs (61%) and the Surrey Docks (16%). Only 9% of the development has occurred in the Royal Docks where 30% of the population lives. 75% of all office space is in the Isle of Dogs and less than 1% of office development is in the Royal Dock area.
The River Thames has become cleaner and now many more species of fish such as salmon and pike are now found in the area. Island gardens and city farms have been established and with the development of nesting rafts, birds have returned to the area such as terns and black redstarts.

## *Movement of producer services to offshore centres*

As well as the movement of offices away from large urban areas, many producer services are now relocating in other countries. This is primarily the result of increased communications and the development of a NIDL in services as well as in manufacturing. Routine data entry and 'back office' functions for banks are two of the main types of producer service that have located 'off shore'. Whilst data entry functions (such as American

Airlines data entry operations in Barbados and British Airways operations in India) have relocated in an effort to reduce costs, banks have relocated to avoid government regulation and taxes. It has been estimated that up to 50 per cent of the total money in the world either resides in or is passing through these offshore tax havens. Countries such as the Cayman Islands and the British Virgin Islands have many producer service firms locating or carrying out business through them.

There is currently debate whether, as with manufacturing, offshore producer service provision will increase in the same way that manufacturing left core areas and relocated in NICs. Whilst some see the expansion into China as symbolic of the movement of producer services, others have noticed that the continued technological advances in data capture and storage such as the use of optical scanners will make routine data operations redundant. Similarly, the complexity of many producer services is increasing rather than decreasing the need for face to face meetings between client and provider. This has already been noted for the continued concentration of producer services in large urban areas and the development of world cities. It seems therefore unlikely that the development of offshore producer services will have the same impact on producer service employment in MEDCs that the development of NICs had on manufacturing.

### Globalisation

FIGURE 4.18 Service setting continuum

The globalisation of services is slightly different from that of manufactured goods. Manufactured goods were initially traded between countries and it was only after developments in communications and government policy that manufacturing firms became globalised through Foreign Direct Investment (FDI) in different countries. Manufacturing therefore utilises both exports and FDI equally to become globalised.

Services, on the other hand, were much slower to become globalised. This was due to the fact that many services are not tradable and have to be provided and consumed simultaneously. In fact there appears to be a service continuum (Fig 4.18). Whilst globalisation in fixed services (such as hotels) can only occur through FDI, tradable services (such as films) do not need FDI and can be traded between countries. Between fixed and tradable services there are goods services (such as the software that comes 'free' with a computer you buy) and consulting services (such as the specialist advice offered by producer service firms) both of which can become globalised through both FDI and by being tradable.

This importance of FDI in the globalisation of services is shown in the fact that services now account for more FDI than manufacturing (Fig 4.5).

The same factors that caused globalisation in manufacturing industries have been responsible for the globalisation of services – developments in technology and communications, the rise of TNCs and government policies (Fig 4.19).

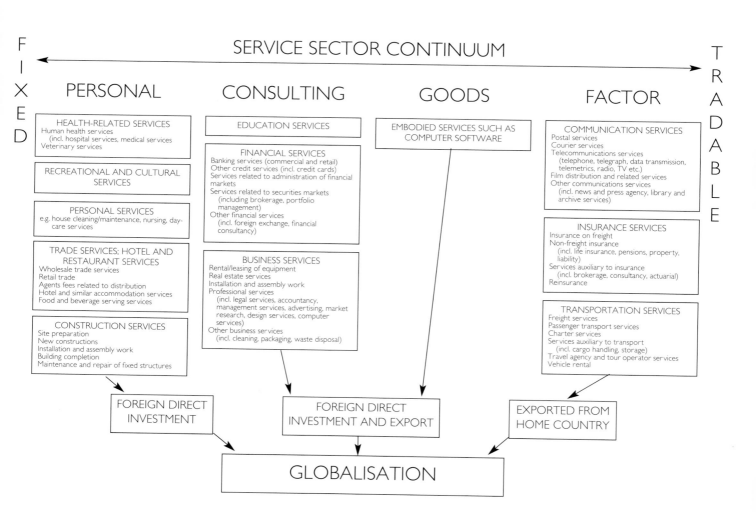

### Government deregulation

Many services are now becoming less regulated and are allowed to be internationally tradable. This is because of developments in the WTO who passed in principle a free trade in service agreement in 1994 and ratified a convention on telecommunications in 1997. Regional trading blocs such as the EU have also assisted the development of globalisation in services. The Single Market Agreement of 1992 allowed the unhindered trade in many services across the whole of the EU and has certainly accelerated the growth of foreign banks in most European capitals.

Money is no longer a means to buy goods and services but has become a commodity in its right ie money itself can now be bought and sold. It is estimated that the amount of money bought and sold is now EIGHT times as much as the amount of other goods and services bought and sold.

### Increases in ICT

Information is both the process and the product of many service industries. With developments in digital rather than analogue transmission and the growth of cable and then satellite communication system ICT services become internationally tradable in their own right.

### The Impacts of TNC

Service firms such as advertising agencies, legal firms, hotel and car rental firms as well as financial services initially globalised so as to offer their services to globalising manufacturing TNC. Saturation of many domestic markets in EMDC with very few new clients available particularly for commercial banking and insurance was also a factor. Service conglomerates particularly the Japanese Sogo Shosha (GTC) and the South Korean Chaebol have also caused the globalisation of services. Japanese Sogo Shosha which are General Trading Companies and South Korean Chaebol are both industrial and commercial companies and are responsible for 8% of world trade, led by Mitsubishi and Mitsui. These Sogo Shosha were responsible for much of the globalisation of Japanese TNC's and provide fmancial services as well as information, risk reduction, organisational and auxiliary services. New products have been developed that can be traded around the world. Euro bonds, Junk bonds, interest rate swaps were all developed in the 1970's and 1980's and can ball be internationally traded.

FIGURE 4.19
Globalisation of services

# Summary

Services and manufacturing are becoming increasingly interdependent and the next generation of students will not learn about 'manufacturing' and 'services' but instead production and consumption, instinctively knowing that in both sectors goods have to be manufactured and services provided. Firms such as Nike and Benetton represent this complete interdependence with service workers such as designers and advertising executives adding more value to the product of training shoes or clothes than the workers who actually make the product.

Services have irrevocably become the dominant industrial sector in MEDCs and will continue to be so. It also appears that despite some evidence of an international division of labour in services, this is unlikely to match that which has occurred in manufacturing. Services, particularly producer services are going to remain largely in MEDCs rather than relocate to NICs.

# Key Ideas

■ Services are now the most important sector of the economy. Producer services primarily serve businesses whilst consumer services serve people.
■ The growth in services is a result of increases in affluence, changes in the production process, globalisation and innovations in technology.
   The location of consumer, producer and public services is determined by an area's cooperative advantages. These comparative advantages have changed over the recent past and will also change in the future.
■ Technology and the development of ICT in particular has been of vital importance in changing the comparative advantages of service work locations.

■ There have been recent increases in producer service work and tourist service industries. There has also been an increase in female participation in the service workforce which is often part time.
■ Consumer services have relocated to out of town shopping centres and producer services have relocated away from large urban areas.
■ World Cities have developed where services operate between countries rather than within the countries they are placed in.
■ Globalisation has occurred in services due to advances in ICT, the development of TNC and through government action.

# 5
# THE DEVELOPMENT PROCESS

*'All are equal, but some are more equal than others'*
*(adapted from Animal Farm, George Orwell)*

What exactly does 'development' mean? Builders develop land, designers develop products, and governments develop their economies. Essentially development involves change, moving forward, improvement, raising a country's standard of living. Our understanding of the term 'development' has moved on in recent decades; the impact of those processes creating that development vary significantly between global, national and regional scales, and between the developed and developing world.

The economies of LEDCs in particular showed few signs of evolving as Rostow predicted. Economic wealth was concentrated in the hands of very few people in LEDCs with an attendant high standard of living while the majority of the population remained poor, their situations unchanged.

A new understanding of 'development' has become accepted. 'Growth' is concerned with rising national income, whereas 'development' is concerned not only with rising national income but also with the distribution of the income. The concept of **social development** includes an appreciation of human needs – the basic provision of food, housing and water for everyone (Fig 5.2).

There has been much environmental degradation in the name of development, in both MEDCs and LEDCs, and by the 1990s the concept of *sustainable development* was in common use. The Earth Summit conferences in Rio 1992 and Kobe 1997 have succeeded in raising awareness and apportioning some responsibility for sustainable development in the future.

| | DEMOGRAPHIC CHANGE | ECONOMIC CHANGE | ROSTOW'S OUTLINE OF ECONOMIC DEVELOPMENT |
|---|---|---|---|
| Increased levels of development ↑ | Ageing population with low growth / High life expectancy / Low fertility | Impact of economic development spreads to whole country | High mass consumption / ↑ Drive to maturity |
| | Low DR. Declining BR / Population growth slows down | Industrialisation and urbanisation in core location(s) | ↑ Take off |
| | High BR. Declining DR / High fertility / Rapid population growth | Low level of industrialisation / Few linkages at global scale / Economic dependency | ↑ Preconditions for take-off |
| | High BR & DR / High fertility / Slow population growth | | ↑ Traditional society |

FIGURE 5.1 The development process is associated with demographic as well as economic change

In geographical terms the concept of development initially focused on **economic development** in which industrialisation was seen as the route to becoming a 'successful' nation with a high standard of living and real economic growth. In the 1950s the economist Rostow outlined a model which described the stages through which nation states would pass in order to develop (see Fig 5.1). The model was based on the evolution of economies in North America and Europe.

By the 1970s it was apparent that other nations would not necessarily conform to the same pattern.

# Basic measures of social development

The following measures are usually considered as the basis of a social development policy:
■ Providing basic health care (including family planning), primary education, food security, clean drinking water and sanitation;
■ Income-generating and income-supporting activities for the poor (especially women): small-scale credit facilities, work-guarantee programs, agricultural extension programs and support to small-scale agricultural production
■ Strengthening social organisations; e.g. farmers' associations, women's organisations, cooperatives, trade unions, human rights organisations.

(Source: World Guide 1997/98)

FIGURE 5.2 Basic means of social development

The United Nations introduced its Human Development Report (HDR) in 1990, a recognition of the need to put people at the centre of development rather than economics. HDR defines **Human Development** as 'development of the people, for the people, by the people'.

It is worth noting that this framework for human development is not only restricted to LEDCs. There are plenty of examples of the need for 'development', social justice and equality in areas of industrial countries.

# *Measuring development*

The **Human Development Index**, first published in 1990, tries to summarise and quantify the human development of nations by combining financial indicators such as GNP and GDP with indicators of health and education. It is an attempt to represent the complex real world in a simple index figure. Highest levels of HDI reach almost 1, but since development can always evolve the perfect society of 1 is never attained, as the HDI points out. Fig 5.3 analyses the difference between the GDP and HDI of some LEDCs. Notice how some countries such as Costa Rica, Vietnam and Tanzania provide a high standard of living for their population given their limited GDP. Conversely, Saudi Arabia has a very high GDP but the wealth that represents is not reflected in the standard of living of the population in general. Economies which have experienced rapid growth such as Indonesia now have the opportunity to use their new wealth to raise the living standards of every person, not just those who have immediately benefited from industrial expansion.

Measuring development is not easy. HDR attempts to summarise development in the Human Development Index (for data see p. 6 Ch 1), but the *quality* of the data to create the HDI is sometimes quite suspect. Lack of data is itself an indicator of development. Even the World Bank does not have reliable, comprehensive data on basic demographic and social indicators from many of the countries it finances. Indeed some countries are so poor that a census is postponed for two or three years to save money! Relatively few countries accurately record births and deaths, particularly infant deaths, and very few note the cause of death.

---

**STUDENT ACTIVITY**

Consider the data in Figures 5.4 and 5.5. To what extent may the figures be unreliable?

---

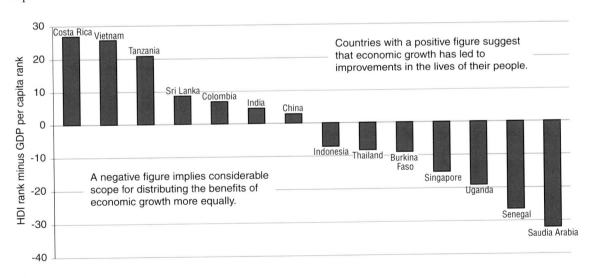

FIGURE 5.3 There is no automatic link between income and human development

FIGURE 5.4 World contrasts in maternal mortality

|  | % of births worldwide | % of deaths of women during pregnancy or childbirth |
|---|---|---|
| Asia | 61 | 55 |
| Africa | 20 | 40 |
| MEDCs | 11 | 1 |

FIGURE 5.5 National contrasts in maternal mortality

| Maternal Mortality per 1000 live births | |
|---|---|
| Sierra Leone | 180 i.e. 1 in 7 women die due to complications in childbirth |
| Afghanistan | 170 |
| Japan | 6 |

# Development and inequality: 'What price progress?'

**Regional development** is an issue for most governments in the world. The inequalities in levels of economic development which result in political tension and social and economic problems of

FIGURE 5.6 Jobless growth

Many parts of the world are witnessing a new phenomenon – jobless growth. Even when output increases, increase in employment lags way behind.
■ Developing countries experienced 4–5 per cent growth in GDP during 1960–73, but employment grew only half as much.
■ Industrial countries managed fairly respectable output growth during 1973–87 but in France, Germany and the UK, employment levels actually fell.
■ Informal employment has increased sharply in developing countries, offering low-wage, non-permanent jobs, instead of remunerative employment.
■ In the United States the recent economic recovery has been a 'jobless recovery'.
Three major causes of jobless growth:
■ labour-saving technology was encouraged by MEDCs as their populations began to decline;
■ rising labour costs and the demands of active trade unions encouraged businesses to reduce their workforces;
■ 20 per cent of the world's population have 80 per cent of world income, i.e. five times more purchasing power, hence rich nations can invest in technology, but ultimately that leads to jobless growth.

Source: HDR 1993

varying degree, are found in every country whether developed or developing, and all governments are bound to address that imbalance to maintain their country's stability.

## Inequality at the global scale

It is unrealistic to expect that any economic growth or development can be equally distributed spatially or socially, that improvements in quality of life can be felt equally across the globe, within nations or even within regions (see Fig 5.6). Consequently one of the characteristics of growth has become inequality. Some places and people benefit while others lag behind to a greater or lesser degree – in both MEDCs and LEDCs. It is here that the policies and role of governments become critical in establishing 'development for all' because the consequences of *unequal* development are far-reaching.

**Globalisation** has tended to erode the power of individual states because large TNCs wield such economic influence, and many governments have become locked into a trade, aid, debt for development scenario so they find it increasingly difficult to make progress in terms of human development. Global industrialisation also means efficiencies and consequently lay-offs, so increasing inequality between those in work and those unemployed. Although one of the main human development strategies is to generate productive employment, global growth of manufacturing output is now greater than the growth of employment. This has produced the 1990s concept of 'jobless growth'.

FIGURE 5.7 Jobless growth: GDP and employment, 1975–2000

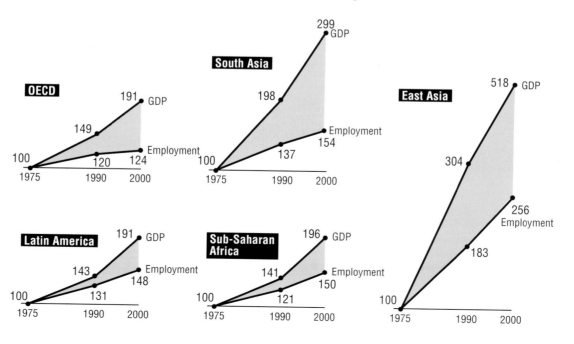

| | Percentage share of income or consumption | |
|---|---|---|
| | **Poorest 20%** | **Richest 20%** |
| Kenya | 3.4 | 62.1 |
| Zimbabwe | 4.0 | 62.3 |
| South Africa | 3.3 | 63.3 |
| Venezuela | 3.6 | 58.4 |
| Mexico | 4.1 | 55.3 |
| Brazil | 2.1 | 67.5 |
| Japan | 8.7 | 37.5 |
| UK | 4.6 | 44.3 |
| USA | 4.7 | 41.9 |
| Netherlands | 8.2 | 36.9 |

FIGURE 5.8 Unequal distribution of income and consumption. Note the contrast with developed countries.

# Inequality at the national scale

## Less Economically Developed Countries

People in rural areas in LEDCs make a very restricted contribution to the economic and social life of their nations with half the urban income and far fewer services. In Ethiopia 87 per cent of population live in rural areas but only 4 per cent have sanitation facilities. This compares with 40 per cent of the urban population. Agricultural development and the much-heralded Green Revolution have also increased inequality in many rural areas of LEDCs. Farmers with better quality land, some education and a little income have access to the system of hybrid seeds, fertilisers, pesticides etc., good storage facilities and personal contacts with middle men. Those very poor farmers with none of these initial advantages are more likely to get into debt and find life even more of a struggle as they are forced to sell their land to repay debts and join the ranks of landless peasants. Other farmers exist on tiny plots with no prospect of self-sufficiency. In India for example 80 per cent of small farms are less than 1 ha in size.

Mechanisation was a 'western' characteristic and, since progress continues to be measured against western standards, has become a typical status symbol of modernisation. It is frequently quite inappropriate that combine harvesters should be introduced into countries such as India where labour is plentiful. Once again it is the rich farmers who benefit, and leave the poor even further behind.

Similarly in urban areas, those workers with some education and skills can find work and slowly move up the financial ladder. The future for those without is bleak. Many workers end up in sweat shops as cheap labour (see Fig 5.9) or even scavenging on rubbish tips.

SWEAT SHIRT

SWEAT SHOP

Oxfam's **CLOTHES CODE** campaign

FIGURE 5.9 Oxfam campaign material from 1996 which helped raise widespread public concern and led to many of Britain's leading clothing companies introducing codes of conduct

There have been many attempts to solve the stark inequalities between rich and poor in LEDCs, and many have failed because programmes have not been sustainable without continued aid or government support. The effectiveness of self-help is now recognised, whereby individuals who can help themselves are more likely to identify their most pressing needs and continue to raise their living standards, albeit slowly.

**Microcredit** schemes are available to give small loans to the very poor to help them out of the poverty trap, or to relieve the worst impacts of crises such as drought. Microcredit allows people to bypass the high interest money lenders and provides credit for the 'unbankable' – those who could never acquire loans through the traditional banking system.

Many nations have become too inflexible to respond to the needs of specific groups within their own countries so the decentralisation of power has become one of the most effective ways of helping people to develop. Where the development gap is huge, people have been inspired to help themselves – grassroots development – supported by NGOs.

There are numerous projects in LEDCs which have small beginnings yet some expand to become very influential in the human development of small communities (see Fig 5.10).

In the rapidly growing Pakistani capital, Karachi, self-help groups have made real progress in social development as local people have organised themselves to improve their standard of living. The Orangi Project focused on providing low cost sanitation and housing, women's work and welfare programmes, and school education. Local leaders on the sanitation programme organised 24 000 families to build 430 000 feet of new sewerage pipes and 28 000 toilets. Local people used their own savings at a quarter of what it would have cost local government. Such spectacular results inspire confidence in local people that they can effectively help themselves – another measure of human development.

FIGURE 5.10 Non-governmental organisations can help people to help themselves

## Inequality among people

As the concept of development evolves to include human development, social development and sustainable development as well as economic development, some groups of people are increasingly marginalised.

- **The poorest people**, through their absolute poverty, are barred from many aspects of social, economic and political life. Familiar scenes of shacks on rubbish tips in developing cities remind us that without an address it is almost impossible to access money, education, health care or exercise the right to vote. Equally the homeless in the UK find it particularly difficult to contribute to their communities (Fig 5.11).
- **Minority groups**, through discrimination, are denied access to education, employment or political representation (Figs 5.12 and 5.13). Castes, tribal groups and indigenous people are more likely to be in low-paid, casual labour jobs. As rural dwellers, many have less access to land – the key to survival. In MEDCs ethnic groups also experience discrimination, as the bitterness of The Balkans in the 1990s so vividly displayed.
- **Rural dwellers** in LEDCs have less access to education, health, water and sanitation. In Ethiopia, for example, 87 per cent of people are rural dwellers but only 11 per cent have access to safe drinking water, compared to 70 per cent of the urban population. Recent trends in development in LEDCs have focused more on agriculture. However, small and marginal farmers in remote or ecologically fragile areas have less access to credit and irrigation. Governments in LEDCs are forced to reduce spending and cut back on rural services. In doing so they increase inequality between small farmers and the influential large farmers and agribusinesses.
- **Disabled people**, 10 per cent of the world's population, are frequently associated with poverty, unemployment and lower levels of achievement.
- **Women** – The Human Development Report 1993 comments that '... women have less power, less autonomy, more work, less money, and more responsibility than men. Women in MEDCs have a higher standard of living than women in LEDCs but nowhere are women equal to men'.

### A woman's place ...

The importance of women to the development process has become better appreciated in the 1990s and disparities between men and women are now more clearly identified. The HDI measures standards of living, health, education, and choices and opportunities for people in their communities. Effective development cannot take place without addressing the gender inequalities in both MEDCs and LEDCs because it is women in all societies who take the greatest responsibility for child care and home management.

## An NGO in Zimbabwe – Organisation of Rural Associations for Progress

The Organisation of Rural Associations for Progress (ORAP), an indigenous NGO in Zimbabwe, acts as an umbrella organisation for local groups, each with five to 30 rural families. ORAP provides funds and technical assistance, but the groups and their regional associations make the key decisions.

Most group members are farmers, so ORAP focused initially on generating income in agriculture. Lately, it has also been engaged in education, sanitation and extension services – and in food security and drought relief. Current projects include grinding mills, gardens, irrigation schemes, sewing and savings clubs, animal husbandry and horticulture.

Now operating in three provinces, ORAP employed 60 people directly in 1990, had an annual budget of around $1 million and covered more than 1000 groups (80 000 families), which were also organised into 16 higher associations.

Also operating in the same area as ORAP, the government is essentially delivering services, while ORAP puts the emphasis on participation and social mobilisation. ORAP's approach is being studied by other groups in Zimbabwe, since it seems successfully to have blended an efficient service organisation with a popular grass-roots movement.

Source: Human Development Report 1993

FIGURE 5.11 Homeless people can be marginalised

FIGURE 5.12 Indigenous peoples can be marginalised

# Inequality among people: the homeless

**M**alcolm had his head 'kicked in' while sleeping rough under cardboard in a multi-storey car park in Worthing, Sussex, over the winter. He had spent two years wandering along the South Coast, nine months of it without even hostel accommodation, after a broken relationship quickly followed a broken 30-year marriage. His business as a contractor laying pipes and manholes for British Telecom had folded, and he had lost his home.

'I was always trying to find a job, but every time you apply, if you are in a hostel or have no fixed address no one wants to know you. You get such a stigma attached to you when you are homeless.'

Extract from Homelessness: Issues for the 90s, pp. 4–5
Independence Educational Publishers, Cambridge

## A bleak future for indigenous people

In almost all societies where they are to be found, indigenous people are poorer than most other groups. In Australia, for example, aboriginals receive about half as much income as non-aboriginals. In developing countries the poorest regions are those with the most indigenous people. In Mexico, for example, in *municipios* where less than 10% of the population is indigenous, only 18% of the population is below the poverty line. But where 70% of the population is indigenous, the poverty rate rises to 80%.

Indigenous people also fare worse in the non-income dimensions of poverty. In Canada the infant mortality rate for indigenous children is twice as high as for the population as a whole. In Peru the Indian population is much more prone to illness than the Spanish-speaking population – and twice as likely to be hospitalised.

In Bolivia and Mexico indigenous children receive on average three years less education than non-indigenous children. And in Guatemala the majority of indigenous people have no formal education – only 40% are literate.

But even when they have education indigenous people still face discrimination in employment. In the United States, for example, around 25% of the earnings shortfall of indigenous people is estimated to result from discrimination.

Source: Pscharapoulos and Patrinos 1994

FIGURE 5.13 Contrasts between black and white population in the US

Women have been described as the 'shock absorbers' of multiple crises – they pick up all the extra functions which hold families together in both rich and poor countries.

Did you know:

■ in LEDCs there are 60 per cent more illiterate women than men;
■ in LEDCs 13 per cent fewer girls enrol in primary education;
■ in LEDCs women's wages are 75 per cent those of men;
■ in MEDCs unemployment is higher among women than men;
■ in MEDCs women make up 75 per cent of unpaid family workers;

So important is the issue of Gender that the United Nations has created the **GENDER DEVELOPMENT INDEX** which is the HDI adjusted for gender inequality. It shows that in every country the GDI is lower than the HDI – no society treats its women as well as its men. Canada has the highest GDI ranking, along with Scandinavia, while Sierra Leone, Niger, Burkina Faso and Mali rank lowest.

## One country, two nations

Almost every country has one or more ethnic groups whose level of human development falls far below the national average. One of the clearest, and best documented, cases is that of blacks in the United States.

Their disadvantage starts at birth. The infant mortality rate for whites is 8 per 1000 live births, but for blacks it is 19. And black children are much more likely than white children to grow up in single-parent homes – in 1990, 19% of white children were growing up in single-parent households, compared with 54% of black children.

Children in black families are also more likely to grow up in poverty. The real GDP per capita for whites in 1990 was around $22 000, but for blacks it was around $17 000.

Indeed, if the United States were divided into two 'countries', the one with the white population would rank number one in the world, according to the human development index, while that with the black population would be only number 31.

Source: HDR 1993 *Inequality in the world's richest nation*

| Country | GDI rank | HDI rank |
|---|---|---|
| Canada | 1 | 1 |
| Norway | 2 | 3 |
| USA | 5 | 4 |
| UK | 13 | 15 |
| Germany | 16 | 19 |
| Singapore | 27 | 26 |
| Poland | 37 | 30 |
| Thailand | 39 | 51 |
| Brazil | 60 | 58 |
| China | 90 | 93 |
| Vietnam | 101 | 105 |
| Zimbabwe | 109 | 110 |
| Kenya | 112 | 114 |
| Bangladesh | 128 | 123 |

FIGURE 5.14 The Gender Development Index and Human Development Index for selected countries. There are 146 countries in the HDR listings

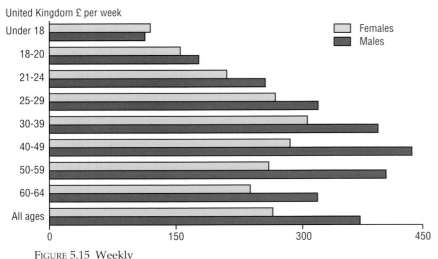

FIGURE 5.15 Weekly earnings of men and women in the UK

FIGURE 5.16 The European contrasts between the earnings of men and women

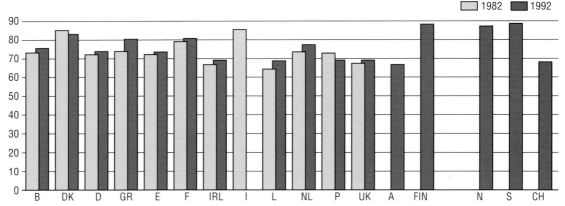

The difference between the wages of men and women is greatest in Austria, and least in Finland, Norway, Sweden and Denmark

## Women in MEDCs

As the industrial world has become more developed, women have fewer children and are more likely to be in paid work. Education has been the key to development. It raises aspirations and gives women the confidence and the skills to work as effectively as men. However it remains the case that women earn less than men (Figs 5.15 and 5.16), and even experience a 'glass ceiling' in the workplace whereby they find it particularly difficult to be promoted beyond a certain level.

It is an indication that such inequalities still exist when government policies in MEDCs are directed to improve the role of women. EU directives state that 'it is important to enable women to compete for stable, highly qualified jobs' and suggest specific measures for child care, training and working hours for women.

FIGURE 5.17 Women in Japan

## Inequalities even in the richest nations

Japan is ranked 7 in the Human Development Index, but only 17 in the Gender Development Index. Does that surprise you? Read the characteristics below then discuss what Japan should do next.

- two in five higher education students are women;
- on average women earn just 51 per cent the salaries of men;
- women hold only 7 per cent of administrative and managerial posts;
- women obtained the right to vote in 1946 but only 2 per cent of parliamentary seats are held by women;
- in 1980 inheritance rights were raised from ⅓ to ½ of their late husband's property (the rest goes to their children);
- the legal age for marriage is 16 for women and 18 for men;
- after divorce a man can marry immediately, but a woman has to wait 6 months.

## Women in LEDCs

In LEDCs the unequal role of women is often circumscribed by culture as well as education. In rural peasant communities women often assume the greatest responsibilities – building homes, collecting fuel and water, cooking and cleaning, childcare and farming – while men are the decision-makers or migrate to find other paid work. Deforestation, soil erosion and water pollution mean that women take longer to reach their fields, collect fuelwood and water. As time demands increase, women share their work with their daughters who are then unable to go to school.

In Uganda 80 per cent of food production is done by women. They do 60 per cent of planting, 70 per cent of weeding, 60 per cent of harvesting and 90 per cent of food processing.
Where women in Uganda have had access to credit, 88 per cent repaid their loans, compared to less than 40 per cent of men.

FIGURE 5.18 Women's work in Uganda

The problem is that women's independence is not always seen as a priority, or their contribution to development recognised in traditional cultures. In Zimbabwe, gender equality was achieved in primary school enrolment by 1990, but when user fees were introduced as part of a structural adjustment programme girls were not sent to school.

In most NICs and LEDCs many employers see women workers as docile, less militant, cheap, and prepared to work in small workshops, sweat shops or at home. In countries such as Myanmar women have little education, few skills and therefore no alternative but to take jobs with poor employment conditions.

In the drive to attract TNCs to invest, countries with export-oriented industries such as Mexico, Brazil, Indonesia, South Korea and Malaysia depended on the promise of union-free, no-minimum-wage labour to attract labour-intensive manufacturing investment. The production process is essentially assembling standardised parts and requires low cost labour with little or no training or experience, but high levels of manual dexterity – conditions of work which women would accept as they try to improve conditions for their families.

Subcontracting and homeworking is also an important part of women's employment, as employers can capitalise on women's needs to increase their income from home work. The range of work is wide – from sub-assembly of electronics to stitching hats, gloves or luggage. In central Thailand villagers produce artificial flowers for export companies in Bangkok: in the Philippines women produce Christmas gift boxes for the USA: in Malaysia women and children in kampongs attach springs and clockwork mechanisms to 'stocking filler' toys for the UK. Developing economies in particular are caught between encouraging industrialisation and condoning the exploitation of women, a typical imbalance in the development process.

At the end of the twentieth century women are seen as a 'flexible workforce' in both developed and less developed countries but their roles vary in different situations (Figs 5.19 and 5.20). Women often work under terms and conditions which would be unacceptable to men. Part-time, short-term labour, with few employment rights now typifies women's work world-wide – a symptom of the spiral of decline. The drive to globalisation appears to lead inexorably towards more inequality.

- A small labour market ensures that women are in demand to maintain industrialisation.
- Government investment in women's education and training.
- Government subsidies for childcare.
- Family members willing to support working women.
- Men encouraged to share household work.

FIGURE 5.19 Role of women in Singapore – permanent part of labour force at every level and sphere of work

- Large workforce therefore less demand for female labour.
- Young women workers travel long distances from villages to work, therefore no family support system.
- Social customs prevent women from seeking help from family or in-laws.
- Household work is not valued.
- Many husbands in poorly paid construction work, taxi drivers, mechanics with low wages.
- Ten per cent of working women involved in industrial home-working using materials delivered from factories. Most tasks are assembly-type: 'finishing' garments by removing threads before packing; sub-assembly of electronics; assembling small toys; sewing luggage, boots, gloves.
- Piece rates of pay i.e. payment by volume not time.

FIGURE 5.20 Role of women in South Korea Subordinate position of women in society limits the work and social contribution of women

The International Food Policy Research Institute has said that 'income in the hands of women contributes more to household food security and child nutrition than income controlled by men'.

'If money is given to women, it is generally used for better nutrition, better clothing, and for the welfare of the household. If it's given to men, it tends to be spent on electronic goods, a new bicycle maybe, or – if we're to be really frank – on prostitution, alcohol and other forms of consumption that don't help the family.'

The World Food Programme (WFP) insists that 80 per cent of its food aid be given directly to households, usually through the senior female member.

Women and girls account for seven out of ten of the planet's hungry, yet it is they whoe produce much of the food. Latest estimates put the proportion of 80 per cent in Africa and 60 per cent in Asia and the level seems to be rising. As men migrate to the cities, the world is seeing 'the feminisation of agriculture and poverty'.

Women often lack the education needed to cope with their new responsibilities. Two out of every three illiterates in the world are women.

There is thus a strong belief that the best way to feed the world's poor will be to educate its women. The WFP in Pakistan began putting that idea into practice with a scheme to give families a can of cooking oil for every month each of their daughters spent at primary school.

The WFP targeted Baluchistan and Frontier Province – poor, arid regions along the borders with Iran and Afghanistan, where purdah is the norm.

'In two years we have doubled enrolment, and the attendance of the girls who are enrolled has increased to 95 per cent,' says WFP's director.

He encountered little resistance on grounds of religion or tradition. Parents had been keeping their girls away for financial reasons – to help with work at home. When the balance of economic advantage was tipped in the opposite direction, they became enthusiastic supporters of their daughters' education.

Source: *The Guardian*, November 1996

FIGURE 5.21 Women, poverty and education

# Industrialisation and development

Since the 1960s many poor nations have strived to industrialise as a way of developing their economies and raising standards of living. Nations have taken different routes to economic growth with a variety of policies applied at different stages in their economic development. In the early stages, in the 1960s, there was state intervention in industry to ensure that a country remained economically independent, and tariffs were imposed to make imports more expensive. **Import substitution** is typical in countries beginning to industrialise whereby locally-made goods replace imported ones. Often the domestic market is small and governments operate forms of protectionism to help their industries in the face of global competition.

When industry becomes more established, exports play a more important role in economic growth. Foreign exchange is earned on exports and the expanded market creates more jobs and wealth in the producer country. This in turn raises consumer spending, generates further industrial development and subsequently money for social development.

Development in the form of industrialisation has 'gone global'. As industries strive to become more efficient, comparative advantage i.e. the resources of labour, minerals and physical location becomes critical. Industries have complex, often global, links (forward and backward linkages) which lead to agglomeration in particular locations. At the global scale the USA, European Community and Japan are the hubs of economic/industrial activity. Even the high profile industrial expansion of the East Pacific Rim nations since 1960 is relatively small compared to the established industrial nations.

These locations can be thought of as the focus **core** of economic activity and become attractive to migrants from less successful **peripheral** regions in search of work. As migrants increase the size of the workforce the core region becomes attractive to companies because, among other factors, it forms a local market for goods. The result is an upward spiral of growth where money earned by industry and the workforce is recycled within the core. Other factors reinforce the concentration – the workforce becomes more skilled, communications improve, personal contacts are made and prestige locations are established. The periphery – those locations where there is less economic activity – tends to suffer as it is ignored by industrialists and it becomes more and more isolated and left behind.

The peripheral region may decline because it is based on traditional heavy industry, and global competition leads to closure, unemployment and out-migration. The once flourishing North East England was faced with this prospect in the 1970s as coal mining declined dramatically along with shipbuilding and engineering (see case study p. 92). South East England, as the core, developed its service industries and became the focus for most investment and growth in the UK.

Some regions maintain their pre-eminence by continually investing in new industries and technology, and successfully combine new manufacturing with service industries despite declining traditional industries.

FIGURE 5.22 The South East Asian economies illustrate the range of policies which countries employ to generate economic growth.

- Strong government support for industry in the form of price protection against imports and low interest rates so that companies could afford to invest and expand.
- Strong export base with government incentives for some industrial products notably shipbuilding, iron and steel, electronics.
- Government restrictions on foreign investments meant that monies generated tended to stay within the Asian economies.
- Active government support for research and development.
- Few restrictions on employment conditions, minimum wages, working hours.
- Heavy investment in education and training to provide a skilled workforce.

# Models of economic growth

The Swedish economist Gunnar Mrydal (1963) outlined a **Model of Cumulative Causation** which explained the main features of unbalanced economic growth. He described the upward spiral process whereby some regions become centres of economic growth. Equally, it is relevant to declining regions which experience increasing difficulty in attracting new industry and have to combat the negative images of economic decline, a supposedly

unskilled workforce, and environmental decay.

Also in the 1960s, John Friedman developed his **Core – Periphery Model** which sought to integrate the different ideas of development in regions, with a clear focus on initial development in the city.

Both Friedman and Myrdal recognised the unequal nature of development and that the contrasts were reinforced by rural/urban differences. As rural areas develop they also change demographically since it is predominantly the young, mobile population who migrate to find work or build new careers in the Core regions, while the settled, older population tend to have more ties and are less willing to move. The ageing of peripheral regions does not make it any easier to overcome the economic forces of development in the Core.

## Global scale

The core – periphery concept is seen at a global scale with North West Europe, North America and Japan at the core of the world economic and political system, and the poorest countries, notably in Sub-Saharan Africa, at the periphery. The change in global patterns has seen the NICs acquiring some core economic status despite the vast geographical distances separating them from the traditional developed regions. In reality, levels of development at the global scale are now a continuum between the extremes of Core and Periphery with *rates* of development also being an important characteristic. Major world organisations such as the IMF, World Bank and UN have a crucial role in the economic, social and political development of countries, particularly over the direction which that development takes.

The World Trade Organisation (WTO) has opened up trade restrictions between many countries. This has particularly benefited the **semi-periphery** economies – those who are developing an industrial base and can trade on the world market. These countries also have money for health, education, transport and infrastructure and are beginning to generate economic growth of their own.

## Continental scale

Within the continent of Europe there is ample evidence of unequal development. Strains inside the European Union reflect this as the poorer countries claim economic support for small traditional farmers and regional aid for infrastructure projects. The political will and influence is there to make Europe strong but economically it is very disparate. The Core economy lies within the 'hot banana' area (see Fig 5.24) between the English Midlands and Northern Italy, while the periphery consists of the Mediterranean region.

Within the Asian subcontinent, contrasts are clearly seen between the affluent and developed economies of Japan, Hong Kong, Singapore and Taiwan and peripheral countries of Cambodia, Myanmar and Vietnam. The 'upwardly mobile' economies of Indonesia, Thailand, India, Malaysia and China aspire to become core economies, but are beset by financial and structural problems, many of which are affecting the rest of the world within the global trading system.

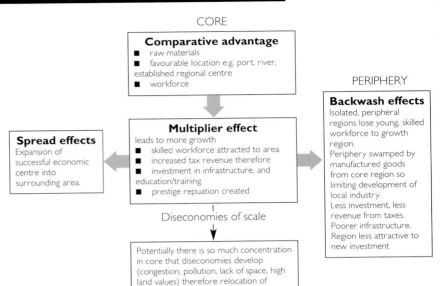

FIGURE 5.23 Relationships between the Core and the Periphery

With its colonial heritage and its struggle against discrimination of every kind, Africa remains on the economic periphery of the global system. Even where there is relatively little industrialisation in global terms, there are still contrasts between isolated core locations in southern Ghana, southern Nigeria and South Africa and peripheral countries such as Ethiopia and Burkina Faso. Such contrasts are as closely linked to the geographical isolation of landlocked states as to the political and economic instability which typifies much of Africa.

FIGURE 5.24 Core periphery areas in Western Europe

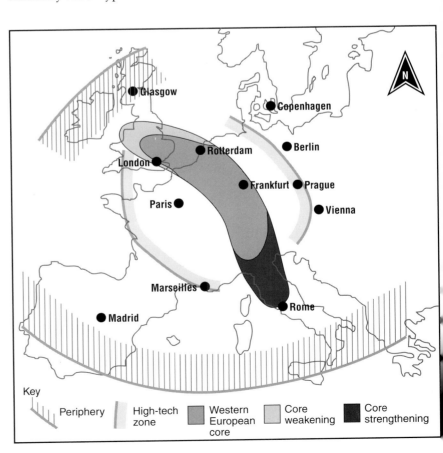

Key

Periphery    High-tech zone    Western European core    Core weakening    Core strengthening

Its 47 countries present a tapestry of national sentiment, underdeveloped resources, environmental pressure and neocolonialism. It remains a global challenge how to support the African nations in their quest for development, particularly as the gap between the wealthy urban dwellers with their westernised lifestyles presents such a glaring contrast to the rural poor. The US has become locked into a debate about the right mix of development assistance, debt reduction, trade restrictions and investment to encourage growth and sustainable development. However it is likely that whatever further industrialisation occurs, especially from TNCs, it will be attracted to the core economies. Rapid population growth in cities creates a consumer market where people earn money, acquire 'western' tastes, and increase their spending power.

## National/Regional scale

At the national scale, core regions tend to focus on the capital city as the main administrative centre, and on ports or mineral locations where industrial development generates backward and forward linkages. Regions without any current comparative advantage retreat to the periphery of economic importance. As the gap between the two widens, governments are bound to consider how best to reverse the status of the periphery.

Regional development in the Developed World, is usually directed to either aid economic development in rural areas or to stem severe decline in old industrial regions. Following the end of the Second World War, established industrial regions in Developed Countries such as North East France, the

FIGURE 5.25  Map of regional inequalities in EU

The last decade has seen quite dramatic changes in the map of Europe and in the extent and character of the European Union. In part, these changes relate to the expansion of the EU eastwards (the East German Länder), southwards (Greece, Portugal and Spain), northwards (Finland and Sweden) and, with the accession of Austria, towards the central European core. With each expansion, the scale of spatial inequalities within the EU has grown.

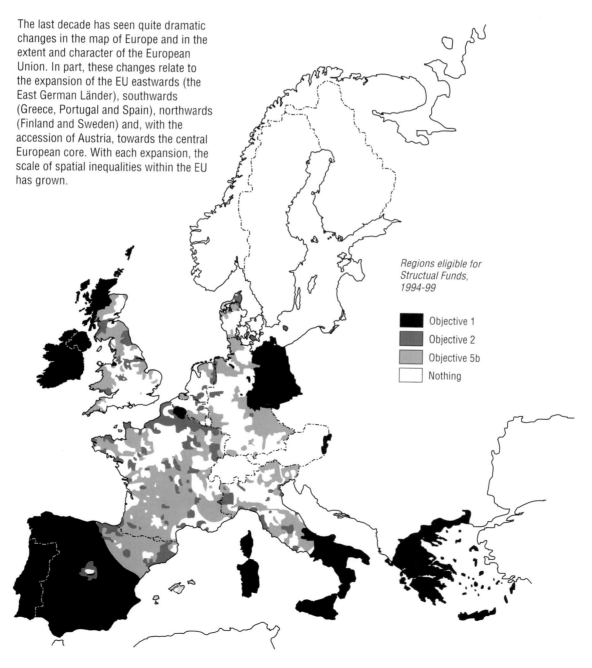

Regions eligible for Structual Funds, 1994-99

- Objective 1
- Objective 2
- Objective 5b
- Nothing

Ruhr in Germany, Sambre-Meuse in Belgium, South Wales and North East England enjoyed a period of industrial growth as the economies of those countries were rebuilt. Since the late 1960s many regions have experienced a period of economic decline, some more dramatically than others, based on the absolute decline of their natural resources such as coal or iron ore, or the decline of their traditional heavy industry such as shipbuilding, steel production, textiles or metal working. The decline of these regions has been all the more marked when compared with the economic expansion of other new areas where **footloose industries** such as electronics and 'high tech' companies have agglomerated. National governments and the EU attempt to revive flagging regional economies by offering financial incentives to attract businesses to these regions particularly through the EU Structural Funds and Regional Policies. Some economic development schemes have proved successful with the result that local economies are now reviving – a cycle of industrial growth, decline and renewal is evident. European aid gives financial support to regions as part of its Regional Aid Policy. Objectives 1, 2 and 5b are the only ones of a specific regional nature, but the others are also relevant to regions experiencing economic and social decline (Fig 5.25). As the EU has expanded, its attention has turned away from deindustrialised cities to the poorer southern regions of Greece, Southern Italy and Portugal.

Some regions in Europe have been fortunate in that they had a diverse economic base in service and financial activities and were not so dependent on traditional industries. The economies of these regions, such as the Ruhr, have remained thriving industrial centres despite the pressures of industrial decline and have benefited from their status as regional or national capitals.

---

**Objective 1 regions in the EU**
whole of Greece
S and W of Spain
Italian Mezzogiorno
Corsica
Nord-Pas-de-Calais
Northern Ireland
Scottish Highlands
Merseyside
Flevoland in Netherlands
Hainault in Belgium
East Berlin
Burgenland in Austria

---

## Types of Regional Development in the EU

**Objective 1 Regions**
Development priorities include promoting the production sector: modernising infrastructure for communications, telecommunications, energy and water supply.

**Objective 2 regions**
Priority given to employment; quality of environment; redevelopment of sites, land and buildings; economic restructuring; improvement in region's image.

**Objective 5b regions**
Aim to diversify economic activity; job creation in non-agricultural sectors especially tourism and small/medium sized businesses.

FIGURE 5.26 Types of Regional Aid to EU member states, 1997

|  | Category | Criteria |
|---|---|---|
| **Objective 1** | underdeveloped regions where development is lagging behind | * GNP/capita is less than 75 per cent of EU average<br>* peripheral regions with relatively little industry<br>* where industry is threatened |
| **Objective 2** | regions experiencing economic conversion or decline | * rate of unemployment above EU average<br>* ratio of persons in industry to total in employment which is higher than EU average |
| **Objective 3** | } long term unemployment |  |
| **Objective 4** | } long term unemployment |  |
| **Objective 5a** | adaptation of agricultural structures |  |
| **Objective 5b** | economic and social diversification, development of rural areas | * GDP/capita<br>* proportion of agricultural jobs to total employment<br>* low level of agricultural income<br>* low population density<br>* substantial depopulation |

## CASE STUDY

### Unequal development – National scale United Kingdom

Development processes are evident within the UK in terms of economic development, human development and sustainable development. An investigation of regional data illustrates broadly the concept of core – periphery, but also the limitations of such a simplistic model.

The EU has had a significant impact on regional patterns in the UK and in other European countries. While London and the Midlands are included in the European core stretching to the Ruhr, Paris and Milan, most of Britain is peripheral within Europe.

From the 1960s onwards the core economic region was dominated by London but included a broad area of West Yorkshire/South Lancashire in the north, most of the West Midlands, and the South East. This region was viewed as having high economic potential with over half the population, low levels of unemployment and therefore high consumer spending power, and good accessibility via the motorway network.

Outside this broad core was the periphery – the rural fringe and pockets of traditional, declining heavy industry facing serious economic stagnation in a downward economic spiral (see Fig 5.27). Successive governments attempted to reverse this inequality through government investments and regional policies.

By the 1980s the North–South divide was firmly established – the 'successful south' being the South East, East Anglia, and the East Midlands. Core periphery application in spatial terms was weakened by the decline of manufacturing in the West Midlands, formerly part of the Core.

As deindustrialisation progressed through all regions, coincidentally there was rapid growth in the tertiary sector especially the service economy – financial and business services, high-tech and research and development. This was fundamentally important in the economic boom in the South East from 1983.

Another trend in the distribution of manufacturing industry was a move from old, congested, inner city sites in conurbations to small town locations and the rural fringe. As industry became footloose and flexible, environmental quality for the workforce became a significant factor in industrial location. The 'Cambridge phenomenon' is typical of this change, and by 1990 the arc around west London from East Anglia to Crawley and Gatwick Airport was established. Outward growth from Greater London could be seen as spread effects from the core.

In real life, economic forces are not the only ones to affect industrial location and regional development. Political policies have also played a significant role in Britain, as in most countries.

FIGURE 5.27 Model of economic growth, decline and renewal.

Uninterrupted economic growth:
Paris
London
Ruhr

Absolute decline
eg. Basque region

International importance
Trade Services Finance

National importance
Route Centre Services

Renewal - economic decline arrested by regional investment. Lille, S. Wales, Central Scotland, NE England

⌒ Established industrial centre
⌒ Continued economic growth
–·–·– Economic decline
·······• Economic renewal

FIGURE 5.28 Contrasts in Regional gains and losses 1979–1990

|  | Gain in service jobs | Loss in manufacturing jobs |
|---|---|---|
| The South | 1.4 million | 0.9 million |
| Rest of UK | 0.8 million | 1.6 million |

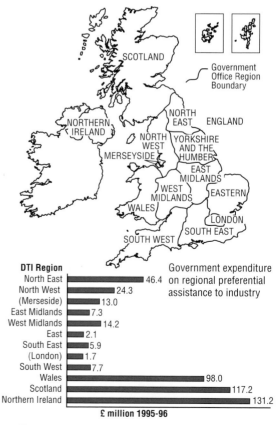

| DTI Region | |
|---|---|
| North East | 46.4 |
| North West | 24.3 |
| (Merseyside) | 13.0 |
| East Midlands | 7.3 |
| West Midlands | 14.2 |
| East | 2.1 |
| South East | 5.9 |
| (London) | 1.7 |
| South West | 7.7 |
| Wales | 98.0 |
| Scotland | 117.2 |
| Northern Ireland | 131.2 |

Government expenditure on regional preferential assistance to industry

£ million 1995-96

FIGURE 5.29 UK Government supports for industry

The demise of regional policies in the 1970s and 1980s reinforced the 'periphery' concept, particularly in Wales, Scotland, Ireland and Northern England, as they became increasingly dependent on the core for economic support through regional aid. But it was political policy too which led to the economic recession of the mid 1990s after the 'boom' years of the 1980s, and in which the south east was particularly severely affected by the decline in services as well as manufacturing. The nightmare of negative equity in the housing market is one which few home owners at the time will forget.

While UK regions can benefit from such economic support, it would seem increasingly unlikely that it will be sufficient to change their peripheral status. Despite a reduction in the importance of real distances it remains to be seen whether the geographical edge of Europe can become an economic focus in a core region.

The Republic of Ireland may be an interesting exception. Strong political support for Europe has drawn in huge inward investment plus substantial regional development monies. GDP is rising and the economic outlook is favourable.

## CASE STUDY

### *Unequal development – Regional scale Northern France*

Within northern France the core region is clearly Paris, the largest city in Europe (8.5 million), and the route focus of the transport network. Paris has experienced continued economic growth as a result of its capital status, good transport by water, rail and road, and its prestigious reputation for innovation, style and culture. Growth in the central core has been matched by population growth in the ring of New Towns surrounding Paris within a 100 km radius. Footloose industries have been attracted to these towns with skilled workforces, pleasant environments and good access – the spread effects from the core. Lille has represented the downward transition zone where industrial decline and outmigration led to economic decay. With sufficient resources and investment it seems possible for some regions to revive and recover from their former decline although the extent and permanence of the current optimism/upward transition remains to be seen.

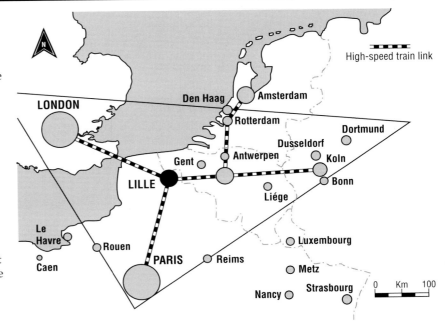

FIGURE 5.30 Map of Lille within Northern Europe

FIGURE 5.31 (a) Aerial shot of Lille in the 1950s; (b) New image of Lille as a young vibrant city

**Lille**, 200 kms north of Paris.
Population: 168 424

In the Nord-Pas-de-Calais region, the hub of a transport network on the canalised Deule River, 10 kms from the Belgian border, good links to Paris and other French cities.

An old industrial city based on the Nord coalfield, the key industries in Lille were coalmining, iron and steel and textiles. Lille was a leading French manufacturing base surrounded by a ring of other cities, Roubaix, Tourcoing, Bethune, Douai all of whose economies depended on coal and the canal network to the English Channel. Since the 1960s the thin, faulted coal seams have become expensive to mine and there was competition from imported coal. The government invested heavily in nuclear energy for electricity production thus removing a major market for coal. Heavy industry declined as a result of competition from cheaper producers overseas and in Eastern Europe, and consequently there has been dramatic economic decline in the region.

Since 1985 Lille has benefited from financial incentives offered in national and regional development schemes. Old blighted industrial areas have been replaced by nearly 100 new factories, new shopping centres and housing, attracted by the 100 million people living within 300 kms of Lille. The key to success has been the position of Lille as a

route focus. The old canal network has been upgraded to take 3000-tonne barges from Dunkerque to Lille and Paris. Six new motorways provide essential communications for modern industries and component firms placing Lille at the centre of the Paris–Brussels axis. New rail links on the TGV network, France's high speed train, make Paris only one hour away, Brussels 35 minutes, and London two hours on Eurostar, the Channel Tunnel link. The Lille–Europe TGV station is central to Euralille, a £2 billion international shopping, office and housing and leisure development, the flagship of the new image of Lille as a young vibrant city. Lille now aims to attract major banks and insurance services relocating from Brussels, Paris or London.

Renewal is not without its continual problems for Lille. Much new office space remains empty and unemployment particularly for immigrant groups such as Algerians and Moroccans, is still above average for France. Workers from the coalfield and steel industries have opportunities for retraining but still struggle to find work. Lille still has to combat it's traditional image as an old, dirty isolated city but good communications and a skilled labour force are the key elements for future success.

The economic history of Lille clearly illustrates the pattern of growth, decline and renewal typical of many industrial cities. At a regional scale Lille also illustrates the Core–Periphery Model.

# Unequal Development – Local Scale

We have seen how, within the UK, there is a broad North–South divide, but *within* regions there are also sizeable centres of growth and decline. Some, like Leeds, have always been successful. Others such as Cardiff, Liverpool and Newcastle have experienced huge economic and industrial growth in the nineteenth and early twentieth centuries followed by rapid and devastating decline. The cycle continues however, with substantial

efforts, supported by European regional aid, to regenerate depressed areas. Inevitably renewal brings conflict – in this case from adjacent areas which do not benefit from grant aid. The Merry Hill Shopping Centre, built on an old steel works near Dudley in the West Midlands, has become a focus of economic activity, but Dudley itself cannot compete and faces gradual decline in shopping and services.

## CASE STUDY

FIGURE 5.32 Location of Royal Quays development

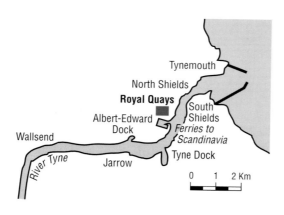

### *Royal Quays, Tyneside*

Royal Quays is the flagship development of Tyne and Wear Development Corporation, transforming a contaminated, derelict river bank site and the acutely socially deprived community of Meadowell. The Albert–Edward dock was the centre of heavy industry, timber trading and coal exporting – a prime south-facing site on the River Tyne within easy access of the Tyne Tunnel and the A1. The Corporation invested £245 million with EU funding as an Enterprise Zone plus the City Challenge initiative, and £160 million from private investment.

FIGURE 5.33 Landscaping includes grassed areas, water features, bridges and walkways

There were four clear themes for the regeneration strategy:

1. **Creating new business districts for both modern office developments and industrial estates**. This includes: the 13 000 m² European Microelectronics Institute serving the microelectronics industry on Teeside; Daewoo motor importers; Twining Tea Blenders; an expanded North Sea ferry terminal; 10 000 m² commercial business space, 20 000 m² of industrial floorspace; £12 million on new roads enhancing access to the area; new investment for the North Shields Fish Quay.

2. **Increasing employment and improving access to jobs through grant aid and advice to local and incoming businesses, and introducing training initiatives**. 200 new jobs anticipated.

3. **Reviving the riverside as a place to live by providing new homes, leisure, shopping and cultural facilities**. Housing regeneration has transformed the area with 1200 mixed tenure homes by private developers; regional attractions such as Wet'n'Wild water park and The Parks sports centre; Royal Quays Outlet Shopping Centre which attracts visitors throughout the region.

4. **Improving land reclamation, landscaping, restoring historic buildings and creating parks, walkways and cycleways**. A 250 berth marina in the former Albert–Edward dock and extensive landscaping has transformed the area beyond all recognition.

---

**STUDENT ACTIVITY**

In what ways do the following terms explain economic changes on Tyneside?
- downward transition
- backwash effects
- multiplier effects
- upward transition zone

FIGURE 5.34 (a) The area before development (b) the area after development.

## CASE STUDY

### National scale China

Although China is poor it has much less inequality and abject poverty than countries such as India and Bangladesh. The transformation of the economy resulted in rapid growth in the early 1990s with a 12.5 per cent increase in GDP in 1992, followed by inflation at 20 per cent in 1994. In such a huge country of 9.5 million km² change is inevitably spatially and socially uneven, but the egalitarian policies and state enterprises of Mao Zedong which ensured strong control over resource distribution have reduced some inequalities between coast and interior, urban and rural societies. One government policy of restricting rural–urban migration stopped the concentrations of poor communities in China's cities and limited the development of shanty towns. Another meant that rural peasants were not paid salaries/wages therefore there was equality within each production unit. State population policies began first for expansion in the 1950s and then for strict control since 1970. Policies have also had repercussions on the economic systems of both rural and urban areas.

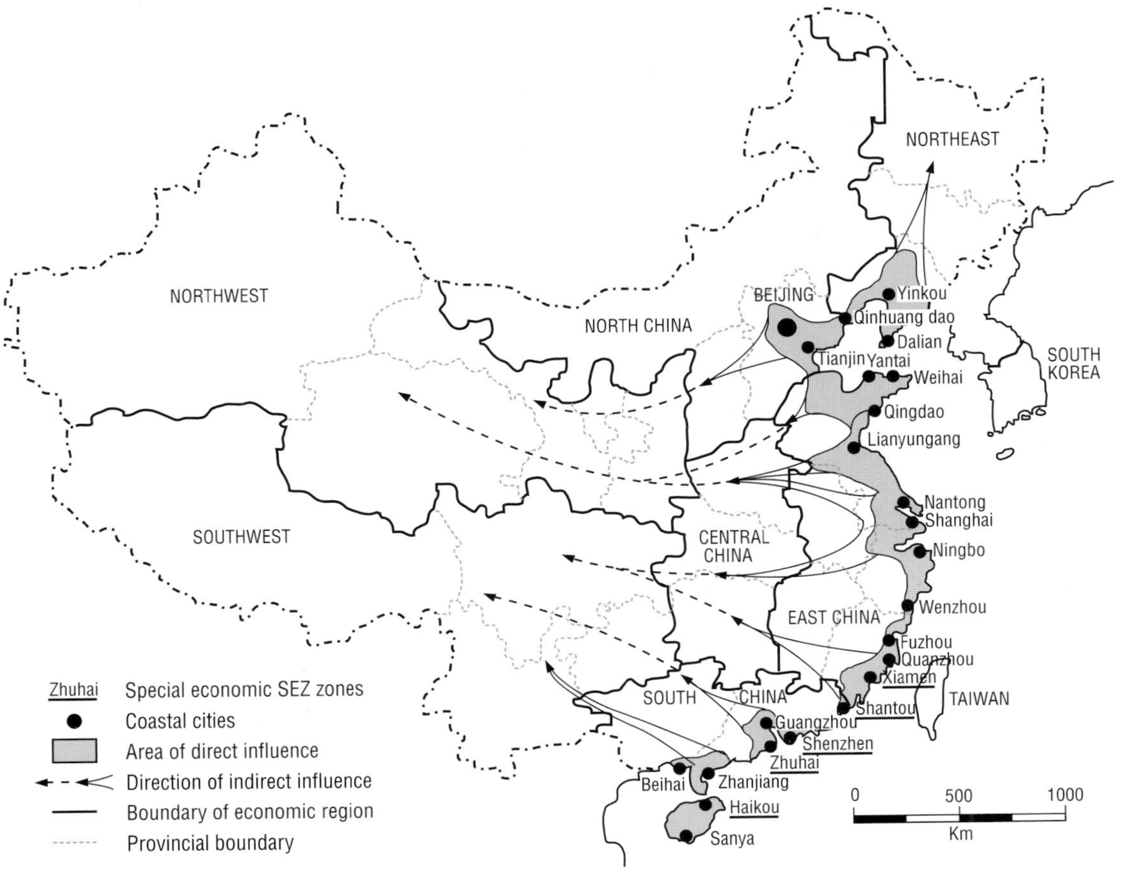

FIGURE 5.35 Map of
China shows the decline
of coastal influence with
distance inland

As China is modernising and becoming integrated into the world economy, inequalities are becoming apparent as a result of lack of centralised controls, and the freedom given to states to pursue the comparative advantages of their regions.

### Inequalities within China

■ In such a huge country there are significant contrasts in the natural and physical resources of the land. The Yangtze valley is rapidly increasing its agricultural output over its fertile floodplain but the poor, marginal areas such as the low-lying salty and sandy plain of North China, the loess plateau in Shaanxi, Gansu and Ningxia, and the mountainous North West cannot hope to compete.

■ Coastal cities have a clear advantage over inland centres when attracting foreign investment, and developing export led growth, and industrial growth is much slower in the north western and south western cities. Communications and transport remain very limited over much of the interior, and as the government draws back its economic responsibilities there is less opportunity for nation-wide transport network schemes.

Inequality is becoming more marked *within* rural economies too. Reforms have pushed poorer peasants off the land to become hired labourers while richer farmers produce more lucrative large scale cash crops. The drive for profit from farming and rural industries has led to some families taking their children from school to work on farms. This goes in the face of calls to increase the numbers in higher education, and also encourages families to ignore birth control policies. The biggest problem is lack of investment in agriculture as large projects such as irrigation and terracing are not undertaken by private enterprise. The Three Gorges Dam is a notable exception. In Mao Zedong's China any food produced was available to the whole nation, but astute regional provinces recognise the value of commercial crops such as silk, cotton and tobacco and the area of grain cultivation has reduced considerably. Serious food shortages in North China in the winters have increased the need for grain imports, adding an unwelcome drain on China's foreign exchange. Because so much development is concentrated at the coast, regional authorities are desperate to develop their own resources. Some coastal provinces such as Guangdong find it hard to get the interior to provide them with raw materials. In an extreme case some Guangdong companies were prepared to pay extremely high prices, and even use army vehicles, to transport raw silk out of Sichuan, in the western region, where various government decrees had prohibited such internal exports. Interior regions can hold coastal regions to ransom to get the transfer of technology and new investment they require.

### China's development strategy

China's development strategy is *coastal* with each region assigned a special role to become internationally competitive and to attract foreign technology and skills (Fig 5.35). Government supports the 'trickle down' effect of the core periphery model. Five Special Economic Zones (SEZs) are key growth poles centred on the southern coastal region. These areas will lead the technology transformation of traditional industries and high value added consumer products. Gradually high energy-consuming and high polluting factories move to other regions. Central region concentrates on energy, raw materials, some machinery, electrical products and agricultural produce while the western region emphasises agriculture, forestry, mineral exploitation and local processing industries. In the 'ladder step' doctrine, regions are equated to steps on a ladder in which the coast, on a higher step, is the first to catch up at an international level, followed in turn by other regions as they develop in turn. Logically, the coast has the resources already, therefore it is easier to modernise than diffuse technology and benefits throughout the economy. The 'anti ladder step' opponents believe that as the coast receives more special privileges the gap with the interior will widen irrevocably. The interior should receive the same encouragement to industrialise so that it can exploit its resources to support the coastal growth strategy. Clearly within China the coast is pivotal in making the country a global economy since it accounts for over 50 per cent of total investment in China. The challenge for the People's Republic is how to encourage even growth within the political climate of decentralised decision-making.

# Debt

## Where did it start?

Since the colonial period of exploitation of natural resources from Africa, Asia and South America the terms of trade have been unfavourable to the supplying countries, and since 1945 prices of cash crops and minerals have not been rising as fast as manufactured goods. Consequently LEDCs export raw materials at a low price thus earning small amounts of foreign exchange, and have to import manufactured goods requiring very large sums of foreign exchange.

FIGURE 5.36 Debt: the new colonialism

In nature's unlucky draw, most developing countries have few energy resources so significant imports of fuel, particularly oil, are required to support the industrialisation which aids their development. This puts a further burden on the small bag of foreign exchange and leads LEDCs to borrow money from international banks. The IMF (International Monetary Fund) is a prime source of loans along with its sister institution the World Bank.

### International Monetary Fund

Makes loans available to countries to help stabilise their economies, restore a viable balance of payments and support sustainable economic growth. Where necessary Governments have to agree to reforms in their financial system, pensions, labour markets, agriculture and energy sectors.

IMF intervention is often unpopular because it only becomes involves in a country's finances during times of crisis, when a government has failed to take unpalatable measures to keep its economy in good shape.

## Causes of the Debt crisis of the 1980s

There were two major international crises in the 1970s which have had the most far-reaching impacts on world economic order. In 1973 the Arab–Israeli conflict seriously interrupted oil supplies from the Gulf to the rest of the world, particularly to the United States and Europe, and in 1979 the Iran–Iraq

war also curtailed oil production. As oil became in short supply prices rose dramatically and developed countries panicked as they realised the implications of the oil-dependence of their societies and economies. Even when the crises were over, oil prices remained high and OPEC producers (including Nigeria and Venezuela) earned huge sums from their 'liquid gold' resources.

Gulf States in particular then invested their vast income in international banks who in turn searched for investment and lending opportunities around the world – principally in LEDCs. At the same time many poor nations with few energy resources were forced to borrow money in order to pay for the expensive yet desperately needed oil which was essential for their industrial development (Fig 5.37).

The world in the 1970s regarded industrial development as the principal way to achieve economic growth and development, so LEDCs were also searching for money to finance infrastructure projects (roads, power supplies, port facilities, education) to encourage industrialisation.

By the early 1980s the developed world was facing rising inflation and interest rates rose to control it. This then triggered economic recession in the developed world. For LEDCs this proved disastrous, as they had borrowed large sums and now could not afford to repay the interest let alone the capital sum. The recession also meant fewer exports to MEDCs and reduced foreign earnings for LEDCs. The result was bankruptcy for Mexico in 1982 with several other countries teetering on the brink of insolvency. The debt crisis had begun, sending shudders around the world as bankers realised how much money was actually tied up in immature LEDC economies.

## Impacts of the Debt crisis

Most LEDCs have been forced to borrow more money to pay the interest due on earlier borrowing, and have also negotiated new terms of repayment on these huge loans. This 'rescheduling' of their debt has frequently been dependent on each country embarking upon economic reforms to reduce government spending and encourage industrial investment and growth.

The statistics make depressing reading (see Fig 5.38). There are 40 Severely Indebted Low Income Countries (SILICS) with a GDP per capita less than $695. Their combined debt totals $160000 per capita, *more* than their combined GDP and more than *double* their export income. LEDCs need to borrow to pay for major projects such as dams, roads and education, but such projects may not generate sufficient revenue to repay the loan. Many people in the poorest countries are too poor to pay taxes, are outside the formal, paid-work system, or evade taxes altogether. Investors have tended to seek short-term gains so there are relatively few institutions who are prepared to take out a long term commitment in the hope that there will be some return in the next century.

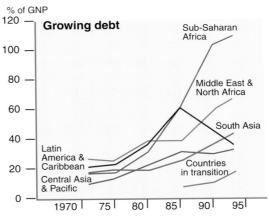

FIGURE 5.37 Growing debt

In the period 1971-1993, the total external debt expressed as a proportion of GNP, increased in every region of the world. The high levels of Latin American debt in the 1980's have decreased since then. The sub-Saharan African debt continues to grow and has already surpassed the regions GNP.

Source: World Bank, World Debt Tables 1994-95, vol. 2 Washington DC, 1994.
Note: In the Sub-Saharan Africa data, South Africa is not included.

FIGURE 5.38 Some countries have accrued vast debts

| Country | Total external debt $m 1994 | External debt $ per capita 1994 |
|---|---|---|
| Argentina | 77388 | 2263 |
| Bangladesh | 16569 | 140 |
| Brazil | 151104 | 950 |
| Chile | 22939 | 1639 |
| China | 100536 | 84 |
| Egypt | 33358 | 588 |
| Ethiopia | 5058 | 92 |
| France | NIL | NIL |
| Germany | NIL | NIL |
| Ghana | 5389 | 324 |
| Hong Kong | NIL | NIL |
| India | 98990 | 108 |
| Indonesia | 96500 | 507 |
| Japan | 22712 | 363 |
| Kenya | 7273 | 280 |
| South Korea | 54542 | 1227 |
| Nepal | 2320 | 111 |
| Netherland | NIL | NIL |
| Nigeria | 33485 | 310 |
| Pakistan | 29579 | 234 |
| Peru | 22623 | 974 |
| Philippines | 39302 | 586 |
| Poland | 42160 | 1094 |
| Saudi Arabia | NIL | NIL |
| South Africa | NIL | NIL |
| Thailand | 60991 | 1051 |
| UK | NIL | NIL |
| USA | NIL | NIL |
| Venezuela | 36850 | 1740 |
| Zambia | 6573 | 714 |

| | |
|---|---|
| FIGURE 5.39 Pro's and Con's of Structural Adjustment | IMF/World Bank suggest that SAPs will increase world trade and therefore reduce inequality within poor countries and between rich and poor countries | Aid agencies claim that SAPs increase inequality since any reduction in education and welfare spending affects the poor most of all. Governments have less money because so much of it is used to pay off debts to MEDCs |
| | Economic progress is linked to globalisation which offers more LEDCs the chance to improve their standard of living | The workforce becomes less skilled therefore less attractive to foreign investors |
| | Countries which have integrated rapidly into the world economy have achieved high levels of economic development – Argentina, Chile, Mexico, Ghana, Hungary, Poland, Czech Republic and Turkey | These 8 countries with high growth rates now absorb most of the foreign investment available for LEDCs |
| | Even where economies have worsened it is difficult to assess whether or not the reforms were instrumental in the process of decline | Countries on the periphery of the world economy are left further and further behind |
| FIGURE 5.40 A critical view of structural adjustment policies | | Repercussions in MEDCs as cheaper labour costs in LEDCs reduce employment opportunities in MEDCs. *Global economy becomes less developed.* |

# Solutions to the Debt crisis

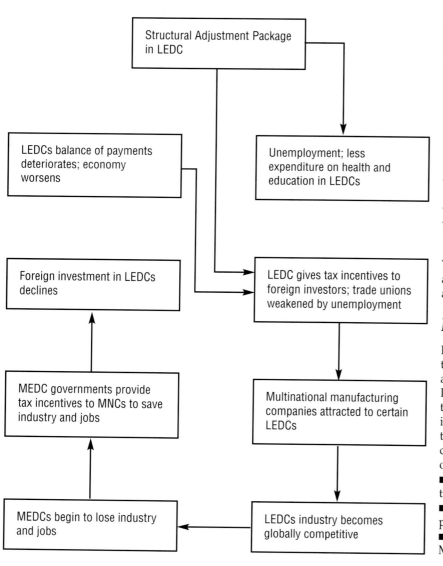

**Structural Adjustment** is the process of economic change required by the IMF and World Bank when they lend money to poor countries. They claim that the more a country is integrated into the global economy the higher the standard of living will become. Most structural adjustment programmes are based on:

■ fewer subsidies and price controls so the industry becomes more efficient;

■ reducing government deficit – commonly this affects education and welfare so that,

– government can reduce taxes on companies and large incomes;

– public companies should be privatised;

– salaries and working conditions should be deregulated so that industry remains competitive in the global market.

There are many conflicting views on the appropriateness and effectiveness of structural adjustment (see Fig 5.39).

## Fairer Trade?

Integrating into the global economy is easier said than done for LEDCs. While much of the world's attention is focused on the amount of Aid given to LEDCs, it remains the case that LEDCs earn many times more through trade. However, because of the inequalities of the global trading system LEDCs are trapped into a pattern of dependency and neo-colonialism (Fig 5.40). The 'trade trap' is the result of many factors:

■ fluctuation of raw material/commodity prices therefore producers are vulnerable;

■ falling world-wide raw material/commodity prices;

■ protectionism and restrictions on imports into MEDCs via tariffs and quotas; through regulations on packaging and labelling; through health and safety issues;

■ farm subsidies in MEDCs to support local farmers to produce at home e.g. sugar beet is grown and exported from the EU even though it is more expensive to produce than in the Caribbean. EU subsidies are no match for small farmers in LEDCs.

TNCs have a substantial political and economic influence on world trading conditions. LEDCs desperate for foreign investment have little leverage to dictate terms of trade.

## Cancellation of Debts

Suggestion from international aid agencies and charities has been to cancel much of the LEDC debt but MEDCs, the rich donor countries, have opposed the economic management in many LEDCs which led to their demise in the first place.

## New forms of Credit

One mechanism which supports the poor is **microcredit** whereby small loans of as little as $15 can be given to the very poor to help them begin to earn their own income. Microfinance is now available to 16 million of the world's poor, providing credit and other financial services. Large organisations such as the Grameen bank in Bangladesh and Kenya Rural Enterprise Project (K-Rep) each have over one million borrowers but there are many small MFIs (microfinance institutions) supported by aid agencies such as CARE, OXFAM and Action Aid. MFIs specialise in providing unsecured loans to individuals, guaranteed only by personal references, or peer group support – a system which would be unthinkable for global financial institutions.

One key aspect is the ability to lend small sums without the high interest rates charged by money lenders or middle men. MFIs are not restricted to the poorest nations and community development banks provide microfinance where there is acute poverty in MEDCs.

Despite its successes even the best-intentioned schemes can lead to inequality. Some of the larger microcredit banks are accused of moving towards supporting the middle and upper poor with lower 'risks', rather than the most desperately poor. Although the sums are small, demand is great, and some aid agencies have been accused of financing microcredit by diverting their limited resources from other primary schemes such as health care.

FIGURE 5.41  The impact of microcredit

Sung Vieng is one of the 8 million people living in Bangkok's 1000 slum communities. Her life has been transformed by microcredit. Two years ago she rented a pedal-powered cart and earned just $4 a day buying scrap paper, metal, and other rubbish to recycle. When the Thai government set up its Urban Community Development Organisation with authority to give poor people income-generating loans, Sung Vieng borrowed $600 for her own motorised cart. Her income has now doubled, and she buys meat and vegetables from shops instead of picking up discarded vegetables from the market floor after it has closed. 13 000 families in 160 communities have benefited from the loans which have also had a major impact on housing, enabling people to buy their own land and escape from the slums.

# Is industrialisation the only route to development?

At the beginning of this chapter 'development' was outlined in terms of economic growth, improving quality of life and social provision for the population, and the sustainable exploitation of resources to provide for future generations. Those countries with some comparative advantage of resources, geographical location, labour or ingenuity, who embarked on the industrial route to development, have been more easily integrated into the global economy and have raised their standards of living. The last decades of the 20th century have been remarkable for the rates at which countries such as South Korea, Singapore, Chile and Argentina have developed. But is industrialisation a realistic goal, even in the medium term, for large areas of LEDCs with lack of resources, poor infrastructure, geographical isolation or political insecurity? Are they to remain underdeveloped, or is there an alternative?

## Development through agriculture

It is possible that spread effects from the industrial/urban core regions could improve social welfare prospects of many rural dwellers. A decline in fertility rates and death rates, and an increase in education opportunities, especially for women, could potentially lead to real strides in human development. However economic development is more challenging. Some governments of African countries actively support commercial farmers who produce for export to huge distributors in MEDCs. While critics claim that this agribusiness is still industrialisation, others point out that the business has come to the people, and that there are opportunities for rural labour to have a regular income and training. In Britain, the major supermarkets have generated consumer demand for crops such as sweet corn, exotic fruits and flowers (Figs 5.42 and 5.43).

FIGURE 5.42 Agribusiness in Zimbabwe

**Zimbabwe:** Tesco's mangetout producer in Maronderra, north of Harare, employs 1700 people who receive regular but low wages all year round. Farm income provides for a school and clinic.

FIGURE 5.43 Agribusiness in Kenya

**Kenya:** Unilever produces 220 million stems of carnations and roses on 140 ha of the Great Rift Valley. Fresh water for irrigation comes from Lake Naivasha, and rain rarely damages the blooms. Cuttings supplied from Europe are carefully accumulated in coldstore then transferred to rooting blocks. One flower picker harvests 200–250 stems by hand per hour which are then graded and packed in cellophane and cardboard boxes, stored at −5°C ready for specialist air freight from Nairobi.

Typically such commercial **agribusinesses** are labour intensive and capital intensive. Highly skilled staff organise a precise, specialist and technical operation with specialist equipment, storage and air-freight transport. Consumers in Europe, with their disposable income, can afford these products, and LEDCs make some development progress. In this way economic development reaches some favoured rural areas, but always at a price.

Where commercial producers take over, subsistence farmers can be forced to more marginal, less fertile land further from their village. To maintain production to feed their families, greater inputs of fertiliser are needed and more irrigation water. Intensification of agriculture requires substantial inputs of agro-chemicals such as phosphates and nitrates which are polluting ground water supplies. This at a time when rainfall in the Tropics is more unpredictable and farmers are forced to rely on ground water for irrigation.

The key for peasant farmers lies in **sustainable agricultural methods** often using intermediate technology which can combine scientific ideas with traditional farming wisdom. In the Philippines, the isolated village of General Nakar has experimented with integrated pest management (IPM). IPM refers to the control of biological plant diseases and destructive insects by using limited chemicals and a combination of botanical, biological and cultural methods. Lamberto Bustonera, a local farmer, uses pest sprays by mixing water, kerosene and common plants like chilli which are known to cause irritation. Spiders, dragonflies, wasps and other insects are encouraged since they also control pests. Other farms in the village now keep ducks on the paddy fields to provide extra income but also to control the snails which breed in the stagnant, moist conditions.

Simple technology has transformed farming methods in Central Honduras with the help of the COSECHA group (the Association of Consultants

for a Sustainable, Ecological and People-Centred Agriculture). The combination of contour ploughing, mulching and minimum tillage has transformed thin tropical soils on steep slopes into productive farms. Planting along the contour instead of downslope reduces soil erosion, green manure helps to protect soil from the sun and slow down evaporation, and provide nutrients for the crops. Minimum tillage also reduces soil erosion.

## Development through Tourism

Tourism can increase incomes by bringing new sources of revenue but it can also destabilise environments and communities by using the limited resources formerly available for local people. Tourism income comes through labour and by encouraging local entrepreneurs to start small businesses selling tourist goods. Tourism also encourages the provision of essential services such as fresh food, clean water, sanitation, electricity supply and transport and it may give an incentive for improving education and learning new skills. In order to make tourism effective and beneficial local involvement is essential and a sustainable approach adopted.

While sustainability is the key to tourism the vexed question of 'how many tourists?' always remains. The overexploitation in Kenya is notorious ('20 vehicles surround a lion'); Botswana has a high-cost-low volume policy; and South Africa uses electric vehicles and one-way systems to control tourist disturbance. The extent to which tourism can be continuously expanded to support further development is a dilemma for countries with few sources of comparative advantage.

## Development through Trade

The World Trade Organisation which regulates world trade had reduced trade restrictions for most countries. This has benefited the semi-periphery economies who can trade in the world market, as well as having the health, education and transport infrastructure to attract investment.

The NICs have achieved development at phenomenal rates through a combination of industrialisation and trade. However the new regulations have still not helped the poorer countries with only primary raw materials to export. Worse still, if the price of raw materials rises MEDCs will seek other suppliers or synthetic replacements because they are not prepared to pay the higher price.

## Development through Aid

While these nations struggle with economic problems, their physical geography continues to make life more difficult. Many of the world's poorest countries are beset by drought, unreliable rainfall, soil erosion, earthquake or volcanic activity – all of which place extra demands on very sparse resources. As a result Aid has become an indispensable part of the economies of the LEDCs and for many forms a significant proportion of their GNP. Aid takes several forms (see Fig 5.45).

There has been much discussion of the effectiveness of aid with some donor countries tending to favour large scale projects which have had questionable benefits to local people. An increasing share of the small aid cake is being allocated to emergency relief and to specifically reduce debt. This means less money for long term development. It seems that poor countries will continue to need aid to support their population at grass roots level to provide improvement in their immediate standard of living.

How effective is the Aid through which donor countries claim they are helping the poor? The success or failure of aid-financed development projects depends on the type of aid, the economic policies of recipients, and the political stability of the region. Countries such as Bolivia, El Salvador, Mali and Uganda have been identified as having effective policies which made good use of aid and therefore achieved faster growth rates than they would have done without aid.

**How much British aid is spent through multilateral organizations?**     **How much aid is fully tied?**

- Bilateral
- EU
- Multilateral (excluding the EU)

| | |
|---|---|
| Aid tied 100% to purchases from the UK | 35.5% of total ODA |
| Aid used officially to subsidize exports (mixed credits) 1990-93 | 8.9% of bilateral ODA |

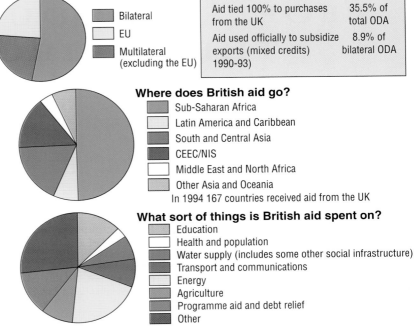

**Where does British aid go?**

- Sub-Saharan Africa
- Latin America and Caribbean
- South and Central Asia
- CEEC/NIS
- Middle East and North Africa
- Other Asia and Oceania

In 1994 167 countries received aid from the UK

**What sort of things is British aid spent on?**

- Education
- Health and population
- Water supply (includes some other social infrastructure)
- Transport and communications
- Energy
- Agriculture
- Programme aid and debt relief
- Other

FIGURE 5.44 The allocation of Aid from the UK

# Summary

The concept of development originally focussed on economic expansion driven by industrialisation as seen in the growth of the MEDCs. Today development is seen as a broader based process which should integrate economic growth, social change and sustainability of resources to provide a focus on *people* rather than *wealth*. The unequal distribution of resources of land, labour and capital results in inequalities in development both spatially and temporally and at a range of scales.

Core – periphery contrasts at the national and regional scale result from major structural changes in economies as markets are integrated and become global. At the global scale the core regions of North America, Europe and Japan continue to concentrate most of the trade, productive capacity and wealth creation, while the gap between the very rich and very poor widens. Although some countries have been able to enter the global trading system, others are increasingly marginalised, becoming more dependent on MEDCs for trade and aid. Solutions to the widening gap are hard to find as economic growth is not easily able to overcome the geographic disadvantages of isolation or poor resource endowment.

The assumption that industrialisation is the only way to development has been questioned and development through agriculture, particularly at grass roots level may be the way forward in the twenty first century. There is now some urgency that a sustainable development approach is adopted in both rural and urban environments world-wide. Most national governments can improve levels of development with resources they already have, but 'globalisation' of co-operation and understanding will be necessary.

# Key Ideas

- The development process should encompass economic, social and sustainable development
- Uneven rates of development lead to spatial inequality within and between nations
- Development leads to inequality between people
- Unequal development has resulted in debt
- There are different routes to development

# 6
# PEOPLE, PRODUCTION AND THE ENVIRONMENT

## *What do we mean by resources?*

Resources are the basis of production and economic wealth. They may be loosely grouped into categories similar to the sectors of an economy:

■ Natural resources include forests, rivers, minerals, solar energy and the sea, associated with the primary sector of the economy and rural locations.
■ Human resources include factories and machinery, offices and infrastructure, the skills and expertise of a local population. These are associated with the secondary (sometimes called manufacturing) sector and urban locations.

■ Less tangible resources include attractive scenery and healthy climates, financial systems and research centres. These are more diverse in location and are mainly associated with the tertiary/service sector and the quaternary sector.

Individual governments look at the resources within their territories as the basis of economic growth and wealth creation. Any country's total wealth is measured as GNP. Wealth generated within its frontiers is GDP. Both statistics are indirect measures of the effectiveness of the people, business and government to unlock resources.

FIGURE 6.1  Exploration for oil

Drilling-rigs are basically of two types. 'Jack-up' rigs used in shallow waters less than 100 metres and semi-submersible rigs used in deeper waters down to 360 metres or more.
If there is enough pressure from water and natural gas under the cap rock, some of the oil will rush to the surface when the well is drilled - such rare wells are called gushers. Primary oil recovery involves pumping followed by injection of water to force out more oil. This is secondary oil recovery. These processes will recovery only about 33% of the reserve, the thicker oils remaining. As the price of crude oil rises more sophisticated methods may be used eg. steam injection to remove about 10% more.
Britain's North sea production in 1995 was 927 million barrels - the equivalent of 360 gallons per head of population. The high output reflects the use of new low-cost technologies to develop smaller fields, and the industry's success in extending the life of existing fields by recovering more of the known reserves. Marine oil pollution is a serious problem affecting fishing, tourism, and marine ecosystems. Some is from tanker spills and pipeline leakage, but most is from onshore ancillary developments such as petrochemical plant and linked processes.

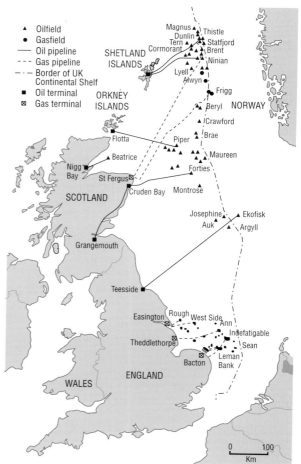

**Semi Submersible Rig**

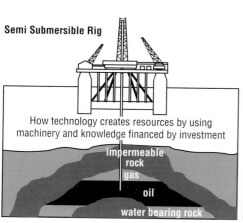

How technology creates resources by using machinery and knowledge financed by investment

Oil is usually a mixture of gas, liquid and solid hydrocarbons trapped deep underground. The cross-section of folded sedimentary rocks shows a common type of situation found in an oil field. Once formed, oil migrates upwards through spaces in rocks (pores, joints, etc). Unless prevented, as in this case by an impermeable layer it will rise to the surface. Lighter oils evaporate, heavier ones persist as tar or oil sands. Detection is done by geophysical prospecting. This means using the seismic, gravitational and magnetic properties of the rocks to work out a probable model structure before putting down exploratory drilling samples.

Resources may be known to exist but remain undeveloped. They are potential not actual.

Technology plays a vital role in unlocking resources. For example, crude oil deposits become valuable resources only when suitable technology existed to produce drilling-rigs, pipelines, refineries, tankers, road systems and the automobile engine. These developments have enabled Saudi Arabia and the Gulf states to accumulate huge sums of money which in turn has revolutionised their economic and political status. Saudi Arabia earns huge amounts from oil exports (GDP) and adds to this by surplus wealth overseas (oil exports + overseas investments = GNP).

Technology is in the hands of business rather than government. Major global businesses (multinational or transnational corporations/TNCs) play an important role not only in supplying technology but also in transferring it from country to country. It was the technological expertise of Royal Dutch Shell which transformed the economy of Saudi Arabia by introducing the necessary technological infrastructure of which the drilling rig is the leading element. See Figure 6.1.

Increasingly, governments are sensitive to economic growth and therefore resource development. Thanks to the diffusion of information by the rapidly developing internet and by global television links, most populations can envisage change and a higher standard-of-living. In practice this means that pressure is put on governments to exploit fully their resource bases. This usually means the rapid development of non-renewable resources and only rarely the more considered management of renewable ones.

## Mineral oil and non-renewable resources

Economically this is the world's single most important resource because it provides the energy underlying present economic development. Its distribution is very uneven. The problem with using oil and oil **fossil fuels** (coal/oil/natural gas) is that they are finite and run out. The **stocks** of these hydrocarbon resources form so slowly, on a human time-scale, that they cannot be renewed, only conserved. Some stocks can be **recycled**. This applies mainly to metals e.g. some vehicle manufacturers have begun to look at their use of steel and earmark it for further use. Fossil fuels cannot be recycled and so there is a constant underlying concern at the rate of **depletion of reserves**, accompanied by a search for alternative energy sources such as tidal power which is renewable.

---

### STOCKS OR RESERVES!

**Stock** describes the total amount of a given item. All the granite in Cornwall is the stock of granite in that county. **Stocks become resources only when there is a demand** for them. If granite is needed for road metal, kaolin, or china clay, then it is not only a feature of the landscape but also a resource. Demand changes its status from stock to resource.

---

## Forests and renewable resources

The view of forests as being renewable is recent. For most of man's history his activities have tended to reduce forest cover, and deforestation continues seemingly unabated in the tropical rain forest areas. In the temperate zone perception has changed. The idea of forests as a dwindling resource has given way to a belief in new planting and forest management by systematic **afforestation** and **conservation**. Managed this way timber can be part of a renewable resource system. Like crops and water resources, it taps an infinite natural environmental flow. Some **flow resources** cannot be managed only tapped. The wind, like the tide, geothermal and solar energy are **non-stockable**. They are unaffected by human actions. In contrast, some natural resources, such as tropical soils can be destroyed by desertification; groundwater can be ruined by the intrusion of sea-water. These systems need careful management to work out the **sustainable yield** – i.e. how much can be taken from a system without destroying it.

# The production of natural resources

## Development – the case of North Sea oil

In the case of **mineral oil** the following sequence could apply:

■ **locate sedimentary basins** where organic products, from which oil is derived, were once deposited, compressed under other sediments and preserved. This may be done by surveying geologic maps and/or satellite images of:
  a) **possible** resources – areas of rock types and structures – (such as anticlines) – similar to those where oil has been previously found

  b) **probable** resources – specific trial locations may then be determined by geophysical surveys – for example using dynamite it is possible to send seismic shock waves (mini-earthquake) through the crustal rocks which will yield detailed information within a given region

**Actual** proven reserves of a resource may be confirmed by a structured point-sample of probable reservoir locations, using trial bores, to establish the physical existence and to identify any mineral oil. There then arises the problem of **attracting investment** for the development of an oil-field. Four factors – other than that of geology – must be considered.

1 **Demand** – is the single most important factor in arousing interest in a resource. The best measure of demand is global prices, for example in the EU the 'spot' market price of Brent (North sea oil-field) crude in Europoort, Rotterdam. Such a price indicates levels of supply. Prices are a kind of index of the balance between supply and demand, and therefore of the economic value of a resource.

2 **Oil qualities** – like its competitor coal, mineral oil is far from being a uniform substance. Simplistically it may be light or heavy, and this will affect its chemical characteristics, which are of practical importance – for example

– is it free from impurities such as sulphur?
– how easily will it distil in a fractionating tower?

3 **Size of the field** – while the geological factors determine size in an absolute sense, markets (**present levels of demand**), and the cost of technology (**methods of exploitation**) fix size in the relative sense of how much oil is worth extracting. The relative size of an oil-field (or any other natural

resource) fluctuates with changes in prices and the technology of extraction. Any estimate of **reserves** will **alter** with any change in the above factors. For example lower prices will reduce the estimated value of a given proven reserve making it less attractive to capital investment.

4 **accessibility of the field:**
– in a horizontal spatial sense – i.e. how far from refineries and/or consumers – compare the North Sea with North slope Alaska;
– and in a vertical sense – i.e. its depth and any geologic constraints;
– and also in the political sense of who owns it – for example the lack of oil in mainland UK, a developed economy, with much capital and expertise made the exploitation of the North Sea oil-field on the European continental shelf much more likely than similar developments on the Patagonian shelf off Southern Argentina.

However, unless inputs of technology and capital investment are available, any oil remains a potential resource. If business can raise the finance to invest in an extraction system, then the resource change status from potential to actual.

Technology's role in the creation of actual resources is very evident in the oil industry. Drilling rigs are very expensive items at the forefront of the extraction process, a technological 'key' unlocking the riches in the rocks. Supporting them are an enormous number of back-up systems, employing a diverse population of helicopter pilots, geologists, many categories of engineers as well as business men dealing with finance (the list is seemingly endless), operating in all kinds of environments. These companies were the forerunners of the modern multinationals, who are key players in the global economy. Oil companies, like other TNCs, have financial resources which 'rival medium-sized national economies'. It is difficult to underestimate their importance in the spread of economic development because they promote locational flexibility.

FIGURE 6.2  Reserves and their vocabulary

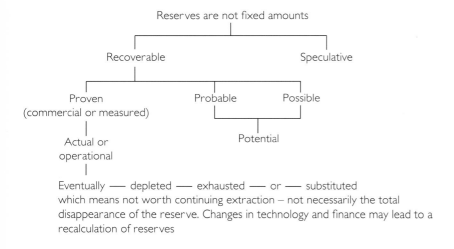

Eventually —— depleted —— exhausted —— or —— substituted which means not worth continuing extraction – not necessarily the total disappearance of the reserve. Changes in technology and finance may lead to a recalculation of reserves

# *Management – contrasting approaches to forestry – Brasil and Sweden*

Modern temperate forest management follows two ecological principles – sustained yield and multiple use.

**Sustainable yield** – the continuous production of forest products from an area by predefined levels using rotational systems of perhaps 100 years, and by careful selection of species and disease control.

**Multiple use** – a forest's yield may be measured in more than its output of timber. Unlike oil, this renewable resource is capable of expansion. There is the option of a production system operating without destroying part of the environmental

framework. The main economic difficulty is that trees are a long-term 'crop', so it is economically difficult to relate supply to demand over several decades. Forests may also have a role as a protection against erosion and pollution, or as a wilderness and/or wildlife area, or for recreation. These environmental values do not fit tidily into the framework of economic development.

As the demand for leisure increases, the role of forests as primarily recreational areas is sure to increase. Given an increased number of picnickers, ramblers and others, it may prove even more

## Contrasting Case-studies

| Development – MEDC | LEDC |
|---|---|
| ■ Sweden – an industrial economy inside EU market-fostering forestry development via large national or state-controlled companies. Timber exported (constructional timber) and processed as raw material e.g. cellulose<br>■ Greater application of science and technology<br>■ Harmonious relations with indigenous nomadic reindeer herders – Lapps | ■ Brazil – a Newly Industrialising Country<br>■ anxious to promote manufacturing and raise capital – by encouraging foreign multi-national exploitation of primary resource-base for export with minimum of domestic processing industries<br>■ 'Leakage' of potential wealth to MEDCs<br>■ Acrimonious relations with indigenous peoples. E.g. Yanomami – invasion of tribal lands |

### Resource base

| | |
|---|---|
| ■ Temperate Swedish Norrland<br>■ dry, cold sub-Arctic environment<br>■ monocultural stands of conifers<br>■ systematic felling of softwood | ■ Tropical Brazilian Amazon<br>■ hot, wet equatorial environment<br>■ enormous biodiversity<br>■ selective logging of hardwoods |

### Economic location

| | |
|---|---|
| ■ outer rural periphery<br>■ marginal fringe and wildscape<br>■ distant from Southern core of Gothenburg-Stockholm 'axis' | ■ outer rural periphery<br>■ marginal fringe and wildscape<br>■ distant from Southern core of Sao-Rio-Belo city 'triangle' |

### Resource policies

| | |
|---|---|
| Sustainable policy on forests deforestation equal to afforestation RENEWABLE RESOURCE | Unsustainable policy on forests deforestation greater than afforestation NON-RENEWABLE RESOURCE |

FIGURE 6.3 The World's forest resource base

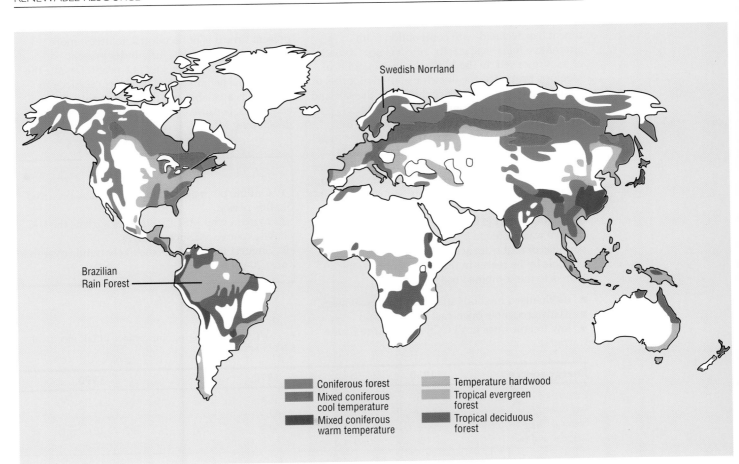

Swedish Norrland

Brazilian Rain Forest

Coniferous forest
Mixed coniferous cool temperature
Mixed coniferous warm temperature

Temperature hardwood
Tropical evergreen forest
Tropical deciduous forest

difficult to maintain a sustained timber flow. Many countries have set aside substantial tracts of countryside for recreational purposes but their management poses increasingly difficult problems which are added to by a shorter working week, falling travel costs and increased leisure time.

Rural land-use systems may not all be compatible e.g. the establishment of National Parks may lead to reductions in the flow of timber or even in its prohibition. In the USA, the development of the very first National Park – Yellowstone Park (1872) – saw an immediate ban on logging. The discovery of the unspoiled natural beauty of this Californian valley inspired the settlers to declare the area inviolate forever. An example of how the development is affected by the values placed on them by society.

*Resource management* in practice becomes a series of decisions which try to plan the development and use of natural and human resources in ways appropriate to the general level of economic and social development. The development context conditions

---

**STUDENT ACTIVITY**

Study the map of the world's forest resource-base, Fig 6.3.
**1** Summarise the distribution and characteristics of Northern coniferous forest and tropical evergreen forest.
**2** Compare the factors influencing production in these natural regions.
**3** Discuss briefly the environmental problems associated with the exploitation of tropical evergreen forest.

---

# Evaluation and change – the rise and fall of UK Coal

## CASE STUDY

### The changing value of natural resources – rise and fall of UK coal

Coal production reached a peak in 1916, from that time it has declined with competition from alternative fuels – especially oil – it is now a shadow of its former self. In the 1980s changes in political ideology promoted the doctrine of market forces in the UK economy. In practice this led to the sale and break-up of the state controlled Electricity Generating Board. The main power supply to industry is now privatised so that companies – such as Powergen — do not have an obligation to buy coal from the National Coal Board for use in power stations. Moreover in newer power stations, natural gas is replacing coal as the favoured fossil fuel – it is said to be cheaper and easier to control. Thus the internal UK market for coal has collapsed. This decline was hastened by the impact of cheap supplies of coal from across the world made possible by increases in the scale of operations thanks to the combined usage of:

■ mechanised methods such as rotary excavators;
■ easily accessible open-cast quarries; and
■ low freight-rates in VLCCS (Very Large Crude Carriers).

There is still a great deal of coal in the UK, but at the present time it is not economic to invest more money in mining it because under present conditions it cannot be sold at a profit. Despite the fact that the technology to transform stacks into reserves is available and the market potential is enormous, because of the demand for energy in a developing MEDC.

---

**STUDENT ACTIVITY**

**1** Outline the major trends which have occurred in this period.
**2** Explain why MEDC countries such as the UK have experienced such changes.
**3** Suggest with reasons the likely trends over the next 20 years.

---

FIGURE 6.4  The changing importance of UK electrical energy sources

| Energy source | 1950 | 1970 | 1990 |
|---|---|---|---|
| Coal | 94.5% | 50.4% | 32.0% |
| Petroleum | 4.0 | 42.9 | 32.6 |
| Natural Gas | 0 | 2.9 | 25.4 |
| Nuclear and HEP | 1.5 | 3.8 | 10.0 |

# *Manufacturing and human resources*

## CASE STUDY

### *The phenomenon of Japan*

The Japanese experience shows clearly that low levels of economic development cannot be put down to a lack of natural environmental resources or to the pressure of population.

### *Inputs to development*

*On the minus side* Japan was not a promising location for manufacturing. The necessary physical inputs were absent. The economy was based on agriculture, there were virtually no fossil fuels to power industrialisation, the low standard of living inhibited the development of a domestic market, and the location was distant from the two main centres of technology, Western Europe and North America. In short there was little to build on. There are few mineral ores which are the basis of heavy industry. Cotton and silk, both of agricultural origin, are virtually the only indigenous raw materials. The physical landscape presents considerable problems for location and communication. There is a shortage of land for industry, roads and railways, so industrial area locations gravitate mainly to the coastal lowlands. Movement inland is often difficult because Japan is a very mountainous country dominated by steep slopes and high peaks. The narrow river valleys take on an added importance, not only for industry but also for agriculture. Much of the landscape is simply too steep to farm unless terraced so there is strong competition for all available flat land. Internal transport costs are also increased by the fact that the country is a group of four large and many smaller islands making up an archipelago, off the coast of East Asia where markets for exports were minimal in the early stages of industrialisation.

*On the plus side* a late start in development can be an advantage because an NIC can build on the experience of its competitors. In practice this means adapting and improving present design, technology and production systems. The Japanese are very good at this and these innate abilities enable them to compete on quality, cost and reliability. In addition they were able to pay only low wages at first because their internal markets were small and standards-of-living low. Low cost goods are a sales advantage.

In Japan social traditions encourage loyalty and this in turn reduces industrial conflict. This is a two-way relationship. Worker loyalty is rewarded by a caring management. There are few industrial disputes. An important practical offshoot of this is very efficient quality control on production lines.

Research and development into improving the effectiveness of the present production system is regarded as critical. Without a constant appraisal of the present the Japanese believe the future will not be secure.

There are close links between:

- the family and the firm;
- the firm and the big corporations;
- the corporations and the government.

This hierarchical social structure is economically efficient because it is disciplined, encourages hard work and respect for the society as a whole, despite the fact that there are many poor, disadvantaged and marginalised groups in Japanese society.

---

the priorities of individual governments, the level of interest of TNCs and the role of targeted regions. In turn these will set the more practicable variables of available capital and technology, infrastructure and labour. Not least is the increasingly important factor of expectation, as the growth of information technology rapidly changes values and attitudes.

### *The industrialisation process*

The earliest industries were textiles and ceramics, based on locally produced raw materials (cotton and clay), so Japan began to build up her own industries by copying and later improving on Western technology.

For example in the West in an area known as Chita Bay lie the cities of Nagoya, Yokkaichi and Toyota. During the 1930s, many heavy engineering and chemical works were opened, based on imported raw materials. The most important though, was a motor vehicle factory opened by Sakichi Toyota in 1936. This has developed into a major TNC. Toyota concentrated on the vertical integration of car making, and so linked industries, including a big steel making plant, in Toyota City, still characterise this manufacturing region.

By the late 1930s, Japan had become an important manufacturing country, challenging the world markets. This growth was not built on local natural resources as in the case of Western Europe and the US. The vast bulk of raw materials, fuel and power have to be imported, and these restrictions create an unfavourable trade balance before manufacturing could begin. World events led to enormous setbacks. Although initially successful the Second World War (1939–1945) ended in catastrophic defeat and destruction of Japanese industrial capacity, symbolised by the dropping of atomic bombs on the cities of Hiroshima and Nagasaki.

A fresh start had to be made and today Japan is one of the world's leading industrial countries with a wide range of products that are household names. Japanese businesses are transplanting into Newly Industrialising Countries and into the territories of their old rivals. In the UK alone for example Japanese car assembly plants are located at:

■ Burnaston, near Derby – Toyota, Japan's largest manufacturer;
■ Swindon, Wiltshire – Honda (Suzuki) linked with the traditionally British Rover;
■ Luton, Bedfordshire – Isuzu, linked with General Motors (Opel/Vauxhall).

Such influence extends beyond motor-vehicles to the full range of modern manufactures flowing from Japanese business corporations

■ heavy industrial goods – steel and ships;
■ consumer goods – CD players, TVs and video-recorders;
■ Information Technology – computer assembly, satellite systems and micro-technology.

Not only are Japanese manufacturers major world 'players', their financial strength is globally important. Tokyo houses one of the most important stock-exchanges.

Economic development is uneven in its effects on regions within any country because comparative advantages vary from region to region. Such large-scale patterns are modelled simplistically as core and periphery, which may be subdivided into inner and outer. In Japan such a pattern is evident (see Figs 6.5 and 6.6).

FIGURE 6.5 Core and periphery areas in Japan

FIGURE 6.6 Map of core and periphery areas in Japan

| Core area | Inner periphery | Outer periphery |
|---|---|---|
| e.g. *Nagasaki-Tokyo* | *Northern Honshu* | *Hokkaido* |
| **Cumulative causation** | Mainly **spread effects** | Mainly **backwash effects** |
| Linked to global networks | linked to national networks | limited regional linkages |
| Economic and political centres | sub-regional centres | economic margins |
| Main transport nodes | high levels of connectivity | movement constrained |
| High-profile perception | upwardly mobile | downward transitional |

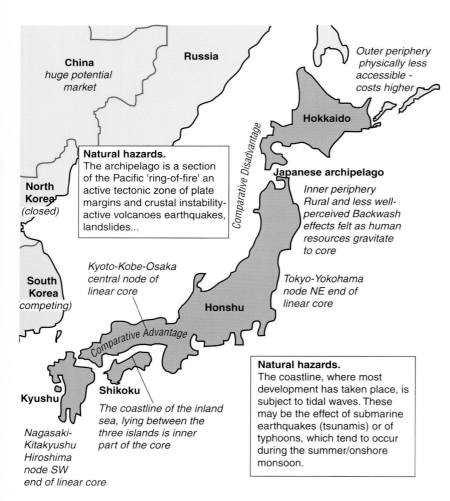

*Trade and comparative advantages*

The uneven distribution of both natural and human resources promotes trade. Japan has built its manufacturing industries on imported raw materials and oil. Saudi Arabia has few manufacturing industries but enormous amounts of oil. Trade between these two is mutually advantageous. While the comparative advantage of Saudi Arabia stems from its natural physical resource endowment, that of Japan derives from its economic strength in having built up capital, labour and access to world markets. It has created its own comparative advantage.

## The impact of the development process

Economic production impacts on the environment directly and indirectly:

Directly, immediately and at specific places – for example the disused Dinorwic slate quarry in North Wales covers 300 hectares of mountainside and has left a succession of quarry faces which rise more than 500 metres from the floor of the quarry. A difficult landscape to reclaim!

*Modern pollution on the atmosphere* has far reaching indirect effects. Although such pollution has been caused for thousands of years, it is only the recent economic development of MEDCs that has been perceived as the main threat. Before industrialisation there were few local production processes which caused widespread pollution. An ancient example was the smelting of ores by the

Romans. Silver smelting produces pollutants containing lead and arsenic, recently discovered in ice-cores in Greenland and Iceland.

The effects of modern industrial and economic development are, wide-ranging and complex. There are a number of confirmed and suspected, direct and indirect environmental impacts. They are:

■ an increase in average annual temperatures;
■ a rise in sea-levels across the world linked to the melting of polar ice sheets;
■ changes to the pattern or structure of the atmosphere itself – for example the shrinking of the ozone layer, under the impact of man-made chlorofluorocarbons (CFCs), by some 10–15 per cent. The greatest damage appears to be over the Antarctic (Figure 6.7), and this has been linked to an increase in skin-cancers in southern South America, Australia and New Zealand;
■ alteration/modification of atmospheric processes e.g. acid rain, and the photochemical action of sunlight on pollutant gases.

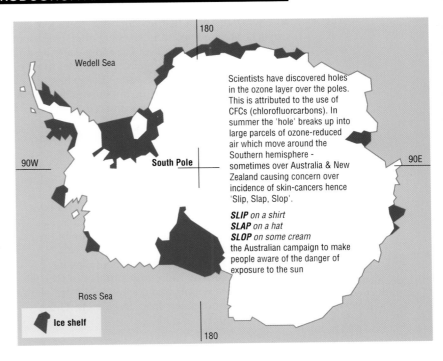

Scientists have discovered holes in the ozone layer over the poles. This is attributed to the use of CFCs (chlorofluorcarbons). In summer the 'hole' breaks up into large parcels of ozone-reduced air which move around the Southern hemisphere - sometimes over Australia & New Zealand causing concern over incidence of skin-cancers hence 'Slip, Slap, Slop'.

**SLIP** on a shirt
**SLAP** on a hat
**SLOP** on some cream
the Australian campaign to make people aware of the danger of exposure to the sun

FIGURE 6.7 Ozone depletion over the S. Pole

## Acid rain and global impacts

Damage to buildings and the decimation of forests in MEDCs is linked to acid rain, which has a high content of sulphur dioxide. This pollutant is emitted by fossil fuelled power stations. Acid rain not only attacks forests but can destroy freshwater ecosystems in lakes and rivers. Areas of impact may be distant from the source of the pollution, perhaps in another country (Fig 6.8). Such transboundary pollutants can only be dealt with by co-ordinated international action by groups such as the G7 countries for example. Apart from the level of economic development, there are several human factors which affect what may be achieved in dealing with this international problem:

■ Government policies – markedly affect the impact of pollutants. In the UK there is no energy policy and the mix of production energy is left to market forces, for example the recent 'dash for gas'. Increasing the consumption of natural gas at the expense of coal, has the welcome but unintended effect of reducing emissions in sulphur dioxide and nitrous oxide, key chemicals in the 'acid attack'. In contrast, policies in France have promoted nuclear energy whose impact problems do not include the emission of these chemicals, although there are risks of nuclear contamination. In Sweden policies are designed to reverse their development and investment in nuclear energy generation systems.

FIGURE 6.8 Acid rain

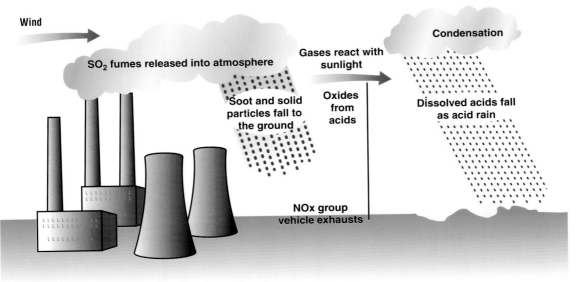

■ Ownership of industries can cause variations in impacts. State-owned industries are often inefficient – for example in former East Germany – and do not invest in newer cleaner technology in order to save jobs. By contrast in the UK water quality has improved since privatisation, but only at the cost of large increases in water prices and reductions in employment.

■ Pressure groups and political will – Germany, Norway and Sweden have important 'green' political parties who can lobby on issues such as acid rain. As a result the emission laws are 'tighter' than in the UK or France, making for a hotly contested debate within the EU. Norway (outside the EU) has the world's first carbon tax to raise revenue for dealing with the acidification of their lakes and forests.

■ The type of physical environment may be important. Norway has a large number of HEP sites (actual and potential), and creates only 5 per cent of its energy requirements from fossil fuels. Thus

FIGURE 6.9 Some environmental impacts of production systems and development

pollution produced within the country is at a low level. However there still is pollution thanks to:

the 'export' of acid rain from the UK, due to the prevailing Westerly wind system

the already existing problems of acidity and poor fertility found in upland environments on non-basic rocks such as granite

the existence of conifer forests which intercept and store the acid rain, increasing the amount which reaches the surface.

Once the acidified water is in the atmospheric system it can then find its way, 'disease-like' into related systems, for example immediately into groundwater and therefore affecting the biosphere and domestic supplies dependent upon aquifers.

It may then pass into the water cycle (Fig 6.9), the planetary 'bloodstream' circulation of many environments, to be distributed around the land by the 'veins and arteries' of the drainage networks. Thus there are 'contagious' effects of this environmental 'disease'.

**Atmosphere**

1. Upper atmosphere - destruction of a natural upper layer, whose value is that it filters out damaging ultra-violet radiation from the sun.

2. Lower atmosphere - ozone here is formed by the reaction of hydrocarbons and nitrogen oxides in the presence of sunlight. The ozone becomes an important component of photochemical smog.

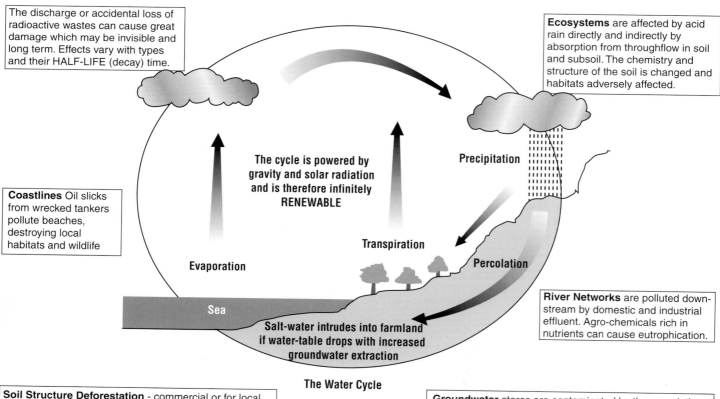

The discharge or accidental loss of radioactive wastes can cause great damage which may be invisible and long term. Effects vary with types and their HALF-LIFE (decay) time.

**Ecosystems** are affected by acid rain directly and indirectly by absorption from throughflow in soil and subsoil. The chemistry and structure of the soil is changed and habitats adversely affected.

**Coastlines** Oil slicks from wrecked tankers pollute beaches, destroying local habitats and wildlife

The cycle is powered by gravity and solar radiation and is therefore infinitely RENEWABLE

Precipitation

Transpiration

Percolation

Evaporation

**River Networks** are polluted downstream by domestic and industrial effluent. Agro-chemicals rich in nutrients can cause eutrophication.

Sea

Salt-water intrudes into farmland if water-table drops with increased groundwater extraction

The Water Cycle

**Soil Structure Deforestation** - commercial or for local firewood - removes the interception store of precipitation, allowing an increase in raindrop impact, leading to overland flow, sheetwash erosion, gulleying, and even desertification.

**Groundwater** stores are contaminated by the percolation of precipitation into pore spaces and bedding planes/joints. Contamination is greater in urban industrial areas especially near heavy industrial estates and leaky landfill sites. Tapping old established underground water sources may have become dangerous.

## CASE STUDY

# *Global warming and the predicament of Bangladesh*

Hypothesis: 'as sea-level rises environmental degradation in low-lying coastal areas increases'.

The mosaic or regional combination of environmental systems in the location of Bangladesh is double-edged (Fig 6.10).
*On the plus side* this is a fertile land capable of supporting many people.

The country consists almost entirely of a large delta formed by the distributaries of the Ganges and Brahmaputra rivers. These two converging river systems rise well-beyond the Bangladeshi frontiers in remote regions such as Nepal, nestling in the Himalayas. The enormous suspended load they transport is deposited at the junction with the Bay of Bengal.

This has created a landscape so flat that during the onshore monsoon, discharge is greater than channel capacity so the rivers overflow their banks and flood. When the floods recede, fresh silt is deposited renewing the fertility of the soil. No artificial inputs are needed. This combination of well-watered flat land, rich silty soil and high temperatures has all the requirements for plant growth. It makes excellent farming land and so it is a valuable natural resource. Most Bangladeshi live in the 68 000 or so villages over the flat plain. They are sited on slightly higher ground and for much of the year they are surrounded by flood water. The landscape is a patchwork of tiny fields, clumps of banana, mango and palm trees, with clusters of huts made from bamboo and mud. The villagers grow rice, wheat and vegetables, or crops such as jute, that is sold to factories in Bangladesh and abroad. The main wealth of Bangladesh is really in its very rich soil and it is the world's largest producer of rice. It has no fossil fuels and few industries therefore making little contribution to the rising levels of global pollution.

*On the minus side* these natural floods do a great deal of damage and cause many difficulties for transport and building. Bangladesh, like India has a monsoon climate with very heavy rain during the summer months. The area also lies in the path of savage and destructive cyclones and tropical storms. These bring torrential rain, powerful winds, thunder, lightning, floods and sometimes tidal waves. In the worst cases as in 1963, 1965, 1970 and 1991, tens of thousands of people lost their lives and hundreds of thousands were made homeless. So the chances of disaster are very high in the delta. To add to these natural hazards, sea-level is rising at a rate of approximately 2 mm per year. It is not clear whether this is a stable rate. The rate may increase and so add to the severity and likelihood of disaster. In such an unstable environment planning rarely gets beyond clearing up immediate disasters. Nor does capital accumulate and provide the means

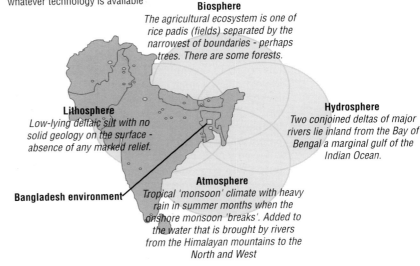

Man lives at the junction of four inter-connected spheres, their varied permutations and interaction make up a mosaic of physical environmental conditions in which he makes his home, using whatever technology is available

**Biosphere**
*The agricultural ecosystem is one of rice padis (fields) separated by the narrowest of boundaries - perhaps trees. There are some forests.*

**Lithosphere**
*Low-lying deltaic silt with no solid geology on the surface - absence of any marked relief.*

**Hydrosphere**
*Two conjoined deltas of major rivers lie inland from the Bay of Bengal a marginal gulf of the Indian Ocean.*

**Atmosphere**
*Tropical 'monsoon' climate with heavy rain in summer months when the onshore monsoon 'breaks'. Added to the water that is brought by rivers from the Himalayan mountains to the North and West*

Bangladesh environment

to a possible solution. It is very difficult to envisage any change.

*On balance* the situation appears extremely difficult. Bangladesh is one of the poorest countries in the world and probably the most crowded. Over 85 million people live in an area the size of England and Wales. Although independent since 1972, development is slow. Agriculture is the main resource, and population the main problem. Other countries have larger populations and are as crowded without it causing a problem. However in Bangladesh, a large proportion of the 85 million people have a low standard of living, and the population is increasing rapidly (Stage 2/DTM). About half the people have no land at all, or so little that they try to earn money by working for wealthier farmers. There are simply too many people to be supported by the country's resources. The cost of adapting to rising sea-level (see Figure 6.11) will be impossible to raise within Bangladesh itself. It is not a 'major player' in international affairs and although clearly a likely 'victim' of global warming, it can only protest at the international conference table .

FIGURE 6.10  The environmental systems affecting Bangladesh

FIGURE 6.11  Estimates of the impact of 1 metre rise in sea-level

| Sample of low-lying countries | People affected (thousands) | % people affected | Capital value (million US$) | Land km² | Land % total | Adaptation cost (million US$) |
|---|---|---|---|---|---|---|
| **Bangladesh** | **71 000** | **60** | **not est.** | **25 000** | **17.5** | **1700** |
| China | 72 000 | 7 | not est. | 35 000 | 0.4 | not known |
| Egypt | 4700 | 9 | 59 272 | 5800 | 1.0 | 13 133 |
| Guyana | 600 | 80 | 4000 | 2400 | 1.1 | 200 |
| Japan | 15 400 | 15 | 807 000 | 2000 | 0.5 | >159 000 |
| Marshall Is. | 40 | 100 | 175 | 9 | 80.0 | >380 |
| Netherlands | 10 000 | 67 | 186 000 | 2165 | 5.9 | 12 286 |
| Nigeria | 3200 | 4 | 18 000 | 18 600 | 2.0 | >1400 |
| Poland | 235 | 1 | 24 000 | 1700 | 0.5 | 1500 |
| Uruguay | 13 | <1 | 1800 | 96 | 0.1 | >1000 |

(Source: *Environmental Management* 20(2), 1996, p. 163)

# Perception and conservation

Resources is a term not so easy to pin down. The main reason for this is that what is considered to be a resource changes with development.

The particular impact made on any one environment depends upon the level of development, which affects available capital and technology, which in turn affects perception and values. For example in the North American temperate grasslands (Prairies), the Old culture was native Amerindians e.g. Sioux, who perceived the environment as buffalo hunting grounds – using horses and bow-and-arrows. The New culture of immigrant Europeans perceive the environment as cereal-producing farms – using the 'iron' horse, ploughs and fences.

Resources then are a **cultural concept**, they do not exist in an abstract way. Moreover concepts may change through time. For example attitudes to trees and forests in medieval Europe have changed:

■ Before the thirteenth century when forest cover was reduced to clear land for farming. Forest was perceived as inexhaustible, if not in the immediate neighbourhood then certainly in the world beyond. Comparative advantage was created by forest clearance.

■ thirteenth century after the forests were perceived as a finite resource. Increasing transport costs and the observable devastation of local landscapes suggested the value of systematic afforestation. The comparative advantage lay with forest conservation.

This changed view is now widely generalised into an anti-exploitation view of development. Keywords in this new view are **sustainable** and **conservation**.

**Conservation** in a strict sense means 'saving' from change e.g. a unique natural habitat threatened by urban development, but in a wider sense conservation implies the planning and management of resources so as to secure their wise use and continuity of supply, while maintaining their quality, value and diversity.

In relation to natural resources, conservation can involve the protection of species from exploitation at one end of the spectrum, to sustaining food production while maintaining or even improving the quality of the environment at the other end.

Four types of conservation have been recognised:
1  **species conservation**, involving the protection of plant and animal species which are under threat from any form of exploitation – e.g. the protection of the panda in Western China, much sought after by Western zoos to add to their leisure attractions;
2  **habitat conservation**, which seeks to maintain representative habitat types over the full, natural ecological range – e.g. the Dorset heath, a rurban habitat threatened by the overspill of development focused on Poole;
3  **land-use conservation**, which seeks to balance the competing forms of land-use with natural ecosystems – e.g. the management of Slapton Ley Nature reserve in the farming and tourist region of South Devon;
4  **creative conservation**, (a general conservation ethic) which aims to make use of landscapes produced by society, from motorway verges to derelict mineral working and spoil heaps.

## Creative conservation – towards sustainability

Today scars on the landscape, pollution of the atmosphere, rivers and seas, deforestation, soil erosion are all inextricably linked with the rise of modern manufacturing and agribusiness. In the old urban industrial regions of MEDCs, impacts of early industrialisation persist. For example, in the UK impacts include:
■ derelict land – land that is so damaged by industrial and other development that it is incapable of beneficial use without further treatment – e.g. spoil-heaps, the waste product of mining in the valleys of South Wales – allied to surface subsidence, associated with disused mine shafts and galleries;
■ scarification – the creation of surface pits, holes and depressions as a direct result of mineral extraction – e.g. between London and Reading in the Thames valley;
■ the abandonment of buildings and machinery, for example disused textile mills in East Lancashire (cotton) and West Yorkshire (wool), and disused infrastructural features associated with these 'smokestack' industries, for example redundant transport networks such as the nineteenth century canal system.

Twentieth century globalisation of production requires a planetary perspective for resource development and creative conservation. We have the means of identifying many problem areas:
■ the technology of space-exploration has given us a new view of **Planet Earth** as a resource-base (Fig 6.12).

■ **remote sensing, information technology and the ecosystem model** have shown us that there is **only one earth** of interacting physical and human systems, a fact confirmed by both natural (e.g. cyclones and tropical storms) and man-made hazards (e.g. tanker oil-spills);

FIGURE 6.12  The Earth as a resource

# ATTRACTIVE DETACHED RESIDENCE BELIEVED TO BE UNIQUE

*This magnificent dwelling has been sadly neglected in recent years. Some outstanding features have been lost. However, it still offers an exceptional home to those prepared to maintain it with care*

**Above all else a new attitude is required replacing the**

**OLD VIEW**

production versus     dysfunctional
the environment    =    development

with a

**NEW VIEW**

production within     sustainable
the environment    =    development

Dysfunctional development disregards the natural functions and limitations of environmental systems hence pollution and related problems

Sustainable development looks at development from the point of view of the planet's 'health' and therefore implies continuity and concern for the environment.

---

Many contemporary economic systems which underpin the development process have a destructive downside. Economic development has reached such a pitch that it threatens the global environment, for example with global warming. It is for this reason that we need to understand how resources may be used sustainably and on a renewable basis. This will enable us to use them in perpetuity, the basis successful **stewardship on this planet earth**.

## The challenge of tourism in LEDCs

Tourism is attractive as a route to development for a poor country, but tourism both uses, and has an impact on, the environment.

### Inputs to development

A unique environmental feature, already in place, may become a resource-base by providing a comparative advantage. For example
- ancient cultures and archaeological sites e.g. Aztecs in Mexico;
- modern culture and anthropological contrasts e.g. Batak civilisation in Thailand;
- unique wildlife as in the Kenyan Masai Mara;
- outstanding physical environmental features e.g. Victoria falls on the Zimbabwe/Zambia frontier, Mount Everest approached from Nepal;
- not least the combination of warmer weather and sandy beaches as in the West Indies, especially attractive in the long winters of North temperate MEDC.

Multinational companies supply the capital to develop chains of hotels and other infrastructural features. Mainly MEDC Airlines and package holiday companies organise the supply of customers. The local indigenous population generally supplies labour at lower skill levels in this new sector of the economy.

The expansion process has its origins in changes within in MEDCs. These include
- increased personal incomes and leisure time and longer paid holidays;
- technological advances in mass-transport e.g. wide-bodied jets, increasing long-haul travel;
- general increases in mobility – e.g. the ability to drive;
- enhanced perceptions through television and advertising;
- growth of effective marketing by the tourist industry, aided by the computer;
- the insatiable demand for fun and relaxation.

Tourism may become far more significant in an LEDC than an MEDC because often there is no other way for local people to be employed. There is simply no work to replace the original occupations these people had before the tourists arrived.

### Impacts

On the natural environment:

- loss of habitat – e.g. destruction of coral reefs in Belize – leading to a move to eco-tourism;
- disruption of wildlife – e.g. game parks on the Masai Mara in Kenya;

- pollution – e.g. by hotel sewage on West Indian beaches.
Social and cultural problems:
- culture conflict – e.g. religious rituals becoming entertainment in Bali;
- social devaluing – e.g. the growth of the sex industry in Thailand leading to the spread of AIDS.
Economic impacts – negative:
- the involvement of multi-national companies is of marginal financial benefit to the host country, since there is a steady outflow or 'leakage' of profits;
- food, drink and even hospitality are imported for tourists rather than met by local suppliers thus consuming more foreign exchange;
- disintegration of the local sustainable economy as an artificial demand for fishing trips, crafts and exotic products produces an apparent 'boom';

- decline of local agriculture and loss of land through tourist expansion;
- an unstable economy based on the seasonability and fickleness of world tourism.
Economic impacts – positive:
- general investment in infrastructure – e.g. the development of an international airport and metalled road network;
- improvement in utilities such as the provision of water and electricity;
- diversification of employment, the transfer of skills – especially the growth of a larger service sector, and an overall increase in the general level of education.
The management of tourism is vital to its success, failure can be fatal.

## CASE STUDY

### Death by tourism in Thailand

Thailand is a poor but beautiful country. It has three basic resources on which to build a tourist industry:

- a cultural legacy of distinctive old buildings such as temples – heritage appeal;
- a warm and attractive natural environment – climate appeal and a long coastline;
- some distinctive native groups – cultural appeal.
It is cheap. The standard-of-living is much lower than in the MEDCs and there are few industries. Employees are willing to accept low wages.

Low wages and a high birth-rate make for poverty. Large families are difficult to keep and educate. There is no social welfare system to support the unemployed or orphaned. The rural North is especially deprived relying mainly on subsistence farming which does not generate capital. Many Thai girls realised that they could solve some of these domestic economic problems by turning to prostitution, and this became a feature of the tourist trade. The growth of this aspect of the Thai economy began during the Vietnam War, when US servicemen made it a mecca for leave. After the war, the situation was exploited by Chinese businessmen who brought organisation and capital. Thailand's main tourist resource became its population. Teenagers with no prospects in their own village migrated to tourist centres such as the capital, Bangkok.

Many social and economic problems ensued.

- An epidemic of sexually-transmitted diseases. Much the most serious of these is AIDS which is making serious inroads into the labour force. Young people cannot afford treatment or even regular check-ups for this and other diseases so their life-expectancy is dropping.

- Population shifts are causing imbalance – rural life is breaking down as the labour force melts away, while in the cities there are the familiar problems of overcrowding and over-stretched services.
- The economic development of the country has slowed down because employers cannot compete with the earning power of the sex industry. Many of those involved will earn more in a night than they would in a month of working in a factory, on a farm or in a hotel.
- State income is affected because most of the income from prostitution is not accountable for tax purposes. It is part of a growing informal economy. Whereas farmers and manufacturers can be taxed on their production, it is impossible to assess accurately how much a prostitute can earn in a given time-slot.
- Bangkok is the focal point for most of these problems, and it has developed a reputation for supplying anything a customer may require including drugs. This further undermines the formal economy because:
  it is more profitable to produce drugs than rice – so the basic food supply is put under pressure;
  drugs are readily, but not legally, exportable. The traders can earn huge amounts of income which is never declared for tax purposes. These traders – drug barons – have enormous powers, which they wield to protect their own interests; dealing with drugs costs money in order to combat organised crime and health-related problems.

The total impact is difficult to quantify, but clearly economic growth is held back and the cultural effects can be devastating.

'In 1989 there were 5.75 million visitors to Hawaii; by the year 2010 it's predicted there will be 11.5 million. The dramatic development of tourism has radically affected the relationship of the local people to the land and sea, which lies at the root of their culture.

It has played a major role in the destruction of ancient Hawaiian burial grounds, significant archaeological site and sacred places, as new hotels and other developments have been built over culturally significant sites.

Many Hawaiians are offended by the exploitation and packaging of their culture for economic benefit. The Reverend Kaleao Patterson of the Hawaiian Ecumenical Coalition of Tourism says 'The culture is romanticized to appeal to the exotic fantasies of world travellers. This perpetuates racist and sexist stereotypes that are culturally inappropriate and demeaning. The issue becomes one of cultural prostitution'.

FIGURE 6.13  Cultural prostitution: Hawaii

In the Lower Casamance region of Senegal in Africa, a 'Tourism for Discovery' project is fostering more personal relationships between tourists and local people, by ensuring that the visitor is treated as a guest rather than an intruder.

Tourists, whose numbers are strictly controlled, are put up in simple lodgings that are built, operated and managed by villagers. Access is by bush taxi or canoe. There are nature excursions, and informal talks by villagers on their history and culture. Tourists are even encouraged to help with agricultural and construction work.

Most food and supplies are produced locally, and meals are prepared using traditional recipes. The scheme has given a boost to the local economy. Returns are immediate, and the profits generated have helped both to create new jobs, and enhance educational and health facilities in the villages.'

FIGURE 6.14  Getting personal: Senegal

## The impact of leisure in MEDCs

Study Fig 6.15. The overall aim of sustainable tourism is to avoid the onset of Stage Four. In UK rural areas sustainable tourism is a movement which seeks to maintain a balance in the countryside, by considering, the pressures on the local environment, the quality of life in the local community, and the enjoyment of the visitors.

The concept of sustainability was boosted by growing concern at the speed with which the Earth's natural resources are being consumed, a view clearly expressed at the world summits in Riot

(1992) and Kobe (1997). The UK Strategy for Sustainable Development (1994) promotes the concept in towns, cities, on the coast and in rural areas. It contains proposals aimed directly at leisure and tourism.

---

**STUDENT ACTIVITY**

Study the three passages above. Compare and contrast the commercial and sustainable approaches to tourism.

---

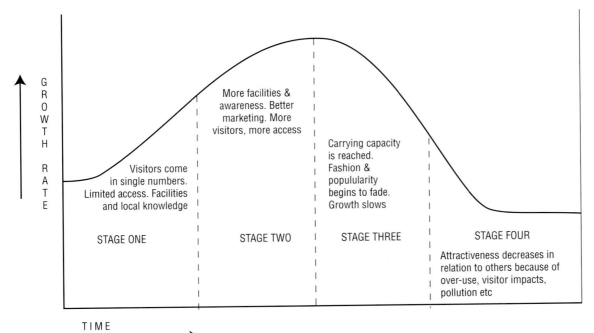

FIGURE 6.15  Model to show the life-cycle of unmanaged tourist development

GROWTH RATE

More facilities & awareness. Better marketing. More visitors, more access

Visitors come in single numbers. Limited access. Facilities and local knowledge

Carrying capacity is reached. Fashion & populularity begins to fade. Growth slows

STAGE ONE

STAGE TWO

STAGE THREE

STAGE FOUR

Attractiveness decreases in relation to others because of over-use, visitor impacts, pollution etc

TIME

## CASE STUDY

### South Hams District Council approach to sustainable tourism (see Figure 6.17)

This is a part of a wider planning initiative (South Devon Green Tourist Initiative) on sustainable leisure and tourism. The overall SD–GTI aim was to move on from the work done in preparation for the 1992 Earth summit. South Devon made a good testing ground because it contains a diverse resource-base:

■ a National Park – Dartmoor;
■ Areas of Outstanding Natural Beauty (AONBs);
■ Sites of Special Scientific Interest (SSIs) – e.g. Slapton Ley;
■ miles of heritage coast;
■ heritage towns e.g. Dartmouth and Totnes;
and is therefore very suitable for assessing the introduction of sustainable leisure and tourism. The pilot project was funded by:
■ local regional bodies such as South Hams District Council, Dartmoor National Park, Devon County Council;
■ the second phase had wider support within the region from national bodies:

1   The Rural Development Commission, the government's agency for economic and social development in rural England. It advises government and its main aim is to create jobs and maintain essential services.
2   The English Tourist Board, the statutory agency for developing tourism. With the British Tourist Authority, it encourages tourists and the provision and improvement of tourist amenities and facilities.
3   The Countryside Commission which works to conserve and enhance the beauty of the English countryside and to help people enjoy it – e.g. in 1994 it began a trial 'run' in the Yorkshire Dales to promote sustainable tourism.
4   Department of National Heritage which has a wide area of responsibility, covering tourism, and aspects of heritage such as the arts, media sport and active recreation, and not least the National Lottery.

■ *South Hams* is very distinctive even within South Devon, and historically has a long record of isolation which promotes individuality. Robert Stanes makes the point that heritage is an aspect of rural landscapes as well as settlements supporting the view that landscapes are cultural with regional and nationalist undertones.
■ He writes, 'The South Hams probably qualifies as a 'pays'. This French word is used by geographers to describe an area having a common agrarian character, a compound of soil, climate and rural culture.' (A Fortunate Place by Robin Stanes – Field Studies Council)
■ French examples of 'pays' might include the Beauce (dry corn growing area around Chartres) and Brie, English examples perhaps the Wirral in Cheshire and the Fylde in West Lancashire.

For South Hams, heritage and the environment are the greatest economic assets. It is a plateau-like landscape of sandstone (with a granite intrusion in the North), well-dissected by rivers whose courses affect trade, communications and settlement patterns. Four heritage towns are clearly affected by rivers and the sea. They are Totnes and Dartmouth on the Dart, and Kingsbridge and Salcombe on the larger ria, named the Kingsbridge estuary. These drowned estuaries provide habitats of international importance for rare species and marine life. There are also diverse coastal habitats (sand dunes, shingle beaches, cliff ledge communities) and country habitats (open heathland, improved arable and moor land, field boundaries of species rich hedgerows). It is this mix of cultural and physical features which provides a resource-base for leisure and tourism. Although farming is obviously the largest land-use, tourism is of great value. South Hams receives on average 12 per cent of the total share of visitors to Devon. The annual value of tourism to this part of Devon is £95m staying visitors, £14.5m day visitors. Customer research shows that South Hams has a high market profile with British professional or semi-professional visitors and retired people visiting as couples or in families. Overseas visitors only make up 5 per cent of the total. The most important activities are all related to the natural attractions of the area, for example going to the beach, strolling footpaths.
    Some constraints are already in place (see Fig 6.18). Designated area controls include:

■ AONB – 121 sq miles;
■ Heritage coast – 58 miles;
■ National Nature Reserve – Slapton Ley;
■ Dartmoor National Park 62 sq miles;
■ Coastal preservation 73 sq miles.

These areas have tended to slow down any change because they tend to enforce what cannot be done rather than encourage what might be done. The thrust of sustainable tourism and leisure initiatives within this protected rural region is to promote growth and regeneration, accommodating changes, which include altering the fabric of rural villages where pressure on house prices from the increase in second homes has increased competition for a limited housing stock.
    Also dealing with day-to-day problems such as road congestion and pressure on infrastructure such as main services and resolving conflicts between interest groups who may wish to innovate e.g. by developing a Virtual Reality theme park, and others who wish investments to be concentrated on enhancing existing accommodation and attractions.
    Decisions have to be evaluated not simply in economic terms but also in terms of
■ the quality of life – what are the consequences of change, can we assess the alternatives, how might people react and respond?

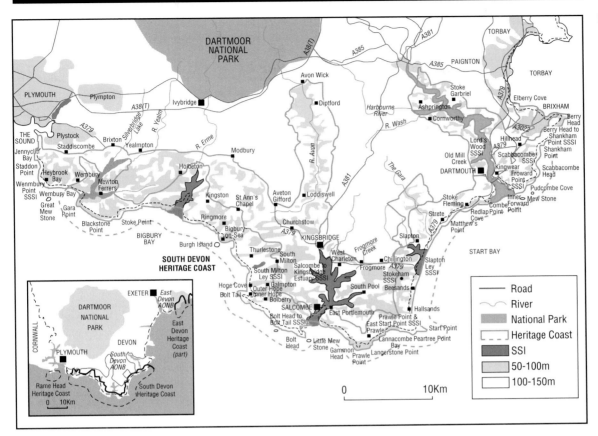

FIGURE 6.16  South Devon

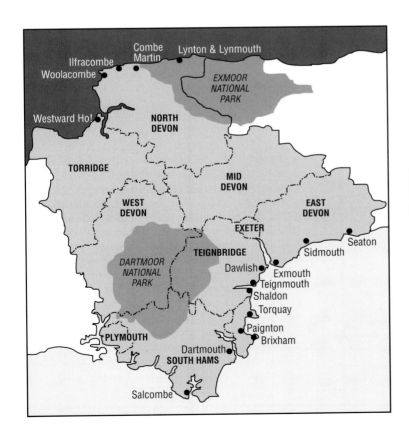
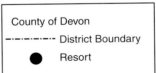

FIGURE 6.17  Controlled areas in South Devon

FIGURE 6.18 Sustainability

## Sustainability is a long-term goal which seeks policies that balance social justice, economic growth and environmental security.

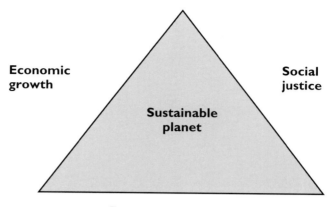

The concept of sustainable development extends beyond care for natural environmental systems. Clean air and water are for the world's population to use. Similarly if there is a right to air and water there are rights to land and resources.

CLEAN AIR + CLEAN WATER + RATIONAL LAND USE = SUSTAINABLE GROWTH

■ the effects on the environment – what will the impacts of change be, what alternative ways of organising space and managing the environment are there? (See Figure 6.19)
This necessitates involving the local population. For example:

**The Green Audit Kit** – The objective was to develop an easy to use DIY manual dealing with the introduction of an environmental policy, mainly for businesses. The principle is to avoid expensive consultants so that the person most familiar with any business will be able to make decisions to reduce environmental impacts. Suggestions range from non-controversial such as fitting low energy light-bulbs to schemes for fund-raising from visitors. The suggestions make up the content of Action sheets which cover Energy, Transport, Purchasing, Waste, Health and the Local Environment. Additionally there are Audit sheets which deal with recording changes. The take-up of the kit was greatly influenced by local key business people who helped spread knowledge of the schemes advantages.
**Green Tourism Awards** – The Merit level of this Award was given to any business which wrote an environmental policy with six or more environmental commitments and a timetable for achieving them. This was a public statement of

approval. The Distinction level set even more demanding criteria. Winners included all types of businesses including a four-star luxury hotel, several small guesthouses and even a small bus company.

These techniques were not confined to South Hams but used throughout South Devon, and knowledge of the Audit Kit and Awards has been promoted both regionally and nationally.
**Green Teams** – were developed to continue funding once the pilot phase was over. They are composed of Local Authority Officers, active business people and other interested parties such as the Field Studies Council Centre at Slapton. The teams raise funds and circulate useful information.

Other initiatives within South Hams included:
■ surveys of resources before making decisions – for example establishing records of trees and orchards;
■ booklets on historic buildings – for example Totnes has the greatest concentration of listed buildings for a town of its size in the South West;
■ promotions – for example 'Making the most of your stay' leaflet.
South Hams Green Tourist team is business led, but it is linked with the whole community trying for a holistic approach to resource development, and one which is flexible to meet future changes.

# Summary

The comparative advantage provided by the availability of resources has produced geographical differences within the economic systems at local, national and global scales. The development that has ensued from those advantages has brought about changes to all our lives and the environment in which we live. However there is increasing evidence that to maintain the patterns of established development, and maintain the comparative advantages which underpin that development, management of resources and the environment is and will be essential. We are all part of the global economic system which uses the global environment but all too often abuse it. We really are 'all in this together'!

## Key Ideas

- Resource development supports the development of economic systems
- Uneven distribution of resources creates locational comparative advantage
- People are also an important economic resource
- Economic and environmental systems are fundamentally in conflict
- Resource development processes have a global environmental impact
- Sustainable economic systems require managed environmental systems

# GLOSSARY

**Core-periphery** – is the concept that describes the spatial pattern and uneven distribution of economic activity, power, and society. The core area is an area of concentrated wealth and economic activity with higher orders of functions. It is a focus for innovation and growth which maintains the core's advantages and influences the rate and nature of development in the surrounding or remote periphery. Cores can decline and new cores develop as the **comparative advantages** of locations change. The principle can operate at the national and global scale.

**Comparative advantage** – is the principle that areas will specialise in the production of those goods and services in which they have the greatest ratio of advantage over other areas. The advantage may stem from physical, technical ,capital or labour resources which may change through time.

**De-industrialisation** – is the process by which the loss of manufacturing industry in an area is not replaced by new activity. This may result in **'rust belts'** of regional decline. At the national level it may result in the loss of a country's manufacturing base. **Re-industrialisation** can occur when **regeneration** takes place. The new industry may be based on well established regional skills, or new and different economic activity.

**Development** – can be defined by a number of different criteria. Economic growth is concerned with rising national income (per capita GDP) but a broader definition includes social development concerning progress towards higher living standards, more opportunities for all and basic human rights for adults and children.

**Environmental externalities** – are social or environmental costs (and benefits) of economic activity which are manifested in the form of pollution or other environmental degradation or in improvements and which are not accounted for in production costs.

**Environmentally friendly technology** – is a label used for cleaner production processes and waste minimisation processes.

**Globalisation** – is the expansion of the functional and financial integration between internationally dispersed activities which creates a web of interdependence between the nations of the world. The process is aided by the influence of **trans-national corporations** in agricultural, manufacturing, and service activities. It creates **a global economic system** of production and consumption.

**Gross Domestic Product (GDP)** – is the total value of the goods and services within a country. Gross **National product (GNP)** in addition to GDP includes wealth earned overseas. The figures are frequently quoted 'per capita' (per head of the population) as an indication of national wealth and development.

**Greenfield sites** and **brown field sites** – are general descriptions of the contrasting sites available for the new construction of built environments e.g. housing, industry, infrastructure. A greenfield site is one previously used by non urban land use; fields, agriculture, recreation. A brown field site has had a previous urban use. It may be derelict, require demolition and clearing. Brownfield is also used more broadly to describe infill sites within an urban area which may not have been built on previously.

**Global shift** – the concept that the concentration of economic activity, particularly of manufacturing is no longer exclusively concentrated in the core of the western world. The centre of gravity of the world manufacturing system has begun to move towards the Pacific and South East Asia. This has influenced concentrations of power, finance and flows of international trade.

**High-technology** – the phrase used to describe post 1960 technology and the nature of new industry. New technologies include: information and communications technology, microelectronic technology, bio technology, materials technology, energy and space technology. Much has been made possible by microchip technology which has aided robotisation, computerisation and miniaturisation. Using CAM/CAD and CNC has revolutionised manufacturing, services and communications. High Tech industries may be those either manufacturing or using new technologies.

**Industrialisation** – the process by which manufacturing industry becomes a dominant part of an economy. It can be spontaneous or planned. It is one means by which a country can create capital and develop. It dominated change in Western Europe in 1750–1850 and the USA 1800–1900. It has been a characteristic of **Newly Industrialising Countries** since the 1960s.

**Newly Industrialising Countries** – (NICs) are countries which have undergone rapid export orientated industrialisation (EOI) in last 30 years. Largely a South East Asian phenomena, the first generation comprised the 'Tiger' economies of Hong Kong, Singapore, Taiwan, Korea. The second generation comprised Thailand, Mexico and Malaysia. More recently Portugal, Greece and Poland have been described as European NIC's.

**NGO** – are non governmental organisations who work to relieve poverty, inequality and environmental problems and can act as pressure groups. They are non profit making and may be financed by fund raising and/or government grants. They vary in scale e.g. Greenpeace, Oxfam, Amnesty international to local scale projects such as ORAP groups in Zimbabwe

**Rural urban inter dependence** – suggests that rural areas dominated by green landscapes of agriculture or wilderness have an economic relationship with the built up areas of urban environments. Rural areas provide, food, resources, leisure environments for urban areas. Urban areas provide goods, services, employment and act as market areas for rural areas. There is increasingly a blurred distinction between the two economies.

**Sustainability** – is a term which came to prominence in 1987 as a result of the World Commission on Environment and Development (Brundtland Report). Sustainable development was described as development by which the needs of the current generation are met while maintaining the same or improved conditions for the next generation. This concept can be applied to agriculture, development, urban living, the use of resources as well as the environment.

**Tertiary Activity** – is service activity. Major categories would include wholesaling, retailing, distribution, transport, administration and tourism. In locational terms such activities are often in shops, offices and warehousing. Service employment can include service to the public, to another industry, another service, or for the state. In MEDCs it is the largest employment sector.

**Trans national corporations (or companies)** – or Multi national corporations are companies with agricultural, manufacturing or service operations in at least two different countries. Control of global operations across frontiers is by strategic decisions usually concentrated in one country. An increasing amount of global trade is **intra** company.

**World cities (global cities)** – are major cities forming the nodes through which run the interconnections of the world economy. The consequences are city economies based on financial and producer services which generate super profits but may be vulnerable to super loss.

Development of global cities is an integral part of the global economic system. Tokyo, New York and London are world cities.

**Quaternary Activity** – developed originally as a sub set of Tertiary activity. It is the service sector which specialises in the provision of information as opposed to a more tangible service or benefit. It is often categorised by the use of computer stored and transmitted communication modes, as in Research and Development, financial services, legal advice, education.

| Some useful abbreviations and acronyms: | |
| --- | --- |
| ASEAN | Association of South East Asian Nations |
| CAM/CAD | Computer aided manufacture. Computer aided design |
| CAP | Common Agricultural Policy |
| CNC | Computerised numerical control |
| EPZ | Export Processing Zones |
| EZ | Enterprise Zones |
| ESA | Environmentally Sensitive Areas |
| FDI | Foreign direct investment |
| HHYV | High yielding varieties |
| IMF | International Monetary Fund |
| NIC | Newly industrialising countries |
| NIDL | New international division of Labour |
| NIS | New Industrial spaces |
| OPEC | Organisation of Oil exporting countries |
| WTO | World Trade Organisation |

# INDEX

# CORONATION ST.

## THE OFFICIAL ANNUAL 2011

by Tim Randall

A Grange Publication

# WELCOME TO WEATHERFIELD!

IN THIS FUN-FILLED
ANNUAL WE CELEBRATE
ANOTHER UNFORGETTABLE
YEAR IN THE STREET.
SO PULL UP A BAR-STOOL,
ORDER YOURSELF A HOTPOT
AND CATCH UP ON ALL THE
GOSS.

ENJOY!

## Things to do

Sort out rota

Speak to Betty re Xmas party

Order lycra microskirt/get roots done

24hr **S** service

STREET CARS

**0161 715 1515**

Airport trips, party bookings, weddings. Fast, reliable and safe

20

23

56

16

10

46

38

30

# contents

INSIDE: ALL THESE CORRIE CRACKERS!

# Tony sets fire to Underworld!

Knicker factory boss Carla Connor's worst nightmare came true in June when her murderous husband Tony Gordon escaped from prison determined to take his revenge on his estranged wife and interfering neighbours, Roy and Hayley Cropper. With a helping hand from ex-cellmate Robbie Sloane, Carla and Hayley found themselves taken hostage in Underworld as an increasingly deranged Tony waggled a loaded gun at their heads. After he'd killed Robbie at point blank range Maria made an unexpected appearance, but Tony eventually allowed his ex-girlfriend, followed by Hayley, to go free. Next he put his twisted plan into action by manically splattering petrol around the factory and setting it alight. In the blazing building a courageous Carla fought for her life and managed to escape in the nick of time, before the whole building went up in flames with only evil Tony still inside.

# No jail for Gail!

When her debt-ridden husband Joe revealed his intention to fake his own death as part of a life-insurance scam Gail McIntyre was understandably horrified. But when Joe drowned for real, Gail was shellshocked to find herself arrested at his wake and banged up on a murder charge. Just when she thought things couldn't get any worse her surprise cellmate Tracy Barlow stitched her up by lying to the police that she'd confessed to the deed. Plus Joe's grieving daughter Tina also gave evidence in court questioning Gail's motives. Despite her loyal family's support, Gail feared the worst as the verdict was delivered — but thankfully the jury wasn't fooled by Tracy's lies and Gail was found not guilty.

# Sally delivers
# Molly's baby!

When Molly Dobbs revealed she was pregnant with his child, Kevin Webster gruffly ordered his former mistress to get rid of it. Estranged husband Tyrone responded very differently – assuming the baby was his he practically did cartwheels down the street. But having decided to give their marriage another go, the overjoyed mechanic was nowhere to be seen when his expectant wife's contractions started. He was miles away attending a breakdown so when Molly's waters suddenly broke it was up to Sally to deliver – unbeknownst to her – her own husband's secret lovechild! Fortunately Tyrone managed to hotfoot it back to Number 9 just in time to see baby Jack being born. Meanwhile Kevin cried as he watched the birth – his emotions in turmoil.

# Deirdre gets caked by Gail!

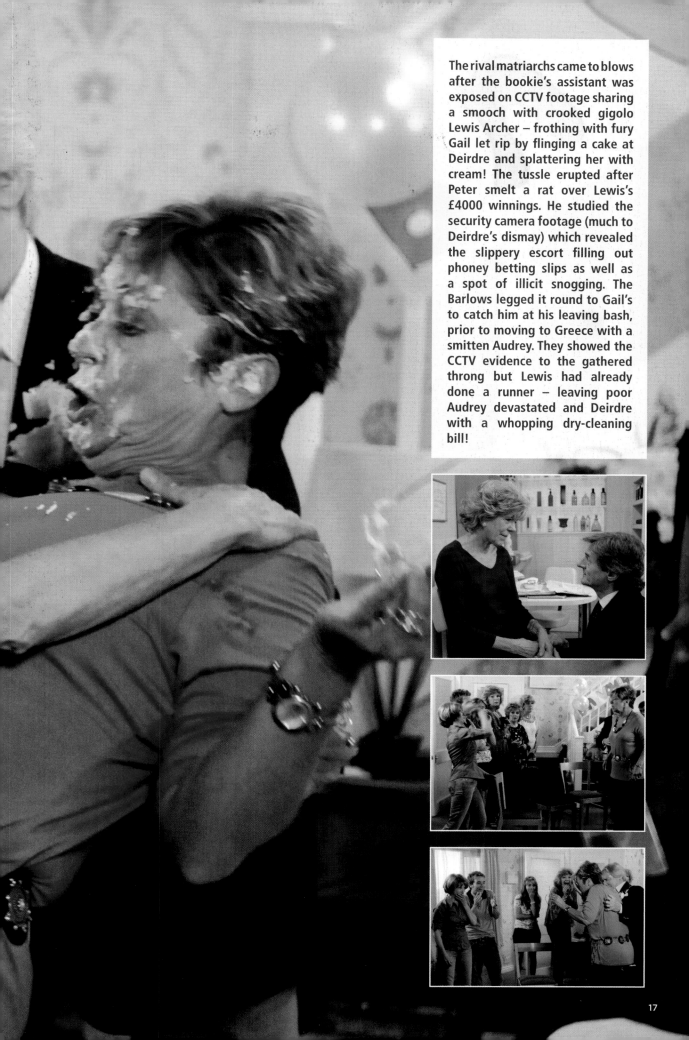

The rival matriarchs came to blows after the bookie's assistant was exposed on CCTV footage sharing a smooch with crooked gigolo Lewis Archer – frothing with fury Gail let rip by flinging a cake at Deirdre and splattering her with cream! The tussle erupted after Peter smelt a rat over Lewis's £4000 winnings. He studied the security camera footage (much to Deirdre's dismay) which revealed the slippery escort filling out phoney betting slips as well as a spot of illicit snogging. The Barlows legged it round to Gail's to catch him at his leaving bash, prior to moving to Greece with a smitten Audrey. They showed the CCTV evidence to the gathered throng but Lewis had already done a runner – leaving poor Audrey devastated and Deirdre with a whopping dry-cleaning bill!

# THE TONY GORDON STORY

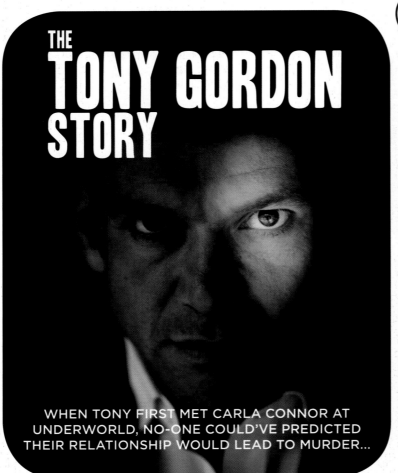

WHEN TONY FIRST MET CARLA CONNOR AT UNDERWORLD, NO-ONE COULD'VE PREDICTED THEIR RELATIONSHIP WOULD LEAD TO MURDER...

OCH AYE DE NOO! SEE YOU JIMMY! DEEP FRIED MARS BAR!

OH YOU ARE SUCH A ROMANTIC, TONY. WANNA GO INTO BUSINESS TOGETHER?

THE YEAR: 2007. THE PLACE: WEATHERFIELD. THE SMOOTH-TALKING NEWCOMER WASTES NO TIME IN CHATTING UP THE WIDOWED KNICKER FACTORY BOSS...

ON HIS STAG NIGHT TONY ARRANGES FOR LIAM TO BE MOWN DOWN BY A SPEEDING CAR...

DIDN'T YOUR MA EVER TEACH YOU THE GREEN CROSS CODE?

I WON'T LOOK BACK IN ANGER...

HOW MANY OTHERS HAVE YOU KILLED!? ENA SHARPLES? MARTHA LONGHURST? LEANNE THE RABBIT?

TONY ADMITS THE MURDER TO DEVASTATED CARLA, WHO FLEES TO LOS ANGELES WITHOUT TELLING ANYONE...

THE PHONE NUMBER IS 999 NOT 666 YOU CRAZY FOOL!

MEANWHILE RELATIONS IMPROVE WITH MARIA AND BEFORE TONY KNOWS IT HE'S DELIVERING HER BABY...

NOW'S NOT A GOOD TIME FOR AN ARM WRESTLE, ROY

BEST OUT OF THREE?

CONVINCED HE'S DYING TONY MAKES A DEATHBED CONFESSION TO ROY...

THIS WOULD NEVER HAPPEN IN DIBLEY

SO HAVE YOU MISSED ME, DARLIN'?

I HOPE THIS'LL BE OVER SOON. ROY'S DOING SPOTTED DICK TONIGHT

IF HE SMUDGES MY MAKE-UP I'LL FLIPPIN' KILL HIM

NEXT TONY TRIES TO DROWN ROY IN THE CANAL BEFORE HANDING HIMSEL IN TO THE POLICE. HE'S BANGED UP BUT THE FOLLOWING YEAR HE ESCAPES AND TAKES A TERRIFIED CARLA AND HAYLEY HOSTAGE AT UNDERWORLD...

# Girls allowed

## YOUNG LOVEBIRDS SOPHIE AND SIAN COME OUT SMILING AFTER A YEAR OF TURMOIL...

Whilst Sean Tully has been cheerfully flying the flag for Weatherfield's out and proud gay men, there haven't exactly been any female role models paving the way for fledgling lesbians Sophie Webster and Sian Powers. As a result the loved-up teenagers kept their relationship a secret for months, until Sophie's worst fears came true at the end of August when she was outed as a lesbian in front of her family.

As the Websters travelled to Roy and Hayley's wedding, Sally started a row with neighbour Claire over what had happened when Sophie was babysitting Dev and Sunita's twins the previous week. But the over-protective mum got more than she bargained for when Claire let slip that she'd caught Sophie snogging Sian when she'd temporarily left the children in her care.

The mortified teenagers looked at each other in panic and denied the accusation, and fortunately Sally remained convinced Claire was lying. In the end an awkward Sophie chose to open up to Kevin. Much to her relief her dad accepted her sexuality without

flying off the handle, but when he insisted Sally should be told Sophie was aghast. By now both girls were terrified of their parents' reactions and decided to run away. They dossed down in a crowded student house, but fled when one of the lads made a pass at a shocked Sophie. Finding themselves homeless as well as penniless the pair realised they had no choice but to head home and face the music.

But as Kevin and Sally sighed with relief, Sian's furious father laid into Sophie accusing her of leading his daughter astray. Sally angrily stepped in to defend the girls, but later confided in Rita she was still struggling to accept their relationship herself.

Meanwhile, Sally allowed Sian to stay at Number 4 and when the headmaster at Weatherfield High refused to take the young couple back because they'd missed the start of term, the factory machinist let rip and accused him of being prejudiced against lesbians! Surely it'll only be a matter of time before Sally's wearing an 'I'm Proud Of My Gay Daughter' t-shirt and marching at next year's Gay Pride...

## FIRST APPEARANCE: 9 APRIL 2010

It was after bumping into former colleague Leanne that good-hearted Cheryl was introduced to Lloyd – the cheeky cabbie who offered the nightclub stripper refuge from her violent builder husband, Chris. But after one tentative night of passion Cheryl put an end to loved-up Lloyd's thoughts of romance when he punched Chris in front of their young son, Russ. Despite gutted Lloyd's apologies she insisted their relationship be purely platonic as Russ's wellbeing was her priority. But with Chris seemingly everywhere she turns, will Cheryl ever be able to move on with her life?

# The Weatherfield Gazette

# CELEBRATING

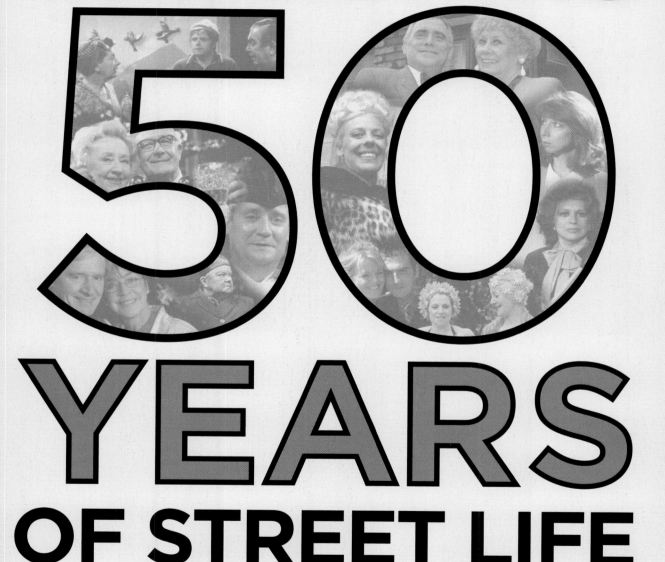

# 50
# YEARS
# OF STREET LIFE

## LOOKING BACK AT HALF A CENTURY OF STORIES, YOUR FAVOURITE LOCAL NEWSPAPER TAKES A TRIP DOWN MEMORY LANE...

**1961**
*Street-brawl...*
Elsie Tanner receives a poison pen letter and falsely accuses Ena Sharples

**1967**
*Congratulations!*
Newlyweds Elsie and Steve Tanner celebrate by cutting their cake

**1962**
*Cheers!* Rovers hosts Jack and Annie Walker celebrate their 25th wedding anniversary

**1968**
*Siege drama;* Valerie Barlow is held hostage by escaped convict Frank Riley

**1964**
*Death becomes her...*Martha Longhurst suffers a heart attack in the Rovers snug

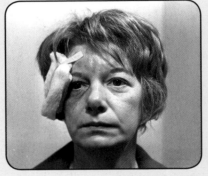

**1969**
*Day-trip disaster...* Hilda Ogden is one of many residents injured when their coach crashes

**1964**
*Fight-club;* Stan Ogden turns professional wrestler for one night only

**1969**
*The arm of the law...* Ena Sharples is arrested during a sit-in at the town hall

**1967**
*Off the rails...*
David Barlow rescues Ena Sharples when a train careers into the street

**1971**
*Hair-raising;* Valerie Barlow is electrocuted as she plugs her hairdryer into a faulty socket

The Weatherfield Gazette

**1972**
*Showtime!* Rita Littlewood does her Marlene Dietrich impression for the Rovers 1940's variety show

**1977**
*Dressed to impress;* the residents celebrate The Queen's Silver Jubilee in style

**1973**
*Chain reaction;* Annie Walker accepts Alf Roberts' offer to become his Lady Mayoress

**1978**
*Violent times…* Ernest Bishop is murdered during a wages raid at the factory

**1974**
*Fun in the sun!* The Weatherfield women win a holiday in Majorca

**1979**
*A lorry crashes into the Rovers;* Ken Barlow and Deirdre Langton search for Tracy under the rubble

**1976**
*What a picture!* Hilda Ogden's beloved 'murial' becomes a fixture at Number 13

**1980**
*Bigamy shocker…* Emily Bishop is shocked to discover new love Arnold Swain already has a wife

**1977**
*It's a girl!* Proud parents Deirdre and Ray Langton pose for a photograph with baby Tracy Lynette

**1983**
*Love triangle…* Deirdre Barlow confesses her affair with Mike Baldwin to husband Ken

**1984**
*End of an era...* Elsie Tanner leaves Weatherfield for a new life in the Algarve

**1989**
Evil Alan Bradley is killed by a tram, marking the end of a nightmare year for Rita Fairclough

**1984**
*Weatherfield's Got Talent!* Ivy Tilsley and Vera Duckworth perform 'We're A Couple Of Swells' at the Rovers

**1990**
*Mum's the word!* Gail Tilsley and Sally Webster pose with babies David and Rosie

**1985**
*A dream come true;* former barmaid Bet Lynch becomes landlady of the Rovers Return

**1993**
*Nanny from hell;* disturbed Carmel Finnan plots to destroy Gail and Martin Platt's marriage

**1986**
*The Rovers is destroyed by fire...* Kevin Webster rescues Bet Lynch from the burning boozer

**1995**
*Goodbye chuck!* Landlady Bet is forced out of the Rovers and quits Weatherfield

**1987**
Warbling pub cleaner Hilda Ogden quits Weatherfield to become a housekeeper in Derbyshire

**1995**
*Under new management;* Vera and Jack Duckworth become proprietors of the Rovers Return

**1995**
*There's no place like gnome!* Derek Wilton discovers Norris Cole is the garden gnome kidnapper

**1999**
*The secret's out…* Fred Elliott reveals to 'nephew' Ashley Peacock that he's actually his dad

**1996**
*Domestic violence…*Liz McDonald is attacked by husband Jim after admitting to an affair

**2000**
*Teenage pregnancy;* 13 year old Sarah Platt is photographed with newborn baby Bethany

**1997**
*Here comes trouble!* The boisterous Battersby clan move into the street

**2001**
*Dancing Queens!* Steve McDonald and Vikram Desai perform as Abba at the Rovers drag night

**1998**
*Free the Weatherfield One!* A campaign is launched when innocent Deirdre Rachid is falsely imprisoned for fraud

**2001**
*It's a boy!* Thrilled parents Emma and Curly Watts are snapped with baby Ben

**1998**
*Save the Red Rec!* Pensioner Emily Bishop turns eco-warrier in a bid to halt the development of the park

**2003**
*'Norman Bates with a briefcase'…* serial killer Richard Hillman confesses all to wife Gail

27

**2003**
*Shelley Unwin's big day…* but bigamist Peter Barlow is already married to florist Lucy Richards

**2006**
*A tragic demise…* Mike Baldwin dies outside the factory in the arms of former love rival Ken Barlow

**2004**
*Who's the daddy?* Wedding day misery for Karen McDonald when Tracy Barlow reveals Steve is Amy's father

**2007**
*The verdict is guilty…* Tracy Barlow is imprisoned for the murder of boyfriend Charlie Stubbs

**2004**
Dev and Sunita Alahan cheat death when Maya Sharma attempts to blow them up inside the corner shop

**2008**
*Goodbye my little swamp-duck…* Jack Duckworth is shocked to find Vera has passed away at home

**2005**
*Older and wiser;* Ken Barlow and Deirdre Rachid tie the knot for a second time

**2009**
*Serial-adulterer?* Ken Barlow plays away from home with barge-living actress Martha Fraser

**2005**
*Doing a runner…* Shelley Unwin jilts bully boy builder Charlie Stubbs at the altar

**2010**
Jailbird Gail McIntyre is shocked to find herself arrested and accused of murdering husband Joe

# Like father like son?

When Ken Barlow decided to dig up the distant past after receiving a long-lost letter from his first love Susan Cunningham, he was unprepared for what he might find – namely yet another offspring he'd failed to witness growing up. When it turned out newfound son Lawrence had ostracised his own child James for being gay, an appalled Ken attempted to act as mediator between his warring son and grandson – but was devastated when homophobic Lawrence refused to soften his stance. On the plus side the floppy-haired patriarch perked up no end when nice-guy James informed him he was just glad to have finally found his granddad!

# A day to remember

The bridal train!

All aboard...hubby in train-ing!

Better late than never!

LOCOMOTIVE ENTHUSIAST ROY WAS CHUFFED WHEN BECKY ARRANGED A STREAM TRAIN TO TRANSPORT EVERYONE TO THE WEDDING, BUT THE JOURNEY DIDN'T GO ACCORDING TO PLAN THANKS TO VENGEFUL MARY TAYLOR WHO WAS STILL SMARTING AFTER BEING LEFT OUT OF HAYLEY'S HEN NIGHT. WHILE ROY SETTLED INTO THE DRIVER'S CABIN, HAYLEY HID IN THE REAR CARRIAGE WITH BRIDESMAIDS FIZ AND BECKY, BUT SOON NOTICED THEY WEREN'T MOVING. IT TURNED OUT MEDDLING MARY HAD UNCOUPLED THE LAST CARRIAGE, LEAVING POOR HAYLEY STRANDED ON THE TRACK! THANKS TO A HANDY RAILWAY PUMP TROLLEY THE FILTHY BRIDAL PARTY MANAGED TO ARRIVE AT THE CEREMONY IN THE NICK OF TIME...

Roy's steamy surprise!

On the right track?

Full steam ahead!

Finally the Croppers say 'I do'!

Happily ever after!

MORE WEDDINGS

# · The Coronation Street Wedding Album ·

Valerie Tatlock & Ken Barlow, 4th August 1962, St Mary's Chruch

Becky Granger & Steve McDonald, 14th August 2009,
Weatherfield Registry Office

Sunita Parekh & Dev Alahan,
25th October 2004, Weatherfield Temple

Sally Seddon & Kevin Webster,
8th October 1986,
Weatherfield Registry Office

Gail Potter & Brian Tilsley, 28th November 1979, St Boniface Church

Sarah Platt & Jason Grimshaw,
31st October 2007,
St Christopher's Church

Deirdre Langton & Ken Barlow, 27th July 1981, All Saints Church

Liz McDonald & Vernon Tomlin,
31st December 2007, Weatherfield Registry Office

Bet Lynch & Alec Gilroy,
9th September 1987,
St Mary's Church

Claire Casey & Ashley Peacock, 25th December 2004, St Christopher's Church

# CORRIE Quiz of the year

SO HAVE YOU BEEN GLUED TO LIFE IN WEATHERFIELD FOR THE LAST 12 MONTHS? TRY OUR FUN QUIZ AND SEE IF YOU KNOW YOUR WINDASS FROM YOUR WEBSTERS...

**1. What special bequest did Blanche make to son-in-law Ken in her will?**

☐ a) Her music box
☐ b) Her dog Eccles
☐ c) Her late husband's watch

**2. What did a tiddly Roy insist he would like to give Mary at Chesney's birthday party?**

☐ a) a kiss
☐ b) a hug
☐ c) a punch

**3. Which familiar face moved back into the street this year and now lives at No 7?**

☐ a) Karen McDonald
☐ b) Shelley Unwin
☐ c) Sunita Alahan

**4. Why did a furious Becky track down her half-sister, Kylie?**

☐ a) Kylie had written a bad reference for Becky's adoption panel
☐ b) Kylie owed her money
☐ c) Kylie was blackmailing Becky

**5. What was the name of the boat Joe used for his fatal attempt to fake his own death?**

☐ a) Gail Warning
☐ b) Gail Force
☐ c) Second Wind

**6. What was Deirdre caught doing on CCTV with Lewis at the bookies?**

- a) Kissing
- b) Arm-wrestling
- c) Arguing

**7. Who did nanny Claire leave in charge of Aadi when he was taken seriously ill?**

- a) Graeme & David
- b) Sophie & Sian
- c) Fiz & Maria

**8. Where did a loved-up Audrey almost open a hotel with fraudster Lewis?**

- a) Greece
- b) Gibraltar
- c) Galway

**9. Beneath which premises did John bury the body of Colin Fishwick?**

- a) Underworld
- b) The Kabin
- c) The Corner Shop

**10. Why did Liz sack Sean from the Rovers ?**

- a) He'd helped himself to pork scratchings
- b) He'd impersonated her on a Facebook-style website
- c) He'd regularly turned up late for his shift

**11. What was the name of Nick's short-lived factory situated under the viaduct?**

- a) Undie Heaven
- b) Nick's Knicks
- c) That's Pants!

**12. What did Anna and Eddie Windass treat themselves to this year?**

- [ ] a) a new kitchen
- [ ] b) a new sofa
- [ ] c) a new bed

**13. Why were Steve and Lloyd forced to apologise to Eileen and give her a pay-rise?**

- [ ] a) For refusing to make her a partner at Street Cars
- [ ] b) For scoffing her stash of snacks
- [ ] c) For making a joke about her love-life

**14. Where did Carla go with boyfriend Trevor to recover from her siege ordeal?**

- [ ] a) South Africa
- [ ] b) Australia
- [ ] c) United States

**15. How did Tina describe Gail when she gave evidence against her during the murder trial?**

- [ ] a) Cruella de Vil
- [ ] b) A Stepford Wife
- [ ] c) A Bond villain

**16. Rita and Emily proved to be incompatible co-workers when they volunteered at a...**

- [ ] a) Soup kitchen
- [ ] b) Charity shop
- [ ] c) Fun run

**17. What had Chesney been doing when Fiz discovered he'd missed his school exams?**

- [ ] a) Hiding at the Red Rec
- [ ] b) Working at the market
- [ ] c) Playing on slot-machines

**18. What did a drunken Rita and Claudia croon at Audrey's 70th birthday party?**

- [ ] a) Je Ne Regrette Rien
- [ ] b) Joe Le Taxi
- [ ] c) I Will Survive

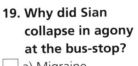

**19. Why did Sian collapse in agony at the bus-stop?**

- [ ] a) Migraine
- [ ] b) Ruptured appendix
- [ ] c) Twisted ankle

**20. Which unlikely venue was the scene of Gary and Kylie's one-off moment of passion?**

- [ ] a) Street Cars office
- [ ] b) Websters' conservatory
- [ ] c) Mary's camper van

**21. What's the name of Blanche's one o'clock club friend who filled Deirdre in on her mother's final days?**

- [ ] a) May
- [ ] b) June
- [ ] c) April

**22.** As she celebrated her 90th birthday, who was Betty's rival for the official title of oldest barmaid in Weatherfield?

☐ a) Bertha Gusset
☐ b) Nellie Harvey
☐ c) Enid Crump

**23.** What was the name of Tony Gordon's former cell-mate and his accomplice during the factory siege?

☐ a) Robbie Sloane
☐ b) Ray Scott
☐ c) Ricky Stone

**24.** Where were Molly and Tyrone going when they were involved in a car crash?

☐ a) To tell Molly's dad about her pregnancy
☐ b) To pick up a cot they'd bought off ebay
☐ c) To have a baby scan at the hospital

**25.** Ken was surprised with a long-lost letter from his first girlfriend. What was her name?

☐ a) Valerie Tatlock
☐ b) Susan Cunningham
☐ c) Martha Fraser

**26.** Why did Rosie pour a pint over Graeme's head in the Rovers?

☐ a) She overheard him calling her a bimbo
☐ b) He refused to buy her a drink
☐ c) He tried to kiss her on the mouth

**27.** What was the reason for Izzy's very first appearance in the street?

☐ a) She applied for a job in the Rovers
☐ b) She was Kirk's blind date
☐ c) She was a friend of Janice's

**28.** What did Mary do to Norris's spectacles while they holidayed at an isolated cottage?

☐ a) She kindly mended them
☐ b) She borrowed them
☐ c) She deliberately smashed them

# Look of ♥ love

## BUT DOES DASTARDLY DAVID ATTEMPT TO WRECK GRAEME AND TINA'S HAPPINESS?

Jealous David Platt totally lost the plot when he finally learnt the truth about Graeme Proctor and Tina McIntyre's relationship – so it was probably wise that his goofy best mate had taken the precaution of handcuffing him to a radiator at Number 8 before breaking the happy news.

Earlier Graeme had been over the moon when he'd woke up next to Tina, however, he soon began to panic when he realised David and Tina's on-off boyfriend Jason would need to be informed they were now together. Whilst David reacted angrily to the coupling of the woman he once described as the love of his life and his oddball pal, a stunned Jason seemed genuinely heartbroken.

But there was no denying Tina and Graeme made a great if unlikely couple. After all she'd been through the Kabin assistant needed someone who'd treat her well – and that's just what Graeme did. First of all proving to be a caring shoulder to cry on while Tina grieved for her father, and once they'd become an item he surprised her with a mystery trip on his rickshaw, flowers and a romantic picnic in the park.

All was going swimmingly for the loved-up pair until the end of September when David badly misread Tina's signals and moved in for a kiss, pinning her to the floor. An angry Tina confided in Rita about what'd happened and fiercely warned David to keep his distance in future. But as the residents of Weatherfield know to their cost, devilish and unpredictable teen David Platt rarely does as he's told and is capable of anything...

'David is gonna kill us!'

Graeme

there's something about **mary**

IT WAS IN 2008 THAT NORRIS SOUGHT OUT MARY TAYLOR AFTER SHE BEAT HIM TO FIRST PRIZE IN A CLIFF RICHARD COMPETITION – A DECISION HE MAY HAVE COME TO REGRET TWO YEARS LATER WHEN SHE WAS HOLDING HIM HOSTAGE IN A LIFE-THREATENING ORDEAL ON THE YORKSHIRE MOORS. HERE WE LOOK BACK AT THE COMPETITION QUEEN'S LOONIEST MOMENTS...

Mary informs Norris that her mother has died. She's pleased because she's free of the burden. Mary returns from her mother's funeral and decides to travel the world in her motor home. A year later, Mary reveals she was lying: 'Mother is alive and well and living in Newton-le-Willows.'

Mary sees a photograph of Norris and Emily's niece Freda in a magazine, after they win a competition together. In a fit of jealousy, Mary squashes her chocolate bar onto Freda's image. Norris frames the photo but Mary smashes it on purpose and throws it in the bin.

Mary entertains Norris in the motor home and attempts to seduce him with a combination of capers and Sheena Easton. A terrified Norris bolts it, leaving Mary heartbroken. She sets off on her round-the-world trip alone, promising to return.

Mary tells Norris she had a passionate love affair on her travels with a Spaniard lemon-grower called Cesaro. When Norris implies she has invented the tale, Mary's face darkens and she hisses: 'The lesions from the love bites have only just cleared up!'

When they go to a cottage in Bronte country as a competition prize, Norris is terrified Mary's going to make a play for him. He's alarmed as she forces him to enter competitions all day, hides his bootlaces, breaks his spectacles, bathes with a duck glove puppet, rubs peppers on her face and manically chops wood in the early hours. He also suspects her of trying to poison him with salad nicoise. He tries to make a run for it but Mary drags him back to the cottage, suggesting they get married. Fearing she intends to kill him, Norris summons the police. Mary's questioned but released without charge.

Mary takes over Hayley & Roy's nuptials by appointing herself wedding planner, until Hayley can't stand her domineering manner anymore and dispenses with her services. A bitter and twisted Mary takes revenge by removing a vital component from the steam engine taking Hayley to the ceremony. This causes the bridal carriage to separate from the rest of the train and Hayley nearly misses her big day!

MARY: What do you wear in bed, Norris?
NORRIS: Oh, pyjamas and an eye mask. You?
MARY: Tweed by Lentheric. And possibly a scrunchy. I tend to heat up at night so I like as few layers as possible after lights out. I just lie there, stroking my Miu-Miu 'til I fall asleep.
NORRIS: Your Miu-Miu?!
MARY: My cuddly monkey.

ROSIE
WEBSTER

CORRIE
*Babe*

42

**OWEN**
**FIRST APPEARANCE: 7 JUNE 2010**

**IZZY**
**FIRST APPEARANCE: 16 APRIL 2010**

**KATY**
**FIRST APPEARANCE: 30 JULY 2010**

From the moment overprotective dad Owen Armstrong set foot in the Rovers looking for his daughter Izzy it was clear there was chemistry between him and pub boss Liz McDonald. He started dating her mate Eileen instead but it wasn't long before the rough-diamond charmer was sneaking off to see the leggy landlady behind her back. When Sean spotted them and reported back to Eileen, the builder showed his menacing side for the first time and threatened the knicker-stitcher. Meanwhile, youngest daughter Katy and boyfriend Chesney were growing closer and older offspring Izzy slept with soldier Gary the night before he left for Afghanistan. Whilst Gary insisted he didn't want a girlfriend waiting for him in case he didn't survive, ballsy Izzy told him she'd be the one to decide if she wanted to wait or not!

**Blanche Hunt**
January 1936 - May 2010

Saint Edmond's Church
Weatherfield

Monday 10th May 2010 11:30am

# Farewell Blanche!

**THERE WERE FOND MEMORIES – AND SCUFFLES – AS BLANCHE HUNT'S NEAREST AND DEAREST GATHERED TO SAY GOODBYE...**

She may have had a caustic tongue and a deep-seated inability to keep her brutal opinions to herself, but as the news of Blanche Hunt's sudden demise spread to the Rovers, the solemn regulars raised a respectful glass in her honour. As if the shock of her mother's passing wasn't enough, next-door a broken-hearted Deirdre was even more stunned as Blanche's friend May revealed the no-nonsense battle-axe had met a man and fallen in love while holidaying Portugal, and was about to return home and share her news when she died of a heart attack.

In the days before the funeral Deirdre worried about what to say in her speech, but she should've been more concerned

## 'Oh I know she could be curmudgeonly at times. Who can't? But the sun on her specs, the breeze in her slacks. She was a different person, Dee Dee.'
### May on Blanche's last days

about Tracy, who arrived handcuffed to a guard. In the pulpit, with tears streaming down her face, Deirdre made a touching, emotional eulogy, but the fireworks started outside when Tracy discovered that Steve wanted to change Amy's name to McDonald and make Becky her legal guardian. A scuffle between Tracy and Becky ensued, resulting in the convicted murderess being man-handled back into the prison van.

At the graveyard Deirdre was in a terrible state and told Ken the sight of Tracy being dragged away had made the day even worse. What Blanche would've made of the commotion is anyone's guess, but as she once pointedly remarked: 'You're going to have to learn to take pleasure in the misfortunes of others, Ken, or you're going to have a very miserable old age!'

MICHELLE
CONNOR

CORRIE
*Babe*

CIARAN
McCARTHY

CORRIE
*Hunk*

47

# Street Talk

**THINK ON AND LOOK SHARP!**

**WILL HE 'ECK AS LIKE!**

WHEN IT COMES TO DISHING OUT OPINIONS THE RESIDENTS OF WEATHERFIELD AREN'T BACKWARD IN COMING FORWARD. BUT CAN YOU REMEMBER WHO SAID WHAT IN 2010?

1. 'I do so love the smell of a fresh pepper. The feel of it against the skin. I'm a sensationalist. Are you, Norris?'

2. 'The one time something happens and I wind up on the telly!'

3. 'She's lazy, she's sponging and she is leading you a merry dance, Steve.'

4. 'My Aunty Monica's mynah bird Paul rocked in time to Una Paloma Blanca.'

5. 'I'm all about loyalty...runs through me like a stick of Blackpool rock.'

6. 'Are you allowed to get married, what with all the to-ing and fro-ing you've had downstairs?'

7. 'Tracy Barlow is a lot of things but she's smart, she's vicious and the best liar I've ever met in my life.'

8. 'What's the view like from that high horse?'

9. 'Who in their right mind would want me for a dad? Happen the turkey baster would have done a better job.'

10. 'You're a family of freaks! You're The Munsters!'

11. 'I hope you don't mind my taking liberties with your peanut brittle balls?'

12. 'If she'd been at the virgin birth she'd have complained the stable were draughty.'

13. 'You've a lovely way with words. You're like a young Bamber Gascoigne.'

14. 'I didn't kill my husband, Tracy. The recession did.'

15. 'Nothing would give me greater pleasure than to deliver a punch to you.'

16. 'It's not a good look, wellies and pedal pushers. I think I've lost the respect of the bus driver.'

17. 'I am officially the oldest barmaid in this town and if this stroppy baggage here don't like it, she knows what she can do about it!'

18. 'I am going to kill you. And I'm going to enjoy it.'

19. 'I'll tell you this: I'm proud of my daughter. Because whatever else she is, she's a good kid, with a good heart.'

# The Weatherfield Puzzler

ARE YOU AN INTELLECTUAL BOFFIN LIKE KEN
OR MERELY MENTALLY CHALLENGED LIKE KIRK?
HAVE A GO AT OUR BUMPER PUZZLE PAGES AND FIND OUT!

# Barmaids wordsearch!

CAN YOU FIND THE NAMES OF THESE ROVERS
EMPLOYEES PAST AND PRESENT?

```
J U D Y M A L L E T T Z H T S
D D O T A I R O L G R I U S U
Z A J E N N Y B R A D L E Y Z
S T N Y G O B E V M K E W T I
A A L E X Q O T V Y N P S A E
M N B L E G Y A R N Y T T E B
A Y V L U G A R A T R O S R I
N A M E E R F E I G N A F M R
T P H H X T L V T H Q I E I C
H O M S A L L Y E R E R I C H
A O T I N A S K D A B A L H A
L L D E N U A C S Q A M A E L
G E H T I C O E D U B F T L L
F Y C W E I G B V E U H A L D
T V I O L E T W I L S O N E C
```

| | | |
|---|---|---|
| SHELLEY | VERA | ANNIE |
| ANGIE FREEMAN | BET | BEV |
| LIZ | BECKY | GEENA |
| VIOLET WILSON | GLORIA TODD | MARIA |
| MICHELLE | BETTY | JENNY BRADLEY |
| RAQUEL | LEANNE | SALLY |
| TANYA POOLEY | NATALIE | SAMANTHA |
| TINA | SUZIE BIRCHALL | JUDY MALLETT |

ANSWERS ON PAGE 60

# Kirk's brainteasers!

## CAN YOU UNRAVEL THESE BRAIN-SCRAMBLING RIDDLES?

1. Everyone has heard it but no one has ever seen it and it only speaks when spoken to. **What is it?**

2. A man works in a fruit and vegetable shop. His shoe size is nine. He is 25 years old. His shirt size is medium and he is six feet tall. **What does he weigh?**

3. I'm the beginning of sorrow and the end of sickness. You cannot express happiness without me yet I'm in the midst of crosses. I'm always in risk yet never in danger. **What am I?**

4. A window cleaner is washing a window on the 22nd floor of a tower block. He suddenly slips and falls. He isn't wearing a safety harness and there's nothing to slow him down. Yet he doesn't suffer any injuries. **How do you account for that?**

5. I can be man or animal. I can be a man or a woman. I don't have a heart so I can't be killed. Tickle my feet, I will not move. **What am I?**

# Who Am I?

## GUESS THE IDENTITY OF THESE MYSTERY RESIDENTS...

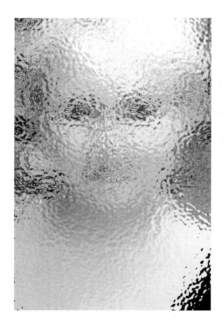

I once had an addiction to cheese and onion crisps
*My ex-boyfriend was called General Custard*
I spend my days using a microphone but I'm not a singer

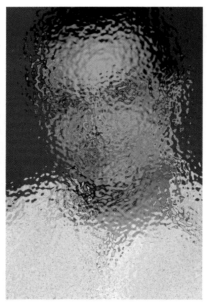

I have many children but I only live with two of them
*My daughter once said I looked like a Seventies crooner*
I have had liaisons with both Deirdre and Tracy Barlow

You saw me for the first time at a hospital disco
*A drunken Kelly Crabtree once tried to seduce me*
My favourite radio show is Elaine Paige on Sunday

# Missing Link

WHAT NUMBER LINKS THIS UNLIKELY GROUP OF LOCALS?

# Go Sudoku kerrrazy with Ken!

JUST FILL THE GRID SO THAT EVERY ROW, EVERY COLUMN & EVERY 3X3 BOX CONTAINS THE NUMBERS 1-9. GOOD LUCK!

|   |   | 6 | 3 |   | 7 |   |   |   |
|---|---|---|---|---|---|---|---|---|
| 7 |   | 2 | 9 |   |   |   |   | 6 |
|   |   |   | 6 |   |   | 7 |   | 1 |
| 3 |   |   |   |   |   | 2 |   | 8 |
| 6 |   | 8 |   | 4 | 3 |   |   | 5 |
|   | 4 |   |   |   | 5 | 6 |   |   |
|   | 6 | 3 |   |   |   |   | 2 |   |
|   | 5 |   | 2 |   |   |   | 3 |   |
|   | 1 |   |   | 3 | 9 |   | 6 |   |

ANSWERS ON PAGE 60

# Spot The Difference!

ANSWERS ON PAGE 60

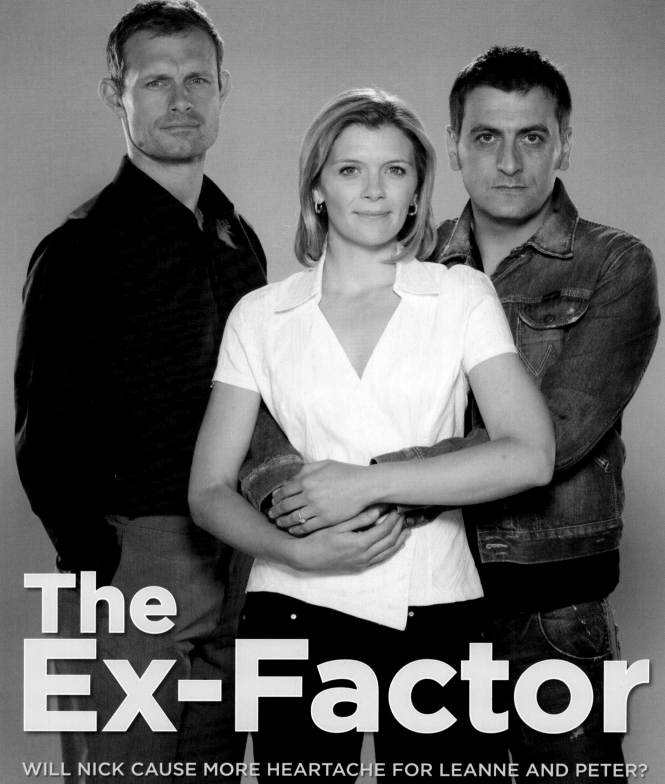

# The Ex-Factor

WILL NICK CAUSE MORE HEARTACHE FOR LEANNE AND PETER?

He was an alcoholic bigamist struggling with single-fatherhood and she was a reformed former prostitute who knew what it was like to have no-one to turn to – so perhaps it was inevitable that friendly support would develop into romance for lost souls Peter Barlow and Leanne Battersby.

They split when Leanne found out Peter had been bonking a rich party girl on her father's yacht while he was supposed to be in rehab, having left Leanne looking after his son Simon. She moved to Leeds but agreed to give their relationship another go when the abashed bookie begged her forgiveness and promised his drinking was a thing of the past.

However Peter fell spectacularly off the wagon at the opening night of their short-lived bar venture, but this time he did face up to his demons and booked into rehab. Back on the street, Peter started acting secretively and Leanne falsely accused him of cheating on her with Michelle Connor. But he'd been preparing to propose, with Michelle merely helping him choose a ring. Feeling guilty for her lack of faith in him and gutted she'd jumped to the wrong conclusion and ruined such a romantic moment, Leanne got down on one knee in the Rovers and proposed.

With Peter's drinking back under control and their engagement to smile about, it was the return of Leanne's ex-husband Nick Tilsley that was to cause further friction in their relationship. Peter was livid when he discovered Leanne had gone against his wishes and helped her ex with a business deal, and having been goaded by Nick in the Rovers he gave the smug factory boss a well-deserved thumping outside on the cobbles.

Meanwhile, unaware that girlfriend Natasha was pregnant, Nick lured Leanne to the factory, pledged his undying love for her and moved in for a kiss just as Natasha appeared and saw them. As a result Natasha went on to terminate her pregnancy, unaware that Leanne had knocked him back. When a suicidal Natasha was later rushed to hospital, Leanne was Nick's rock as he kept vigil by the critically ill hairdresser's bedside.

At the beginning of October Nick decided to give up on Underworld and open a bar on the site of Turner's Joinery. Leanne was furious he'd pinched her idea and turned him down flat when he surprised her by offering her the manager's position. But she had a change of heart when Peter generously pointed out it was her dream job and that just because he couldn't run a bar there was no reason why she shouldn't. But as the couple begin their wedding preparations, old flames Nick and Leanne forge an easy working relationship and it looks like Peter has unintentionally pushed Leanne towards temptation...

**FIRST APPEARANCE: 26 AUGUST 2010**

The McDonalds' hopes of starting a family were dashed when the adoption panel received a bad reference for Becky from her estranged half-sister, Kylie. Livid Becky tracked down her gobby teenage sibling (who it later turned out had a son in foster care called Max) and fisticuffs ensued. After raking over their abusive past, Becky invited her troublesome and homeless sister back to the Rovers to live with them. But could this be a good deed the whole McDonald clan come to regret?

# Gossip King

WHEN IT COMES TO CURTAIN-TWITCHING NO-ONE CAN OUTDO BUSYBODY NEWSAGENT NORRIS COLE. HERE'S WHAT HE'S HEARD IS ON THE CARDS FOR THE COMING MONTHS...

WHICH MATRIARCH'S LIFE WILL BE TURNED UPSIDE DOWN BY A BLAST FROM THE PAST?

THERE'S A MAN WITH A SECRET IN THE STREET... BUT WHO WILL BE THE FIRST TO DISCOVER IT?

LOVE IS IN THE AIR FOR THIS YOUNG BUCK... BUT IS HIS OTHER-HALF JUST STRINGING HIM ALONG?

A BRUNETTE SHOULD BEWARE OF HER LATEST FLAME... HE'S NOT WHAT HE SEEMS

WHO DECIDES A CHANGE IS AS GOOD AS A REST... AND SWIFTLY PUTS A PLAN INTO ACTION?

A TRIP DOWN MEMORY LANE WILL LEAD TO TEMPTATION FOR THIS REDEEMED RESIDENT

A WEATHERFIELD VETERAN IS HAVING THE TIME OF HIS LIFE... BUT ULTIMATELY IT WILL END IN TEARS

TRAGEDY IS AROUND THE CORNER FOR THIS NICE GUY... HOW WILL HE COPE WITH THE AFTERMATH ALONE?

SSSHHH! DON'T TELL ANYONE I TOLD YOU...

# WEATHERFIELD PUZZLER ANSWERS

## Barmaids Wordsearch

```
J U D Y M A L L E T T Z H T S
D D O T A I R O L G R I U S U
Z A J E N N Y B R A D L E Y Z
S T N Y G O B E V M K E W T I
A A L E X Q O T V Y N P S A E
M N B L E G Y A R N Y T T E B
A Y V L U G A R A T R O S R I
N A M E E R F E I G N A F M R
T P H H X T L V T H Q I E I C
H O M S A L L Y E R E R I C H
A O T I N A S K D A B A L H A
L L D E N U A C S Q A M A E L
G E H T I C O E D U B F T L L
F Y C W E I G B V E U H A L D
T V I O L E T W I L S O N E C
```

## Sudoku

| 1 | 9 | 6 | 3 | 5 | 7 | 4 | 8 | 2 |
|---|---|---|---|---|---|---|---|---|
| 7 | 8 | 2 | 9 | 1 | 4 | 3 | 5 | 6 |
| 5 | 3 | 4 | 6 | 8 | 2 | 7 | 9 | 1 |
| 3 | 7 | 5 | 1 | 9 | 6 | 2 | 4 | 8 |
| 6 | 2 | 8 | 7 | 4 | 3 | 9 | 1 | 5 |
| 9 | 4 | 1 | 8 | 2 | 5 | 6 | 7 | 3 |
| 8 | 6 | 3 | 4 | 7 | 1 | 5 | 2 | 9 |
| 4 | 5 | 9 | 2 | 6 | 8 | 1 | 3 | 7 |
| 2 | 1 | 7 | 5 | 3 | 9 | 8 | 6 | 4 |

## Kirk's Brainteasers

1. An echo
2. He weighs fruit and vegetables
3. The letter 's'
4. He was on the inside
5. A shadow

## Who Am I?

Eileen Grimshaw, Dev Alahan, Sean Tully

## Missing Link

They have all lived at No 7 Coronation Street

## Spot The Difference

1. Vera's nail varnish colour 2. "Coronation" is spelt wrong on the banner 3. Man behind Hilda is wearing a Fez 4. Drainpipe colour 5. Style of window behind Bet 6. Vera has acquired a broach 7. The beads on Bet's necklace 8. Hilda's headscarf

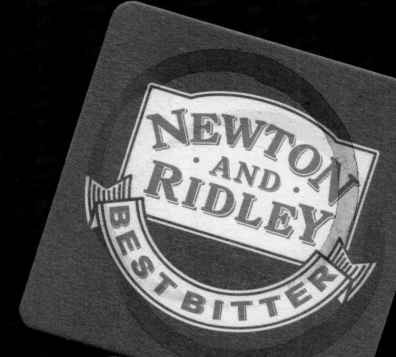

STREET CAB

All drivers are very friendly and polite

Most areas are covered/Weatherfield, Urmston, Stretford, etc.

**Special rates to the airports**

If you are unhappy with our service or feel that you have been overcharged, please contact the office as soon as possible.

**RECEIPT**

From _Weatherfield_ To _Airport_

Date _____ Drivers No _____

Received (with thanks) £ _30_